Wm. R. Corbishley

Profitable Catering

Profitable Catering

by
A. B. Barrows, F.Inst.B.B.

author of
Everyday Productions of Baked Goods

Maclaren and Sons Ltd

LONDON

85334 008 0
'PROFITABLE CATERING'
BY A. B. BARROWS
FIRST PUBLISHED 1967 BY
MACLAREN AND SONS LTD
7 GRAPE STREET LONDON WC2
COPYRIGHT © 1967
A. B. BARROWS

PRINTED IN GREAT BRITAIN
BY BILLING AND SONS LTD
GUILDFORD AND LONDON

Foreword

CATERING of all types has increased at a tremendous rate over the past few years, including that which may be termed "outside catering."

It was originally intended that this book should be a means of introducing bakers and confectioners to the lucrative field of outside catering. Some owners of businesses in the industry already have their own catering sections, finding this more profitable—and satisfying—than by expanding further into retail trade. Whilst many people are under the impression that the baking and catering industries are similar, such persons are correct to only a small point. Here is the meeting place.

Although complete in itself, it is not merely a recipe or cookery book, but one that will assist from the initial customer inquiry to the successful completion of the largest buffet or the smallest wedding party. From a children's party to a hot pot supper—all details are within. Knowing that many good recipe and cookery books are available (including many ideas from allied traders) it has been a deliberate policy to keep some chapters reasonably concise, so that the ideas and instructions may be followed more easily. It is hoped that members of both industries mentioned and, indeed, all concerned with catering in its many and diverse forms will find useful and worthwhile ideas to add to their own specialities.

The entire contents are the experiences of the author over the years, in several businesses having a catering section, whilst they have also formed the basis of the successful "Catering for Bakers" course, offered by the Department of Baking and Food Manufacturing, Hollings College, Manchester 14. All details, thoroughly tried, are only given as a result of personal experience, and may be relied upon to give satisfaction and enhance reputations.

My grateful thanks must be extended to Mr J. Figgins, Editor of *The British Baker*, for his enthusiasm for all things concerning the baking industry, and for suggestions which greatly assisted in the preparation of this book.

July 1967   A. B. BARROWS

Contents

Illustrations

CHAPTER 1

Introduction and Children's Parties

It is in the very nature of things that nothing remains static. Progress on the one hand or decline on the other—this applies probably more to businesses than other things in life. Often, then, does the owner of a business find himself at the crossroads. More production and industry are possible with overheads mostly remaining constant, but where shall the market be found to absorb the increased production?

Sometimes the answer may be found in opening another shop, sometimes by introducing another retail round, or again it may be found by introducing wholesale work of various types, i.e. shops, canteens, restaurants, hotels, etc. Whilst these outlets are in many cases very commendable, all have one drawback, and that is the need for extra capital to purchase property, vans, etc., about which little need be said.

For the business at the crossroads, with little capital available, I would commend the idea of outside catering as being one to be given careful thought. Before the reader hurries to find twenty reasons why this is not practicable in his particular case, I would urge that he gives the matter very careful consideration, for in this book I shall deal with the subject from all angles, including menus for different types of functions, quantities required, staff, etc.

All the ideas and menus to be given will be easily handled by the average baker and confectioner and, should he also handle cooked meats as an additional sideline, then the whole job will be considerably simplified.

I commence with a few warnings. Remember that most functions are held in the afternoons or evenings, so that "free" time will be considerably reduced. When accepting an order, do so wholeheartedly, determined to give the customer every satisfaction and value for money. Remember, too, that you are now, in effect, running two businesses—a confectioner's and a caterer's. Therefore, in your costings, any baked goods used should be credited at the full price to the bakery, for it is easy enough to work for nothing. If in any doubt about accepting an order, remember that it is preferable to refuse at the outset rather than to disappoint a customer, for a bad name will be hard to lose.

When booking an order, obtain all the relevant details from the customer, i.e. name and full address, type of function, date, time and venue; the menu desired, and here give every detail as to what the customer may expect and exactly what service you will give. Should the function be for a date some weeks or months in the future, stress that the price quoted is as then ruling and may be subject to variation in the light of future prices. Refuse to be pinned down on this, for to quote for a function at, say, 10s. a head, and then to present a bill for 12s. a head would only cause bad feeling. By explaining to the customer exactly what she will get for her money, and obtaining from her the maximum information as to her requirements, a good working platform is established, together with the very necessary confidence in each other.

I do know of one confectioner/caterer who arrived at a wedding and, only when the guests were seated, was it discovered that he had forgotten to book and produce a wedding cake. Whilst we all make mistakes, one of that magnitude is inexcusable, for every guest is, for that short time at least, a customer, and satisfactory catering will bring in extra retail customers.

The effect of the incident just mentioned can well be imagined, for at any function no second chance is available, everything must be there, in the correct quantities and at the right time.

Should an enquiring customer appear at all hesitant, send or give her a list of menus at varying prices, and allow her time to discuss the details with others intimately concerned. Never rush her, or she will always wonder whether the other menu would not have been better after all.

Before booking a definite order, obtain a suitable deposit, and request that you receive the exact number to be catered for three days beforehand. Your bill should be based on this guaranteed number, plus any extra attending at the last moment. Never, in any circumstances, charge less than the guaranteed number, for, if this is allowed to become a constant practice, much food will be wasted and the caterer will bear that cost himself.

Crockery and Cutlery

As regards crockery, cutlery and table linen, most functions are held in church halls, town halls, political clubs and similar types of premises. The hire charge for the room is borne by the customer and normally includes crockery, cutlery and linen. Should this, in any particular order, not be the case, then a hire charge should be made for these having to be supplied by the caterer.

Whilst it should be the aim of every individual to have his own equipment, at the outset this may not be possible until the money has been earned. However, most towns have at least one firm that hires catering equipment and initially this may be necessary. For the address of such a local firm, a few minutes with the classified telephone directory will often produce results.

Prices to be charged are, of course, a problem for each individual to solve for himself, but I would recommend at least twice the cost of the food, allowing for bakery goods at full retail prices, plus any hire charge of cutlery, crockery and linen, and a corkage fee of, say, 5s. per bottle for all wines served.

This latter charge can, of course, be varied to suit the amount of wines served. For instance, it will be found that at some functions the customer will desire to supply drinks to the guests *ad lib*. Alternatively, perhaps, only two bottles may be produced for the toast, the guests afterwards being expected to buy their own. In the first place, one or two of the staff will be required to operate the bar as a full-time job, whereas in the second the waitresses will be able, comfortably, to charge the glasses as part of their normal duties. Again, the customer should be consulted as to the amount of wines to be served to each guest and this, of course, will vary considerably. Indeed, the writer has had experience of catering at weddings where the bar has been "free for all", and, at the other end of the scale, where a soft cider drink was served as the toast for a wedding of upwards of 100 guests.

Whilst on the subject of wines, it will generally be found a better practice to let the customer purchase her own, but if the request is made for the caterer to supply these, then do buy good wines, informing her that is what you intend to do. At so many of these functions have I seen the cheapest of ports and sherries served for the toast. That, of course, is quite all right for the customer to supply, but the caterer should always pin his faith on quality. If in any doubt, a good wine merchant will be of great assistance.

Staff

Now to the problem of staff: assuming that the reader is commencing outside catering for the first time and has no knowledge of anyone suitable, then I would advise him to start looking first in the finishing room. The head girl there is the most likely person for, in the

B

1.1 Students of the "Catering for Bakers" course, Department of Baking and Food Manufacturing, Hollings College, Manchester, preparing to serve an afternoon tea buffet just prior to Christmas. The neat uniform of nylon royal blue overall, with white roll collar and cuffs, is quickly laundered, clean in appearance and becoming. The dainty white tea apron enhances the effect.

majority of functions, one solid, reliable and dependable girl is the whole foundation and will be of great assistance in organising the others. She is used to your ways, and *vice versa*, and having prepared most of the food knows what she is serving. She has pride in the goods she has produced and handles them with care, unlike, for instance, many shop assistants who merely "go to work". If properly inspired, she will suggest others, maybe sisters, relatives or friends who will assist. She should, of course, have some knowledge of the etiquette of serving, but a girl of this type falls naturally into the way of it.

You, for your part, have a responsibility to her. This should include supplying overalls, or whatever uniform is decided upon, and these should bear some name or insignia of the firm, and all the waitresses should be similarly attired. These overalls should be kept solely for catering, laundered properly by the firm; a small apron should be supplied for preparation and the laying of tables, which can be taken off before the guests arrive.

Sufficient food should be taken to enable the staff to have the same meal as that given to the guests. If, for some reason or other, the staff do not have their meal whilst there, then allow them to take it home, for these things are appreciated.

Finally, and most important, remember that they do not work solely to become tired and sleep well, so see that they are well paid for their efforts. If you give the staff a fair deal you are entitled to expect one in return, and very rarely will the right type of person let you down.

It will often be necessary to have someone in the preparation room for making tea and coffee, washing up and so on, and here you may find a niche for the elderly aunt who, if of a cheerful temperament, will prove to be a boon. Again, explain to her exactly what is required and rarely will you find cause for complaint.

As many functions finish late it is also your responsibility to see that the staff arrive home safely, either by bus or your own transport.

Finally, and of the utmost importance, remember that you are working as a team. Whilst your main function is to tie up all the loose ends and to see that everything is satisfactory, that does not mean that you have some special dispensation and do not have to do anything. Do not be afraid to roll up your sleeves and lend a hand. Let the staff see that, although you are captain of the team, you are one of them and will pull your weight with them. They will then appreciate that you are human after all, and will produce suggestions and ideas to help further. This way you will get the maximum effort from each of them and all will be well.

Should the reader be requested to cater at a hall of which he has no knowledge, then he should contact the caretaker prior to the date and see what facilities are offered. Make friends with him, see that his tea is provided on the date, and offer a little commission—say so much per head—for any introductions he can make. That quite often works, and I have known some caretakers to give a hand in loading and unloading vans, packing and washing up, etc.

With thoughts on Christmas, it may perhaps be of service to deal with children's parties. Though they just come within the scope of outside catering, normally no service is required, and quite often different works' and offices' managements arrange an outing to a circus or pantomime for the employees' children, or, alternatively, arrange entertainment on the premises. Normally only food is required, the employees getting a great deal of pleasure from doing the actual service.

The first two menus are designed to be pre-packed on cardboard plates, each plate then being enclosed in a transparent cellulose bag or wrapper. This idea makes for ease in service, for all that is required is for a plate to be placed in each child's place. The tea, sugar and milk are supplied separately to all three menus to enable the meal to be completed.

MENU 1

Meat or fish paste finger roll	Mince pie
Dinky pie	Cake
Tea	

MENU 2

Ham roll	Jelly
Sausage roll	Cake
Tea	

MENU 3

This menu is more suitable when supplying the individual items separately and does not lend itself well to pre-packing on account of the extra item and to the fact that the jelly and fruit has a cream topping.

Ham or tongue roll	Cake
Dinky or bridge pie	Jelly, fruit and cream
Mince pie	Tea

In catering for children's parties, remember to keep everything small, for it is the unusual that appeals to them. The cake, for instance, should not be anything too fancy or strongly flavoured. The

1.2. *Table setting for a simple children's party, more suitable for younger children. As in the next illustration, all utensils are disposable.*

varieties I have found to be most popular are various coconut types, such as madeleines and coconut macaroons, pyramid meringues in various colours with bases chocolate dipped, and queen cakes simply iced with fondant and a cherry on the top.

The jelly is preferred brightly coloured and poured into individual soufflé cases containing a small amount of tinned fruit in the bottom of each, such as pear, mandarin orange, peach, etc., and topped with a nice whirl of whipped and sweetened fresh cream, with a spot of raspberry piping jelly to complete.

The three menus given are arranged for three different prices, but additions can easily be made. These may include an animal short-bread biscuit upon which the child's name can be piped in royal icing to form a place card.

For 60 cups of tea, 4 oz. tea, 5 pt milk and 5 lb. cube sugar will be ample; more or less, of course, *pro rata.*

It has been mentioned earlier that service will probably not be required for the majority of children's parties, but, nevertheless, some service will have to be given, if not from the caterer, then from the organisers. The fun of a children's party is being with the children, so the chores should be cut to a minimum.

Cardboard plates have already been mentioned and, if the reader has not kept up to date with current trends from catering suppliers, then he can expect a pleasant surprise. Gone is the starkness of the original cardboard plate, for many attractive varieties are offered today. Some are specially treated to provide for hot meals, but that aspect does not concern us at the moment.

Disposable cups may also be used; that dry cardboard feel to the lips has been banished. Again, these are produced for hot and cold drinks, so the caterer should be careful that he supplies the correct type.

1.3. A more elaborate children's party setting, perhaps more suitable for older children. Soufflé dishes are in a representation of characters from TV shows, with crackers incorporating motifs from another TV programme for children. These novelties make an immediate appeal to children, whilst animal biscuit place-names are also used.

Paper tablecloths may also be supplied. These are generally of a size 36 in. by 36 in. in a fancy pattern, obviously paper, but it is now possible to buy white paper tablecloths in 17½-ft rolls. These latter are of damask finish and, when the tables are laid, they are almost indistinguishable from linen at quite a short distance. Whilst these would be unsuitable for some functions, they could be ideal for others and children's parties are a case in point. An adequate supply of paper serviettes should be provided.

Soufflé cases can add very much to the gaiety of the table, and these are obtainable in many varieties. Included here must be the coloured types, made in a representation of characters from TV children's programmes, which are instantly recognisable by the children. The above also applies to crackers generally acceptable at a Christmas party. Though some of the younger children may not like the bang, the caterer should certainly suggest supplying these. No effort should be spared to make the party a success—and profitable to the caterer.

Apart from tea to drink, which is not always acceptable to children, cordial and milk should be offered. Straws are cheap enough, and a supply could be provided, for it is strange how such small details can transform the party from the "ordinary" to the "super".

The offer should also be made to supply ice cream part way through the party, at a time convenient to the organisers. Large tins of sweets for distribution could be required, as could also be smaller tins, together with blocks of chocolate, etc., as prizes for games-winners. Balloons are always in great demand.

It is quite usual for each child to receive a gift at the conclusion of the party. For a pre-Christmas party, why not suggest a small moulded chocolate figure? (Illustration 9.35, p. 160). These may be wrapped in transparent cellulose and tied with a festive ribbon ready to be fastened to the Christmas tree. Alternatively, a fancy shortbread biscuit, star or crescent shape, again wrapped and nicely presented, could be offered.

Probably very few customers would be agreeable to all the foregoing suggestions for one reason or another, but the caterer, at the initial interview with the organiser, should be able to bring some ideas and enthusiasm to bear, to the benefit of both parties. It should be pointed out how much more convenient it is to the customer to only have one supplier to deal with.

It should be relatively simple for the caterer to quote a price per head, inclusive, rather than itemise, and this will assist the organisers who are generally working to a budget.

Recipes for all the items mentioned will be found elsewhere in this book, whilst for older children a more comprehensive menu could be requested. Menus as given for cold meals or buffets could, therefore, be used.

CHAPTER 2

Wedding Parties

THE majority of enquiries and orders will usually come for wedding parties, and here the reader will have to decide on general policy—whether to cater solely for high-class functions or to tackle any job, provided that it is a paying proposition. It is, of course, pleasurable to cater for the high-class functions where, figuratively speaking, expense is no object, but these enquiries are generally spaced widely apart. The greater majority come from the ordinary, down-to-earth people who, whilst not wishing to skimp, have only a certain amount of money to spend, realise that a wedding is a costly business, and want value for every penny spent.

I feel that it is preferable, from all angles, to tackle any job offered and, provided that the customer is given value for money, everyone is satisfied and, furthermore, the firm can, in the course of time, gain a good name from adopting an all-embracing policy. Indeed, it rather stirs the customer's vanity that a firm, well known for high-class catering, caters for her particular "down-to-earth" functions.

Most enquirers for weddings will want a cold meal of the "high tea" variety, and that provides a good starting point for the first menu. Hot meals do provide problems of their own, and these will be dealt with later. The cheapest menu in the cold meal class will read:

COLD MEAL MENU 1

Ham and tongue	Buttered tea scones
Salads in season	Cakes
Condiments	Individual trifles
White and brown bread and butter	Tea

These are the quantities required: $2\frac{1}{2}$ oz. meat should be allowed per head, and this should be sufficient to provide each person with a generous slice of ham, not too thinly cut, and a half slice of tongue taken from a 6-lb. tinned tongue. One fair sized lettuce will generally be sufficient for eight persons, and one tomato of average size between two people.

One hard-boiled egg, sliced on the egg slicer, between four people, and $\frac{3}{4}$ oz. of boiled beetroot should be allowed to each person. This should preferably be small, to enable it to be sliced neatly. One box of salad cress should be sufficient for 24 people, whilst one small tin of potato salad will allow one heaped teaspoonful to each 10 guests. Allow 1 in. of peeled, thinly-sliced cucumber to five people, allowing two slices per person.

For the bread, an allowance of 16 people to one 1¾-lb. sliced loaf will be ample, whilst one 1¾-lb. sliced brown loaf will be sufficient for 24 people. With these quantities it will generally be found that there is some surplus bread. I do believe, however, that "cheese-paring" on this commodity is utterly wrong, for a loaf, and the amount of butter required, is negligible in cost when weighed against the broad outline of "value for money".

The tea scones should be split and buttered, and a half scone per person will again give a surplus. Three-quarters of an ounce of butter per head should be sufficient both for bread and scones, and again it is "cheese-paring" to use, either completely or partly, margarine.

The cakes should offer as wide a variety as possible, and one per head should be allowed. Individual trifles should be prepared in stemmed trifle glasses, and for this menu a simple trifle could comprise jammed sponge; raspberry, strawberry, or orange jelly; a layer of well-beaten vanilla custard; a whirl of fresh cream finished by a half cherry and a sprinkle of green almond nibs. Should these stemmed glasses not be available, then prepared trifle cases, suitable for a festive occasion, may be used.

For tea, 4 oz. of a good quality dry tea should be used to a 3-gal. urn, and this will be ample for 60 cups of really good tea—another "must" in catering. Two pints of milk and 1 lb. of cube sugar should be allowed for every 10 guests; this amount of milk will be sufficient for it to be supplied to a child if requested.

All preparation should be completed before leaving the bakery. The meat should be cut and sufficient for 10 people placed in grease-proof paper. This is done for two reasons: it prevents it sticking together, which would happen were it merely piled up, and it assists the waitress in serving the meal, for she knows that 10 portions must be served from each paper.

The salads will be prepared by breaking, washing and drying the lettuce, slicing the tomatoes, hard-boiled eggs, beetroot and cucumber, placing all these separately in suitable trays or dishes, and adding a dash of vinegar where required.

The bread should be buttered, cut diagonally, and arranged neatly in small piles on a board, afterwards well covered with wax wrapping or greaseproof paper to prevent drying. Scones should be buttered,

2.1. *The serving of a cold meal, on the occasion of a Prizegiving for Manchester Bakery Students Society, with tables horse-shoe formation, suitable also for a wedding or similar type function. See also 2.2, 3 and 4.*

the tops replaced very lightly, and also covered with greaseproof paper. A few slices of dry bread should also be taken, for, quite often, this is requested by a guest and is one of those details that can be greatly appreciated.

The cakes and trifles should be packed on boards, taking great care that the latter are securely packed and will not roll about during transit.

Some time during the previous week, the room where the function is to be held should be visited and a note made of the facilities offered, together with the arrangements for obtaining boiling water necessary for making tea and for washing up afterwards. A loading list should also be prepared containing everything necessary, not forgetting such things as dishcloths, soap powder, washing-up liquid (detergent), and tea towels. This list should be used when loading the van to prevent anything being forgotten.

Flowers should also be ordered, the varieties depending upon season; the money allowed should be enough to purchase sufficient. Strangely enough, only recently did I read a letter from a reader in my local Press complaining about flowers in butchers' shop windows, which allowed "insects to crawl all over the meat". That is a point of view from a member of the public, but I have never heard it expressed at any function at which I have attended or catered for. Indeed the opposite has quite often been the case, and I have many times over-heard the guests remark favourably on the floral arrangements.

On arrival at the hall it will generally be found that the tables have been arranged in horse-shoe formation, and chairs in position (illus. 2.1.). From this point on the job is yours.

Check the water boiling arrangements, remove the infuser from the urn, half fill with boiling water and replace the lid which is, in effect, "warming the teapot". Meanwhile, the silver cake-stand should be placed in position, the cake set up and the staff kept busy laying the tables. First the cutlery and side plates, cups, saucers and teaspoons, then salad cream and condiments are placed on, with sufficient in one position for each 10 guests, and ash trays with one between each six guests.

Flowers should be arranged with one vase at each end of the top table and one vase midway down each of the legs. Only 1 in. of water should be used in the vases otherwise, should an accident occur and a vase be knocked over, the area of damage will be greatly extended.

Bread and butter, scones and cakes should be placed on plates and stands, all covered with doilies, white for bread and scones, gold for cakes, and all sited strategically to prevent the guests having to do a lot of passing this and passing that.

The trifles should be arranged, one at the top of each fork, and wine glasses, each containing a folded serviette, at the top of the knife. Sugar basins may be placed with one between eight guests.

It may be that you are requested to put place cards in position. This is a job to avoid if at all possible, for seldom does the plan agree with the cards given, and it is so easy to seat two relatives together who have not spoken to each other for years, causing much heartache. If no opportunity presents itself of shedding this responsibility, then request that a member of the family or organisation is present to guide and assist.

This type of menu falls in the "plate service" category, so, as soon as the tables are laid, the staff should be employed on setting out the meal on plates. Set out 10 large plates, checking each for cleanliness, cracks, and chips, and commence by laying on one side of the plate ham and tongue. Follow with the lettuce on the other side, and the remainder of the salad, arranging attractively and completing with a sprinkle of the cress. As each 10 plates are completed place on the table, meats nearest the fork.

The urn should now be emptied, tea placed in the infuser, and refilled with boiling water. When filled, replace the lid, allow to stand for 10 min. or so, then draw off a few teapots full and pour back into the urn to ensure that the tea is of the same strength throughout. When satisfied that the strength is correct, remove the infuser, and the tea will keep hot for several hours without tasting "stewed". A few minutes before serving, fill the teapots with hot water to keep them warm. One teapot should be allowed for each waitress, plus one extra teapot to every three waitresses. For serving this menu, one waitress is sufficient to every 20 guests, with one person supervising and generally assisting in the preparation room.

Just prior to the guests arriving, all lights in the hall should be switched on and the maximum possible done to give the impression of brightness and welcome.

As the guests take their seats the teapots should be filled, with milk put into the teapots. Any guest requiring tea without milk can have this straight from the urn, the waitress bringing this particular cup from the table. As each waitress empties her pot, she will return to the preparation room, the "spare" will then be taken and her original pot refilled. Hence, there will only be a space of a few seconds in between a continuous service.

2.2 *The setting shown in Illustration 2.1, seen from the President's seat.*

2.3. *Another view from the top table.*

2.4. *A view from "leg".*

As soon as each guest has been served with tea, the waitresses should be left on duty to see that, if possible, the slightest want is supplied before it has to be requested. This includes refilling cups, replenishing bread and butter plates, etc. As the first course is finished the plates will be removed, handed in to the preparation room where they should be immediately scraped, and put straight into the sink containing very hot water and detergent or soap powder. The forks may also go in, but knives should be placed in a separate empty bowl for later washing to prevent loosening of handles.

Meanwhile, the meal is proceeding satisfactorily, the service being as unobtrusive as possible with no hint of "rush" given to the guests.

When the trifle dishes are removed, the waitresses should start to serve the wine for the toasts. If a choice is given, one waitress should start by asking the chief guests their preference, serve as required, and move on. The waitress following then charges the empty glasses and follows on.

In the case of a wedding, the bride and bridegroom now break the sugar of the cake, and the cake is removed to the preparation room for cutting. For this, cut the cake straight across the middle of the bottom tier, and then into $\frac{1}{2}$-in. slices. Lay each slice downwards and cut again into $\frac{1}{2}$-in. slices, the waitresses placing the cut portions on to a tray or plate covered with a doily and serving each guest with a piece. Remember to serve the bride and "mothers-in-law" each with a favour or memento.

The waitresses should then withdraw to enable the speeches to be made. All that then remains is the clearing and packing up, remembering especially to leave everything clean and tidy in the preparation room. The actual clearing of the hall is the responsibility of the caretaker. Quite often at a function of this type, a light supper is also required and this will be dealt with later.

The serving of higher-priced menus should allow for an increase in table decorations.

A narrow strip—say 8 in. wide—of red satin or, if this is not available, red crêpe paper, laid along the centre of the top table, adds a touch of brightness and gaiety. If using paper, obtain a sheet, remove the centre band, and, before opening out, cut to the width required. Using forefinger and thumb of both hands employ a "tearing" motion to both ends without actually tearing the paper. When opened out it will be found that a serrated edge appears on both ends, and the paper may then be laid directly in position on the tablecloth. Also to be considered carefully is the use of smilax fern, obtainable to order from a good-class florist or greengrocer. A remarkably attractive effect is obtained with 5-ft lengths laid along the centre of the tables.

The use of some pieces of good quality silver, especially candelabra, complete with red candles, also helps tremendously to lift the function out of the ordinary. A pair of these may be hired, if necessary, from equipment hirers, and may be used at either end of the red satin or paper, with the vases of flowers then placed at the ends of the top table, the smilax forming a connecting link by running from end to end. Such an arrangement, with highly-polished silver cake stand in the centre, upon which stands the wedding cake, has brought much praise at many wedding receptions. If costs permit, the smilax may be extended down the centre of the "legs".

Following the ham and tongue menu mentioned previously the next menu in price and popularity will include chicken and a choice of meats to accompany, and sweets.

It should be stressed that the choice must be decided by the customer prior to the date of the function, the guests then having the set choice. To offer a choice at the function itself will inevitably lead to waste, the cost of which will be borne by the caterer himself, and, unless carefully watched, utter chaos.

MENU 2

Chicken and stuffing	White and brown bread and butter
Roast pork and apple sauce	Buttered tea scones
or	Fancy cakes
Ham and tongue	Individual sherry trifles
Salads in season	*or*
Condiments	Fruit salad and cream
	Tea

Allow one large chicken, 4–5 lb. dressed weight to each 10 guests. Wash thoroughly, place in a large pan or other suitable vessel, cover with cold water, add a small amount of salt and bring to the boil. Then turn down the gas and allow to simmer gently until cooked, which usually takes approximately 2 hr. Whilst every care should be taken that it is thoroughly cooked, do not leave on for too long, otherwise the chicken may fall to pieces and be wasteful and difficult to carve. It is a wise plan to cook the day before required, remove from the pan and allow to cool, leaving in the refrigerator overnight. This prepares the bird for firmer carving.

Remove the skin, legs and wings; if properly cooked, this will be a simple matter. Carve one side of the breast, placing the slices on greaseproof paper, turn the chicken round and repeat the process, afterwards carving the meat from the legs and wings. Again, one

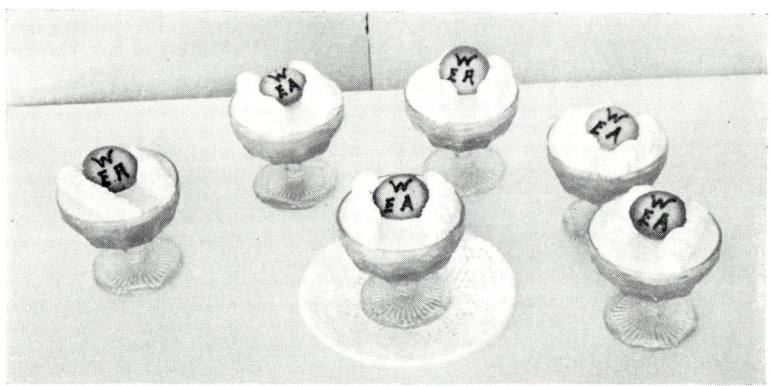

2.5. Individual trifles, using langue-du-chat biscuits upon which the initial letters of the organisation have been piped in chocolate.

paper of chicken will be sufficient for 10 guests, and care should be taken that each guest receives some from the breast and some of the meat from the legs.

Each guest will require ½ oz. of stuffing, and apple sauce if pork is chosen, and 1½ oz. meat will be necessary. Should the alternative, ham and tongue, be decided upon, then that same amount will be required.

The remaining quantities of food will be as already detailed. The cakes, once again, should be of as wide a variety as possible in taste and flavour, as well as appearance.

For the sherry trifles, place a small amount of jammed sponge in the bottom of each of the glasses, make up a simple sugar syrup and, when cool, add sufficient good-quality sherry to give a definite flavour. Pour enough syrup into the sponge to moisten without allowing it to become soggy. Add a layer of well-beaten, cold, vanilla custard and complete with whipped and sweetened fresh cream. Finish the decorations, if possible, with some motif appertaining to the organisation for which you are catering.

I have in mind doing this on one occasion for a certain women's organisation, the badge of which took the form of three letters within a circle. It was a simple matter to pipe these three letters in the form shown on the badge—taken from the official notepaper—in piping chocolate on a round langue-du-chat biscuit, placing one biscuit on each trifle. Such small details bring home to the customer the fact that you have taken interest in their particular order and, all other things being equal, it is sufficient to ensure that you obtain any repeat order.

Should fruit salad be decided upon, the choice lies between fresh or tinned. Allow 4 oz. fruit, including syrup, for each guest, and in this instance take it in bulk, for it is a simple matter to weigh out the required amount and to fill the dishes in the preparation room. Take, also, sufficient whipped and sweetened cream, a savoy bag and tube, to enable you to complete the sweet properly.

The procedure for serving this menu is as detailed for the first, and, once again, one waitress should be sufficient for each 20 guests, with one person extra to assist in the preparation room.

MENU 3

Grapefruit *or* tomato soup	Condiments
Chicken and stuffing	White and brown bread and butter
Roast pork and apple sauce	Pineapple savarins
or	Petits fours glacés
Ham and tongue	Cheese and biscuits
Salads in season	Coffee

As the reader will notice immediately, this menu will entail more service than the previous two, and here one waitress will be necessary to every 15 guests. Should the number to be served exceed 60, then an extra pair of hands in the preparation room will be needed.

Should fresh grapefruit be decided upon, cut in halves across the fruit, cut round between fruit and rind, sprinkle with plenty of sugar and place a tinned maraschino cherry in the centre of each, serving in sundae glasses. The use of fresh fruit does entail extra labour.

If tinned grapefruit is decided upon, then 4 oz. per guest, including syrup, will be required. No sugar should be necessary, but once again serve in sundae glasses, placing a maraschino cherry in the centre of each.

If tomato soup is served, allow 6 oz. per head, and a small, fancy-shaped, well-glazed dinner cob.

To make the soup slice three each of medium-sized carrots, turnips and onions. Add a small quantity of chopped ham, place in a stewpan with 3 oz. butter and a small amount of parsley. Stir over a gentle gas for 10 min., add 3 qt of good stock and 15 medium-sized, ripe tomatoes. Simmer gently for $2\frac{1}{2}$ hr, pass through a hair sieve, return to the stewpan and, if required, thicken slightly with a little roux and add a spot of colour. Season to taste and serve on very hot plates.

The quantities required for the main course will be as already detailed.

The savarins, for catering service, should be glazed with boiled apricot purée, a segment of fresh or drained, tinned pineapple

c

placed in the hollow, covered with a whirl of whipped and sweetened fresh cream, topped with a piece of crystallised pineapple and pinch of green almond nibs. These should be served on small sweet plates.

Of the petits fours glacés as wide a range as possible of both fillings and finishes should be employed.

A total of 1 oz. of cheese should be allowed for each guest, and this should be of three varieties. Each should be arranged neatly on a board or platter with butter, allowing ⅓ oz. per head. Biscuits, again, should include a variety, i.e. cream crackers, savoury cheese biscuits, water biscuits, etc., and three biscuits per guest allowed.

Of the varieties of cheese, a gorgonzola or Danish blue should be one, a fine white Cheshire and, if obtainable, a Leicester or Cheddar, to complete the choice. If costs permit, a few radishes, sticks of celery, slices of cucumber, gherkins, olives, silverskin onions, pickled walnuts, etc., may also be placed alongside the cheese together with a bundle of cocktail sticks. This is a touch that can be greatly appreciated.

The coffee, to be successful, should be carefully made by using between 1 oz. and 2 oz. coffee to each pint of boiling water, depending upon the quality. If ground coffee is used it will be necessary to strain it, but many of the proprietary brands of tinned ground coffee on sale today dissolve quickly and easily and do not require this operation. The water should be allowed to boil vigorously, add the coffee, and stir well. If not required for immediate use, it should be poured into a well-warmed urn until required. An equal quantity of fresh milk should be boiled, and a combined total of 5 oz. per guest will be required. Each waitress should be supplied with two pots, one containing coffee and one containing the boiling milk, each pot being well warmed before use. The guests will then have the choice of "black" or "white" in the proportions desired.

Now to some general hints on the service of a menu of this type.

If grapefruit has been chosen, this will be on the table as the guests enter, the extra cutlery already being set out, together with bread and butter and petits fours glacés on doily-covered stands.

Should soup be the choice, plates should be warming and the soup hot as the guests arrive. After they are seated, this should be served immediately and, when all have finished, the empty plates removed.

The main course, previously set out in the preparation room, is then served, and, when finished, the plates and cutlery removed, and the sweet served, which, again, may have been previously set out in the preparation room.

These plates are then removed and the cheese and biscuits served;

these may be placed on the tables for the guests to help themselves or, alternatively, may be served individually by the waitresses. Personally, I favour the former idea, placing the food on the table strategically for the guests to help themselves. Meanwhile the waitresses can be employed in setting out the coffee cups, saucers and spoons, together with basins of demerara and small cube sugar. The coffee is then served and, finally, any liqueurs or wines desired.

Quite often, with a menu of this type, wine is also served during the meal, and should this be the case additional staff will be required to serve it at an additional charge.

For higher-priced menus, a course comprising salmon may be requested, and the following two menus include this:

MENU 4

Grapefruit	White and brown bread and butter
Salmon mayonnaise	Fruit salad and ice cream with
Beef, tongue, ham	cream
Salads in season	Cheese and biscuits
	Coffee

The quantities of grapefruit required have already been dealt with.

The amount of salmon per guest will depend upon the price that can be obtained for the meal, but as this is a very expensive item the amount will have to be very carefully watched. It is suggested that the ideal will lie somewhere between $1\frac{1}{2}$ oz. and $2\frac{1}{2}$ oz. per head.

To cook, fillet the salmon and cut into thin slices or oval fillets. Wrap in greaseproof paper, place into a buttered pan or dish, season with salt and pepper, just cover with fish stock or water, add a dash of vinegar, replace the pan lid and cook either in a cool oven or over medium to low gas until cooked, usually 20–30 min. being sufficient.

For the mayonnaise, place two raw egg yolks into a clean, cold basin, add a teaspoonful of dry mustard and mix with a spatula. Very gradually, stirring continuously, add a little salad oil taken from a total of $7\frac{1}{2}$ oz. Add one teaspoonful of vinegar, then, gradually, the remainder of the oil. Add the sieved yolks of two hard-boiled eggs, salt and pepper to taste, and gradually add two tablespoonfuls of vinegar. If preferred, a very small amount of castor sugar may be added.

The salmon should be served on a lettuce leaf with a small amount of the mayonnaise poured over. It is normal and usual for thin slices of brown bread and butter to be served with this item, but as it is included as a subsidiary to the main course, it is assumed that it will be on the table at the start.

Of the main course little need be said, as this again has been dealt with previously. Although three types of meat are given, the choice from any two should be decided before the function is due to take place.

For the first time, ice cream is featured on the menu. Should the reader sell this commodity as a sideline then no problem exists. For the reader having to purchase it, the choice will have to be made whether to buy the factory type or from the smaller manufacturer. My experience has been that, where it has been requested, preference is fairly even.

Should the factory type be decided upon, then I would recommend the reader to purchase the family-size bricks in three colours, which may then be served as "Rainbow Ice". This may be cut into slices, placed on the fruit salad and surmounted by a whirl of fresh, whipped and sweetened cream.

One advantage to be gained from purchasing from the smaller manufacturer is that the ice cream can be supplied in a container in bulk. The loan of servers, together with the supply of spoons and sufficient wafers, is generally included in the price. Should a good supplier be found, then it is always an advantage to ask the customer if she would like this to be supplied during the less formal part of the function, thus providing another source of extra profit. It entails very little extra work for the staff, for it is a simple matter to place it in the sundae glasses, set the wafers in position and serve.

Staff needed for serving the above menu should be one to each 15 guests, provided that the preparation room offers sufficient space to enable the salmon and main courses to be set out prior to the guests arriving. If space does not permit this, then allow one waitress to each 12 guests, plus two people in the preparation room should the number of guests exceed 60.

MENU 5

Grapefruit	Potato salad
Salmon mayonnaise	Green salad
Cucumber salad	White and brown bread and butter
Chicken and stuffing	Charlotte russe
Pork and apple sauce	*or*
or	Charlotte royale
Ham	Cheese and biscuits
	Coffee

For serving this menu, one waitress will be required for every 12 guests, with two assistants in the preparation room. The general

2.6. *An alternative table layout, with "top table" for principal guests, and the remaining tables separate. Set for dinner, the tables await floral decoration.*

pattern of serving as already detailed may be followed. Cook and serve the salmon as previously indicated, this time including cucumber salad.

To make this, having removed the rind, cut a fresh cucumber into thin slices, lay on a flat dish and sprinkle with salt. Allow to remain for $\frac{1}{2}$ hr or so, drain off any water that has exuded and pour over some salad oil and a little vinegar. Season as required with salt and pepper and serve on the lettuce leaf round the salmon.

For the potato salad, to be served with the main course, peel and cook thoroughly, without breaking, sufficient small to medium-sized potatoes. When cooked, drain and allow to go quite cold. Dice, cover with mayonnaise, add some chopped parsley, a little finely chopped onion, and mix all carefully, taking care not to break up the potatoes.

To make the green salad, wash and dry the most tender parts of either cabbage or cos lettuce. Break into small pieces and mix with mayonnaise to which a little finely chopped onion has been added. Serve on a whole lettuce leaf, and decorate with a few small pieces of beetroot and slices of hard-boiled egg.

The sweet, in this instance, may be served directly to the guests or, alternatively, served on to the dessert plates in the preparation room, ready for the waitresses to take to the tables on completion of the main course. Whichever method is decided upon, however, I do feel that such an attractive sweet should be seen by the guests before being served and to this end may be used as a table decoration, to be removed before the main course is served or, alternatively, set out on a side table where the guests can easily notice it.

The general pattern of the serving of cold meals has been fairly comprehensively dealt with, and the reader should now be able to compile different variations to suit his own particular requirements. It will, perhaps, be of some assistance if this chapter is concluded with details for the production of different types of salads. These, used with a combination of meats, can provide attractive and "different" menus, thus enabling the reader to save his menus from becoming stereotyped. On such things are businesses built.

French Salad

This consists of a mixture of endive, lettuce, a small amount of mustard and cress, chervil and tarragon being mixed with mayonnaise. Decoration of the salad may be carried out with beetroot, cucumber, sliced, peeled tomatoes and slices of hard-boiled egg.

German Salad

Mix carefully boiled and cold vegetables, such as "button" brussels sprouts, pieces of cauliflower, boiled and diced potatoes, and broad beans, so as not to crush, with mayonnaise, chopped parsley, seasoning and a little vinegar. Practically any type of vegetable may be included.

Lobster Salad

Wash and dry leaves of lettuce and endive and place alternately on to a dish of suitable size, preferably silver, and season lightly with salt and pepper. Remove the meat from a fresh lobster, cut into slices and arrange on the leaves, afterwards spreading lightly with mayonnaise. Decorate the base with small, round slices of beetroot and peeled cucumber, arranged so that the slices overlap. Arrange a border of alternate slices of hard-boiled eggs and cucumber round the edge of the dish, finishing with a sprinkle of chopped parsley.

Tomato Salad

Mix with sliced tomatoes a plain dressing comprising salad oil, vinegar and finely chopped onion. If desired, thin slices of spanish onions may be included. Before serving, add a sprinkle of chopped parsley.

Italian Salad

This usually comprises a haphazard mixture of cooked vegetables, such as cauliflower, sprouts, french and haricot beans, and a small amount of diced potato, peas, etc., to which may be added pieces of fowl, or any other kind of meat. Mix, without crushing, the vegetables into mayonnaise to which has been added some chopped gherkins and silverskin onions, arrange on a silver or glass dish, placing olives on the top. Complete the decoration with circles of beetroot, stamped out with $\frac{1}{2}$-in. plain cutter, and a few capers.

Macedoine Salad

Prepare and cook french beans, carrots, turnips, green peas, white pieces of cauliflower, asparagus tops and haricot beans, with a little celery heart. Turnips, carrots and celery heart should be cubed before cooking. Drain and dry well, then mix in mayonnaise, to which a little cream has been added. Arrange in a salad bowl or dish, finally decorating with various coloured vegetables and chopped parsley.

Table Preparation

Illustration 2.1 shows the room as found on arrival, with sufficient tables set up to accommodate the number of guests expected. This is generally arranged by the caretaker, but there are occasions when the confectioner will find that this has not been done.

Finishing Touches

The finishing touches to the tables constitute the placing in position of wine glasses, each containing a serviette, and, finally, the straightening of the chairs. Illustrations 2.3 and 2.4 show the finished tables, awaiting the arrival of the guests, with all now ready for serving.

Light Supper

Quite often, when the original order is booked, a request is made for a light supper to be served. This is usually required between two and three hours after the main meal has been served, and is an additional source of income.

At the higher-priced type of function, the supper may take the form of a buffet, but by far the greater number of requests will probably be for a "plate service" light refreshment.

The following are some suggestions:

No. 1
  Bridge roll with ham and cress
  Fancy cake
  Tea or coffee

No. 2
  Bridge roll with egg and cress
  Bridge or "Dinky" pork pie
  Fancy cake
  Tea or coffee

No. 3
  Meat patties
  Buttered scone
  Fancy cake
  Tea or coffee

No. 4
  Filled vol-au-vent
  Sausage roll
  Bridge roll with cheese and cress
  Fancy cake
  Tea or coffee

Lines such as vol-au-vent and sausage rolls should only be included and offered provided the caterer is certain that facilities exist at the venue to warm them thoroughly so that they are served hot.

If space permits, the plates can be set out on a table, and tea or coffee served from an adjoining table.

If this is not possible, then arrange the prepared plates on confectioners' boards, and cups, with saucers separate, on another. These may, of course, be laid in position as the washing up from the main meal proceeds, so that much of the work is done well in advance.

At the pre-arranged time, the staff may carry the boards through, food first, and serve the seated guests. Follow with the tea and, in this instance, the writer has always found it most practicable to pour the tea, already containing milk and sugar in the teapots, into the cups prior to serving. Any guest desiring tea without milk or sugar may have it straight from the urn; as this percentage is usually very small, it is very little trouble.

CHAPTER 3

Buffets – simple and medium-sized

CATERING for buffet functions does, I feel, give the confectioner more cause for satisfaction than any other type of catering. He has complete control over the goods from the initial purchase of the raw materials, through all stages of manufacture, to the actual setting out of the buffet and its eventual consumption. What a glorious opportunity presents itself in the setting out of a high-class buffet!

He does, I know, have the same control in all forms of catering, but he does not have the same chance to produce the "different" type of goods demanded at this type of function or the chance to display so many of his goods to the best advantage.

A buffet may take the form of a main meal, or may be more in the nature of refreshments during a social evening. As in all other forms of catering, a menu can be presented to satisfy the customer and show a reasonable profit margin.

For the lower-priced and smaller function, one large table will generally be sufficient, with savouries at one end and sweets at the other. The larger and more expensive function will demand two tables, one for savouries and one for sweets, distinctly separate for preference. The positioning should be such that the tables are displayed as conspicuously as possible. Remember, eye appeal comes first, and it is quite permissible to sacrifice a little convenience to yourself to achieve that aim, so that the guests, as they file in, will see the buffet at its best.

To set the tables, cover with well-starched white cloths, pulling down to floor level at the front. The overhang at each corner should be lifted and pinned up at either side of the table. At the front of the table, and hanging down to a depth of approximately 8 in., should be a strip of red satin, or, if this is not available, red crepe paper pulled tight may be used, keeping the fixing drawing pins hidden. A further narrow strip of the same material should be placed half-way across and running lengthwise along the top of the table. Smilax fern can again be used very advantageously, with a length running along the centre of the red satin or crepe paper strip on top of the table, and further lengths looped against the red material pinned to the front of the table.

To set out the food, divide the table mentally in halves; right-hand side for savouries, left-hand side for sweets. Take two ordinary confectioner's boards, turn them upside down and cover completely with tablecloths or serviettes, tucking the ends underneath, and setting one on each side of the table, raised slightly at the back and at an angle to the front of the table. Cover the cloths on the boards with doilies, white on the right-hand side for savouries, gold for sweets on the left, and set out the food in rows as neatly and attractively as possible. Use silver dishes, or, if these are not available, doily-covered plates for the remaining food, remembering to keep the display properly balanced, and using sprigs of clean, fresh parsley to decorate the savouries.

Two vases of flowers and fern could be placed at the back of the buffet, taking care that these do not overhang the food and, if at all possible, silver candelabra, complete with red candles, to finish the decoration. The buffet, when completed, should look clean, bright, attractive and alive, with the finest possible goods that you are capable of producing shown in a perfectly balanced setting.

Sufficient plates should be at the end of the table near the savouries. Each guest will take a plate, help himself to savouries, move on, take the sweets and a serviette placed at the furthest end of the table. He will then move on to a separate table for tea or coffee before sitting.

The only service that you should be expected to provide would be for setting out the buffet, serving the tea or coffee and clearing away afterwards. With a higher-priced buffet, however, it will be found advantageous if waitresses serve the beverages after the guests have obtained the food and sat down. Normally, and other than this, actual waiting on at the tables is not included. Any wine served should be charged extra. This is known as "corkage" for so much per bottle served. In the case of catering at a function where a "free" bar is provided, there should be an "all in" charge, depending upon the number of staff engaged solely upon this task and the amount of drinks served.

Sufficient seats should be arranged at either separate or long tables. The latter should be covered with tablecloths and set out with whatever cutlery is necessary, together with any seasonings or condiments. Flowers for these tables are very desirable. Should the number of seats be less than the number of guests, then two sittings would be required, and here the caterer must be very firm and as tactful as possible. Should the function be in the form of a ball or dance, he should insist that the supper tickets be marked "1st Sitting" and "2nd Sitting", and, if the meal is of considerable proportions, a separate "sweet" ticket attached, to enable the guest to make a second journey to the buffet.

Arrange to have a reliable and authoritative person at the entrance to the room, and, if the function is of any size at all, erect a nylon or rope barrier running parallel to the buffet, so that all guests going for food have to pass the ticket collector. Anyone not bearing the correct ticket or "coming again" should be quite firmly and courteously turned away. In the case of several sittings, the food must be divided out equally, so that the buffet can be re-set immediately the first sitting is over. As always, the caterer must demand and receive a guaranteed number on which to base his final account.

It is usual at functions of this type to provide a supper for the cloakroom attendants, doormen and band, etc. It is strange when, comparing notes afterwards, the doormen have increased, according to the number of suppers served, from two to five, band from seven to 13, and cloakroom attendants from four to eight. As the organisation holding the function usually pays for these, there is room for argument in the final assessment. To obviate this it is wise to set these meals out beforehand and take them to the various places where they are to be consumed, giving the staff strict instructions that on no account must any more be served without your knowledge and consent.

Whilst these latter points may, in print, seem somewhat harsh, they are extremely necessary, for all too often can chaos develop. The blame

3.1 *Simple supper–dance buffet.*

3.2. Separate sweet buffet, utilising paper buffet flags.

is then placed fairly and squarely upon the caterer, who is left in the unhappy position of trying to re-establish some sort of order.

It is a good plan to use buffet flags on each of the separate items, and a good, reliable and pleasant member of the staff should be posted at the savoury and sweet ends of the buffet to assist the guests by explaining the answers to any questions that may be asked concerning the food. This service should, as in all types of catering, be as unobtrusive as possible, with the aim to keep the queue moving without apparent haste.

As regards the food, this is always a talking point at any social function, and the aim should be to provide something "different" and unusual. All too often do caterers at this type of function start off with sandwiches which, though often very nice in themselves, are too "ordinary". Produce and offer the guest something that she cannot make herself, and immediately you have found a worthy ambassador. Similarly, vol-au-vents and sausage rolls produced from puff-paste should only figure on the menu provided facilities exist for these to be served warm. Sausage rolls made from a good-quality pie paste can, however, be eaten and enjoyed when cold.

Of the prices to be charged, everything, of course, will depend upon the menu. Unlike the cold meals previously dealt with, although the number of items are increased with higher price, it does not necessarily mean that each guest will expect to have one portion of everything.

In the menus to follow, starting with lower-priced ones and increasing in price and variety, the amounts required will be indicated by a percentage: 100 per cent will be regarded as the total number of

guests, and the percentage against each individual item the number
required.

MENU 1

Savoury	Per cent	Sweet	Per cent
Tongue rolls	50	Buttered cherry tea	
Ham rolls	50	scones	100
Bridge pork pies	100	Fancy cakes	100
Cheese mirroars	80	Tea and coffee	

The rolls should be small bridge rolls, nicely glazed and baked,
split and buttered, and containing a reasonably generous amount of
the desired meat filling. Mustard should be provided.

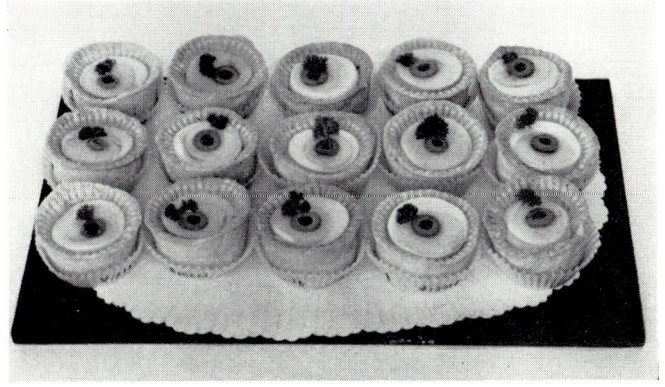

3.3 *Cheese mirroars.*

Cheese mirroars are actually of Continental origin, and consist of
an empty pastry case baked in a round bridge pie tin. The pastry may
be puff or good-quality pie paste, and though the original demands
puff, I must express my personal preference for pie paste, being easier
and quicker to block, and, to me, better eating.

When baked and cold, remove from the tins, and half fill with a
mixture comprising equal quantities of butter and baker's powdered
cheese. If the latter is not available, then finely-grated cooking cheese
of good ripe flavour will be suitable. Cream both materials well together before use, adding, if desired, a small amount of celery salt. A
little fresh cream may be added to give a softer filling.

On the top of each place a disc of hard-boiled egg, and transfer the
prepared cases to a draining wire placed over a tray. Fill the cases to
the top with aspic jelly only slightly above setting point, and place in

the centre of each a whole roasted and de-husked hazelnut, or slice of stuffed olive.

By now, some of the aspic jelly will have been absorbed, and the mirroars should be re-jellied, with the jelly once again only slightly above setting point. Should the jelly be used hot, it would seep into the pastry case, giving soggy and unsightly goods. Complete with a small pinch of parsley on each, place in greaseproof paper cases, and the goods are ready for dispatch.

Of the cherry tea scones, only one half constitutes a portion.

The cakes, once again, should be of the widest possible variety in finish and flavour, and should be set out on the buffet in a manner similar to the illustrations appearing in the previous chapter.

Quantities of tea and coffee are similar to those already published for cold meals.

The following four menus are all reasonably close in price range, and are in the "no man's land" between functional refreshments and a main meal. Once again the percentage figures indicate the number of servings required for the average buffet.

MENU 2

	Per cent		*Per cent*
Continental ham gipfels	100	Cheese mirroars	75
Sausage rolls	80	Buttered tea scones	100
Bridge pork pies	90	Fancies (various)	100
		Tea and coffee	

The Continental ham gipfels are simple to produce and delightful to eat, their crispness evoking many expressions of pleasure.

The method of producing gipfels, similar to that for croissants, is given on page 197.

To finish, split and butter normally, having previously added 2 oz. of dry mustard to each pound of butter during creaming. Place inside a good filling of nicely cooked lean ham and replace the top, taking care that no butter smears appear on the outside of the roll. When setting out on the buffet, decorate with a few sprigs of clean, fresh parsley.

MENU 3

	Per cent		*Per cent*
Chicken or turkey rolls		Cheese mirroars	75
with onion stuffing	100	Various gateaux	75
Continental ham gipfels	100	Individual sherry trifles	90
Bridge pork pies	75	Fancies	100
		Tea and coffee	

It will be obvious that in this menu slightly more emphasis is placed on the sweets, thus making it more suitable for a 21st birthday party, or dance menu, where the guests can reasonably be expected to be predominantly in the younger age groups and whose tastes lie more in this direction.

For the gateaux, I would recommend a variety of bases; e.g. sponge, butter sponge, sugar batter and high ratio, baking in 10-in. hoops, the finished base to be of a depth of between $1\frac{1}{2}$ and not higher than 2 in. Any deeper than this will make the finished article look far too clumsy.

Perhaps the most satisfactory type of finish is that of the torten; but instead of removing the centre in the normal way, divide straight across, each gateau then providing 18 portions and each portion being finished and decorated in a similar manner.

Imagination in the decoration of the bases should be given full rein, and the flavour of the individual gateau should be given as much attention as, or even more than, the finish. The widest possible range of materials should be used and I would advocate the use of glacé pineapple and other fruits such as pears, apricots, peaches and orange peel from which all the pith has been removed, all being boiled in sugar syrup in the same way as pineapple. The syrup thus produced is ideal for flavouring the buttercream, which is immeasurably improved for layering by the addition of a small amount of chopped fruit.

Two other varieties of gateau that always find ready favour are kirsch and rum.

Assuming that this plan is adopted, it is a simple matter for one of the waitresses assisting on the buffet to serve the guest, using a pastry server, a portion of gateau already cut.

The method of producing sherry trifles has been described previously, but it should not be forgotten, when these appear on the menu for a buffet, that dessert spoons and forks will be required.

MENU 4

	Per cent		Per cent
Mushroom or shrimp		Cheese mirroars	50
vol-au-vent	100	Various gateaux	100
Ham rolls	50	*or*	
Tongue rolls	50	Individual sherry trifles	100
Bridge pork pies	75	Fancies	100

Tea and coffee

MENU 5

	Per cent		Per cent
Continental open sand-wiches	100	Cheese mirroars	60
Continental ham gipfels	100	Charlotte russe	50
Sausage rolls	75	Charlotte royale	50
Bridge pork pies	75	Petits fours glacés	100
		Tea and coffee	

This is the first occasion on which continental open sandwiches have appeared on our menus; so popular are these, they are deserving of a fair amount of description. Always attracting a great deal of attention on buffets by their colourfulness and the variety it is possible to produce, they are as delicious to eat as they are delightful to look upon.

It is possible to use bread for the base, but I would most strongly advise against this, for the bread becomes soggy and thus the sandwich falls short of expectations.

Using full virgin puff-paste containing a portion of cuttings, roll out to an approximate thickness of $\frac{1}{10}$ in., dock well with the roller-docker and cut out with a 3-in. plain cutter. Set out carefully on sheet tins, allow a good rest and bake off in the usual manner, ensuring that the discs are thoroughly baked out.

The varieties may now be divided into four groups:

(1) Salad
(2) Fish
(3) Meat
(4) Cheese

All varieties are thinly buttered, then the fish varieties are spread with a good quality fish paste and meat varieties with meat paste: the cheese variety may be spread with a cream spreading cheese, and the discs for the salad variety are just left buttered.

This may seem a deal of trouble, but it is really time well spent, for one of the outstanding features of these goods is variety in flavour, the pastes helping immeasurably in this direction. As all the discs are so prepared it is only necessary now to describe some of the infinite variety possible to produce. I have no hesitation in saying that the craftsman will derive great pleasure in giving his imagination full rein in their production.

Continental Open Sandwiches

(1) *Vienna Sausage:* Small vienna sausages are split lengthwise, with a few sprigs of salad cress placed between the halves on the prepared

3.4. *The use of a simple hand spray to give the Continental open sandwiches an adequate, but thin, coat of aspic jelly.*

disc. A few pieces of chopped beetroot are placed at the opposite end to the cress and a small portion of potato salad is placed in the centre.

(2) *Cheese:* A liberal amount of cheese is grated on to the prepared disc and slices of pickled gherkin placed in a row across the sandwich.

(3) *Beef:* Thinly sliced, lean beef is cut with a cutter slightly smaller than the disc and placed in position. Complete with four halves of silverskin onions and a sprig of parsley in the centre.

(4) *Tongue:* Prepare this as for the beef. Decorate with three discs of boiled new potatoes, placing a small disc of beetroot in the centre to provide contrast.

(5) *Shrimp:* Using the cutter as previously, cut out a disc from a good, clean lettuce leaf. Place the shrimps in a row across the widest part of the disc, and finish with a small amount of potato salad between the "claws".

(6) *Sardine:* Prepare the lettuce as previously and lay on to the prepared disc. Decorate with a good sprig of clean, fresh parsley.

(7) *Sardine and Shrimp:* Prepare the lettuce and base as previously, arranging a sardine along the centre with shrimps, this time opened, at either side. Decorate the edge of the sandwich with very small sprigs of parsley.

D

3.5. *A variety of Continental open sandwiches ready for setting out on a buffet.*

(8) *Salad* 1: The disc of lettuce is placed in position and finished by using half slices of egg and tomato, with a thin strip of peeled cucumber placed over the joint; a small amount of chopped beetroot is placed at each side.

(9) *Ham and Potato Salad:* A disc of ham is put on to a prepared puff-paste disc and four small portions of potato salad added. The centre is finished with green peas and a butter bean.

(10) *Salad* 2: This comprises butter beans and potato salad placed alternately round a disc of beetroot on lettuce. In the centre of the beetroot pipe a small star of mashed potato.

(11) *Beef and Salad:* Here, the disc of beef is garnished with potato salad, peas and beans.

(12) *Ham and Salad:* Place a disc of lettuce over the disc of ham, and garnish with sliced egg and tomato, beetroot and cress.

As the reader will readily gather from the above varieties, very many more are possible. Such items as lobster, salmon, chicken and salami, etc., have not been included.

After all have been prepared, place on draining wires over a bowl, and ladle over aspic jelly, only slightly above setting point, repeating the operation after the first glaze has set. This will ensure an attractive gloss. Alternatively, a spray may be used.

At first, these goods are a little trouble to produce, but, from that negative viewpoint, is not everything in life a little trouble? It is to the confectioner and caterer who is willing to take the trouble to produce the "different" article and give a better service that the customer naturally turns. After these have been produced once or twice and the staff have got the idea, then the production will be comparatively simple.

As to price, that is up to the confectioner. Cheese, vienna sausage, etc., are cheaper to produce than, say, salmon or chicken; when a customer requires a menu containing these, the choice is invariably left to the caterer. Again, were these meant for retail sale, a high price would be necessary, but as part of a menu, some cheaper items can be added so enabling the caterer to present them on a reasonably priced menu.

The number of varieties required will vary with the number of guests, but a total of, say, two from each of the four groups, giving eight in all, will be found sufficient both to satisfy all tastes and provide the colour necessary for the average-size buffet.

CHAPTER 4

Large Buffets

It is now time to deal with buffets of higher price. The number of guests to be served should be taken into consideration when quoting, for the lower the total, so, correspondingly, slightly higher will be the charge for each individual. As always, a guaranteed number will be required, whilst two buffet tables will usually be necessary to set out the food, as detailed previously.

SAVOURY BUFFET 1

	Per cent		*Per cent*
Sliced roast ham*	66⅔	Cheese mirroars	50
Sliced sirloin of beef*	33⅓	Bridge pork pies	75
Ham gipfels	100	Sausage rolls	100
Continental open sand-wiches	100		

* On skewers to enable ease of handling

SWEET BUFFET 1

	Per cent		*Per cent*
Charlotte russe	33⅓	Black Forest gateau	33⅓
Charlotte royale	33⅓	Petits fours glacés	100
Kirsch gateau	33⅓	Tea and coffee	

Oblong biscuits are required for the ham and beef, and for these full virgin puff is required. Roll out to $\frac{1}{10}$ in. thick, dock well with the roller docker and cut, with either the seven-wheeled pastry cutter or suitable stick and knife, into oblongs of approximately $2\frac{1}{2}$ by $1\frac{1}{4}$ in. Transfer to a clean sheet, allow the usual period of rest and bake to dry out thoroughly.

To make up, butter each biscuit reasonably, mixing in a small amount of dry mustard when creaming the butter. After slicing the meat, cut into oblongs and wrap entirely round the biscuit, spearing the end, when finished, firmly to the biscuit with a cocktail stick. Set out on silver dishes, garnish with sprigs of clean parsley, and place a shallow dish of silverskin onions along with a number of cocktail sticks in close proximity.

4.1. *Individual tables set ready for a large buffet.*

The reason for the differing quantities of meat is that I have found that ham enjoys by far the greater popularity.

The cutlery required for this sweet buffet will be dessert forks and spoons.

Full-scale Meals

Both the following menus are full-scale meals, and for these the tables for the guests should be set with cutlery, crockery, bread and butter, and such condiments as may be necessary.

Whilst the guests will still be expected to collect their own food, first from the savoury buffet and, when that has been consumed, from the sweet buffet, waitresses should be employed serving the tea and coffee after the guests are seated. The replenishing of bread and butter plates, etc., should be done automatically.

For buffets of this standard, full floral arrangements should include flowers on the individual tables to blend in with those arranged on the buffets. Often the task of entire floral arrangements will be handed to the caterer and the easiest way I have found is to contact the director of the local council parks committee. For quite a small consideration it can usually be arranged for the parks department to take over. Besides

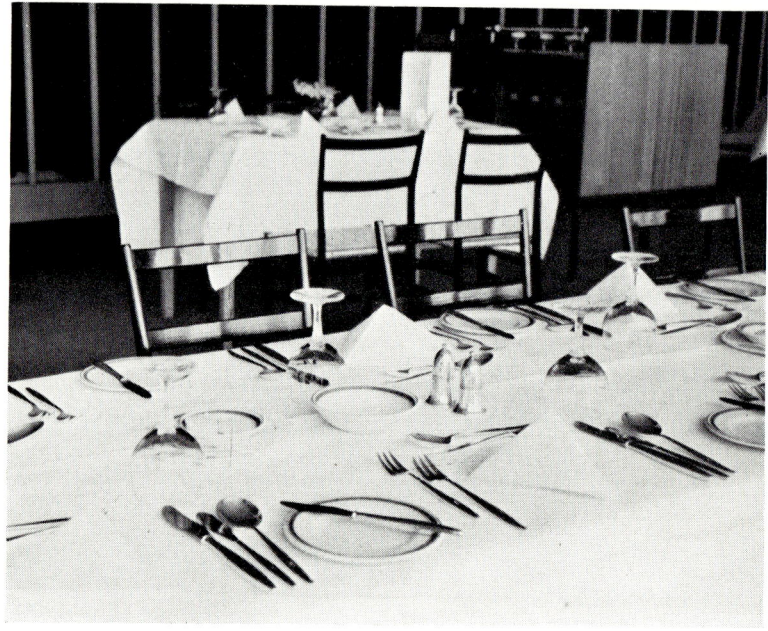

4.2 and 3. *Varied arrangements of tables for a large buffet.*

4.4. *Floral arrangements should include small vases of flowers for the individual tables. Spring flowers with a variety of ferns and evergreens are entrancing.*

the general arrangements in the hall itself, plants and ferns will usually be used to decorate staircases and alcoves, etc. Indeed, I well remember one occasion at which I catered where the very co-operative parks department included in the arrangements at the entrance a portable lily pond, illuminated and complete with fountain and gold-fish. The whole effect was entrancing and the objective of the scheme—that of putting the customers in the frame of mind to enjoy thoroughly their evening out—was achieved even before coats were handed in at the cloakroom. The cost of this whole service was slightly less than fivepence per head.

To raise further the tone of the function, a chef should be employed on the savoury buffet to carve as required. To a business that also employs a restaurant with resident chef, this presents no problem, but to any business without, a problem arises.

My advice here would be that, if the business is in a town of any size where civic functions are normally held, then often a chef may be found in the local town hall. A box of cakes and a word in the town hall attendant's ear will usually effect the necessary introduction, and very often it will be found that he will be willing to assist for a consideration. Failing this, a contact with a hotel employing a chef will often prove fruitful, or, again, a catering school, if in the vicinity, would be happy to recommend an advanced student desiring further experience.

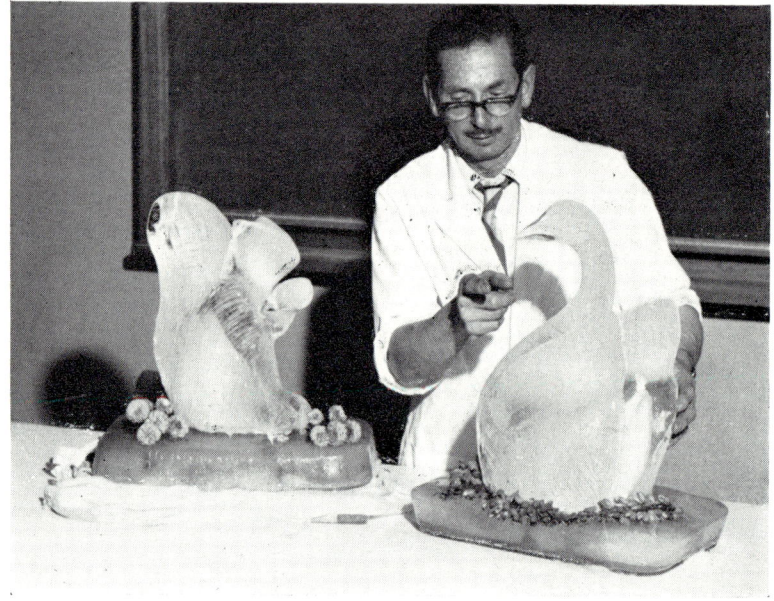

4.5. *Ice carvings are particularly admired as buffet centre pieces. Probably the foremost expert in this field is Mr E. Storer of Coventry, here shown putting finishing touches to a swan and squirrel during a demonstration given to Manchester Bakery Students Society, whose permission to use this photograph is greatly appreciated.*

4.6. *Chefs carving at a large buffet.*

Once a chef has been found, then the rest is usually simple, for even if he is not available when required, he will quite often be in a position to contact another. It has been my experience that these men are of tremendous assistance, and to see them carving as required, calmly dealing with the queue of guests, giving each full attention and forgetting nothing is a truly uplifting experience. Dressed in spotless "whites", with conventional tall hat and neckerchief, they certainly help to provide that "something different" to any function.

SAVOURY BUFFET 2

	Per cent		Per cent
Roast ham*	75	Continental open sandwiches	100
Tongue*	75	Bridge pork pies	75
Chicken*	100	Sausage rolls	75
Roast beef*	50	Cheese mirroars	50
Continental ham gipfels	100	Fancy-shaped dinner cobs	200

Onion stuffing and condiments

* Chef in attendance to carve

SWEET BUFFET 2

	Per cent		Per cent
Charlotte russe	$33\frac{1}{3}$	Fancies	50
Charlotte royale	$33\frac{1}{3}$	Petits fours glacés	50
Kirsch gateau	$33\frac{1}{3}$		

Tea or coffee to guests' personal choice

4.7. Part of the savoury buffet.

4.8. A section of the sweet buffet. Note the use of smilax fern.

With regard to the meats, 1½ oz. each of cooked ham and tongue, 1 oz. of beef and 2 oz. of actual chicken meat will be required, worked out to the percentages indicated. Depending upon the number required, at least one chicken, nicely browned and glazed with aspic jelly, should be displayed whole on the buffet, whilst the rest may be carved beforehand.

The ham, after roasting and allowing to become quite cold and set, should be skinned, partially defatted, and rolled in either dried and sieved bread crumbs or fine rusk, previously coloured slightly by the addition of a few spots of egg colour, rubbed through the hands and dried out in the oven.

The beef, if desired, may be lightly glazed with aspic jelly and garnished with a little parsley, sliced cucumber and tomato, whilst the tongue, usually of the tinned variety, may also be thinly glazed. For the confectioner handling cooked meats as a sideline, this is an invaluable opportunity to make a really wonderful display of meats, all set out to obtain maximum advantage.

One and a half ounces of onion stuffing should be allowed for each guest, and this should be a firm mixture comprising meat juices or stock, boiled chopped onion, seasoning, sage and thyme, with a binder in the form of bread crumbs or rusk. If desired, a proportion of it may be placed in a roasting tin containing a small amount of hot fat and cooking completed in the oven to give a crispy finish.

Staff

The chef, as a king-pin of this particular buffet, should occupy the most prominent position. He will normally provide his own set of carvers, but arrangements for a carving board will probably be required. If only one sitting is required, then one waitress to every 15 guests will be sufficient, but if two sittings are necessary, then one waitress for each 10 guests, excluding any wholly employed wine waitresses or bar attendants, will probably be needed. Much depends upon the venue, convenience, and facilities available, but in the case of more than one sitting, tables must be cleared and reset as quickly as possible. If crockery and cutlery are at a premium, speed and efficiency will be required to prepare for the second sitting, for undue delay will give rise to justifiable irritation.

SAVOURY BUFFET 3

	Per cent		Per cent
Soup	100	Tongue*	50
One whole lobster*		Roast beef*	40
Lobster mayonnaise	100	Continental open sand-	
Smoked salmon*	100	wiches	100
Chicken*	100	Sausage rolls	75
Roast ham*	75	Bridge pork pies	50
White and brown bread and butter		Salads in season	

* To carve as required

SWEET BUFFET 3

	Per cent		Per cent
Vacherin	$33\frac{1}{3}$	Petits fours glacés	75
Charlotte russe	$33\frac{1}{3}$	Gateaux, various	25
Fruit salad and cream	$33\frac{1}{3}$	Tea or coffee	

The serving of soup may be queried, but this is an ideal prelude to a wedding buffet, where the guests may arrive in a haphazard fashion, and the serving of this, in cups, helps to break the initial frigid atmosphere. It is a touch greatly appreciated during the earlier months of the year when the weather is anything but kind, and when many weddings are held to "beat the tax man". The methods of producing various types of soups will be dealt with in another chapter but 5 oz. per head should be allowed.

The whole lobster should be cooked, of course, and used initially as a buffet decoration, but be available to the chef if required. For the lobster mayonnaise, allow $1\frac{1}{2}$ oz. of lobster meat per serving. Place good, clean, fresh lettuce leaves in position on a silver dish and divide up the cooked fish, retaining to one side a few of the best pieces. Place the remainder in position on the lettuce, and cover all over with mayonnaise to which a small amount of aspic jelly, almost at setting point, has been added to stiffen it slightly. Decorate with the portion of lobster set aside for this purpose. Complete by garnishing with sliced cucumber, tomato, egg, etc.

Allow $1\frac{1}{2}$ oz. per serving of smoked salmon, ready for serving. Set out on a shallow silver tray on the buffet, garnish with cucumber and parsley, slicing as requested.

Of the meat, 1 oz. each of roast ham, tongue and beef, after cooking, will be required for each portion, whilst 2 oz. of chicken meat should be allowed, that is approximately 10 portions per average-size chicken.

Quantities of bread and butter will be as already previously detailed under the "cold meals" title, whilst 5 oz. fruit salad, including a small quantity of syrup, will constitute one portion.

CHAPTER 5

Setting out the Buffet

HAVING dealt fairly comprehensively with buffets of varying prices, illustrations of the setting out of an actual buffet may assist in clarifying the previously written word. These photographs were taken at an actual function, at a reasonable cost, the menu being as follows:

	Per cent		Per cent
Continental open sand-		Tongue rolls	40
wiches	100	Ham rolls	40
Continental ham gipfels	100	Fancies	100
Bridge pork pies	80	Gateaux, various	80

Tea or coffee

It should, perhaps, be stressed that the minimum expense was incurred in the use of decorative materials, in order to illustrate that it is not necessary to spend fabulously to achieve a tastefully laid out buffet. Hence, the minimum of silver was used, and crêpe paper instead of the more usual satin.

Illustration 5.1 was taken from the door of the hall where the guests would enter. The position was chosen so that the maximum number would see it exactly as illustrated. The impression should be one of perfect balance, with buffet flags used to indicate as clearly as possible the nature of each item, with all flags pointing in the same direction. The method of serving was for the guests to walk to the left-hand side, obtain a plate from the pile, help themselves to savouries (Illustration 5.2), then sweets (Illustration 5.3), before obtaining tea or coffee from a separate table and finding a seat at the tables set out for this purpose. A total staff of three handled this function quite comfortably, one member being stationed on the buffet to render any assistance required, the other two pouring and serving the tea and coffee as required.

Illustration 5.4 shows the buffet in "skeleton" form. Two trestle tables, each $2\frac{1}{2}$ ft wide, were put together against the wall. They were then covered with tablecloths down to floor level at the sides and front, using drawing pins as necessary, the heads of the latter not being allowed to show. A roll of red crêpe paper was cut before unfolding, and the edges serrated by employing a "tearing" motion to either end without actual tearing. The paper was then opened, laid

5.1. *View of the buffet from the entrance.*

along the top of the table and approximately $\frac{1}{2}$ in. brought over the front edge and pinned with drawing pins, tightening up the paper before the insertion of each pin. After all these were in position, the paper was carefully turned over to hang down the front of the table.

The buffet centre-piece, therefore, took the form of a flower basket, complete with red tulips and sufficient green to produce a picturesque whole; the flower basket stood on a silver cakestand.

Two confectioner's boards were turned upside down, covered with tablecloths and placed in position at an angle of 45 deg. to the centre of the table, thus, in the mind's eye, dividing the table into halves, the rear of the boards being very slightly raised. White doilies were set out on the right-hand board for savouries, and gold on the left-hand board for sweets.

Two trails of smilax fern led from the basket, one going to the farthest edge of the savoury board and one, similarly, to the sweet board. This was joined to a further length and draped along the front of the red paper, straight pins being used as necessary to hold in position.

The setting out of the food was done to give the result shown in illustration 5.5.

Eight varieties of open sandwiches were set out on the savoury (right) board, each variety being kept to one row, with each row

5.2. *The guests obtaining savouries.*

5.3. *Selecting sweets.*

5.4. *The buffet in skeleton form.*

5.5. *Buffet completed and awaiting the guests. Note the use of smilax fern and, at the base of the basket, the plastic "Catering by * * *" sign, which ensures that guests are aware of the caterer, which can be a good advertisement.*

5.6. *A corner of the buffet, showing the open Continental sandwiches. Note the use of buffet flags.*

arranged to give the maximum effect as regards contrast, colour and attractiveness with its neighbours.

As it was not possible to arrange all these on the board, those remaining were laid out attractively on a large doily-covered dish and placed to the front left of the board.

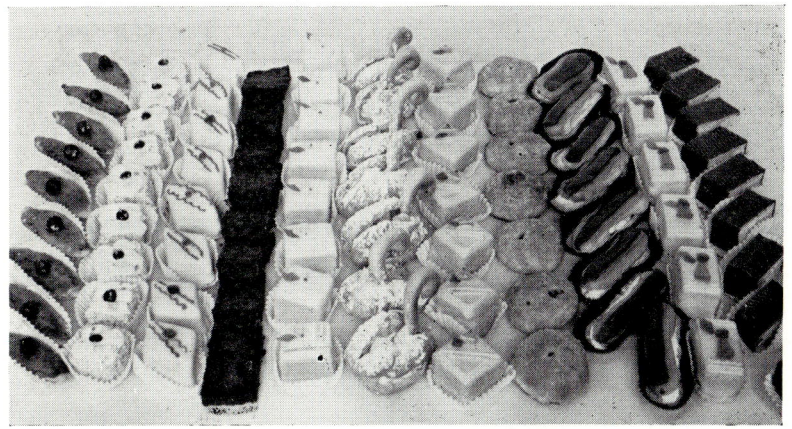

5.7. *A selection of fancies as they could be arranged for a buffet. Note how the odd éclair, slightly out of position, spoils the whole appearance.*

E

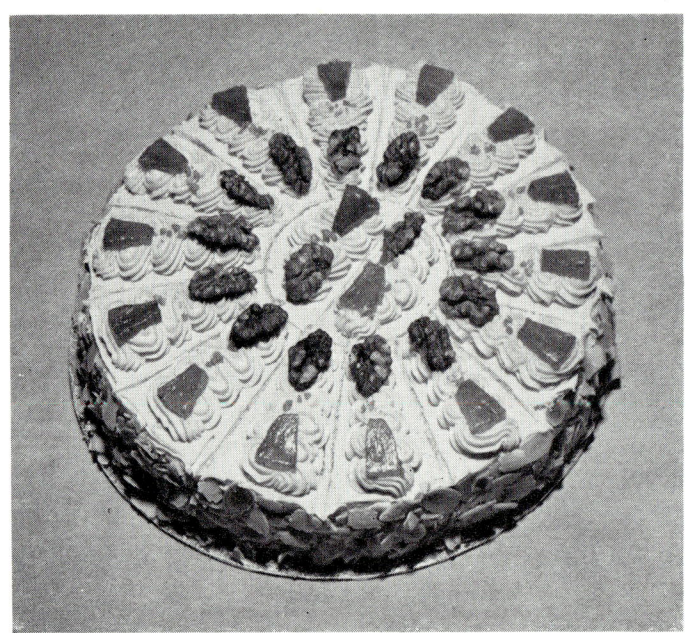

5.8. *Pineapple torte.*

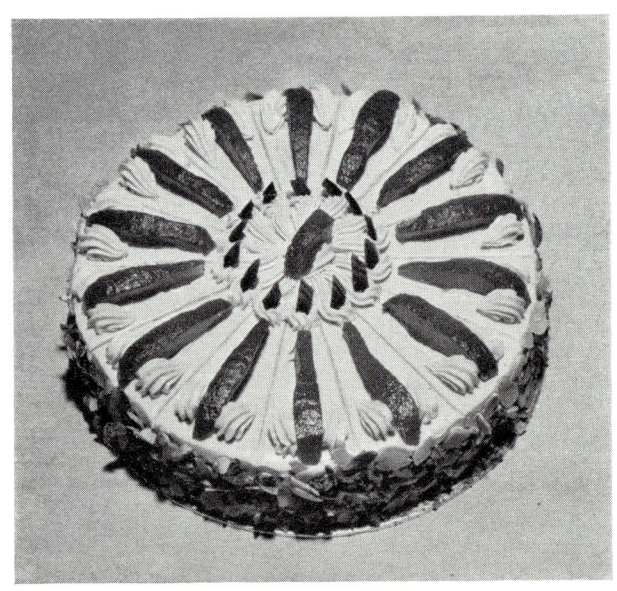

5.9. *Pear torte.*

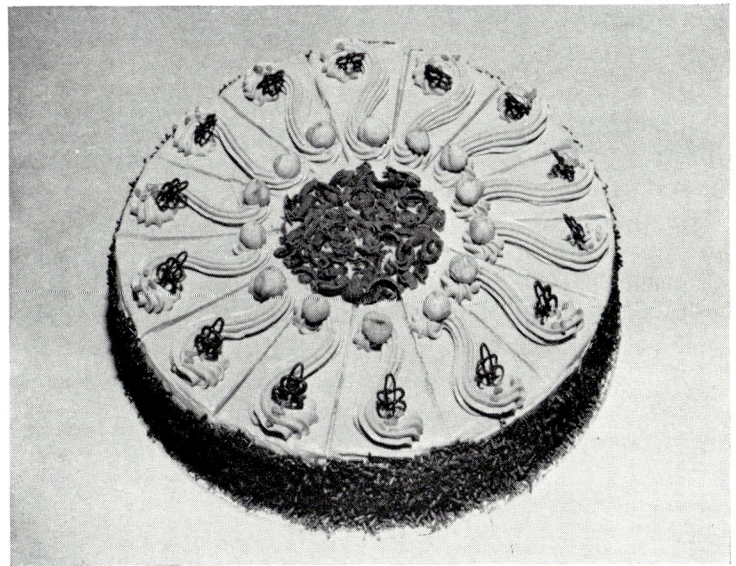

5.10. *Coffee torte.*

Tongue and ham rolls were set out on silver trays and placed respectively left and right of the centre-piece, in front of which stood a large dish holding the bridge pies. Again, in front of this stood a shallow silver tray holding the ham gipfels. A garnish of small sprigs of clean, fresh parsley, to decorate the various savouries, together with the insertion of the buffet flags, completed this section.

Turning to the sweets, the fancies were set out, continental fashion, in neat rows, on the sweet board to balance the open sandwiches, whilst the three gateaux, the rear two being slightly raised, provided the connecting link between savoury and sweet. Two vases of flowers, at the rear and not overhanging the food, completed the setting out.

Illustrations 5.8, 9 and 10 show the different types of gateaux used.

Pineapple Torte

Illustration 5.8 was a pineapple-coloured and -flavoured buttersponge base, split and sandwiched with buttercream flavoured with glacé pineapple syrup and, for contrast, containing a reasonable amount of chopped, ordinary tinned pineapple. The top replaced, it was then masked with the pineapple-flavoured buttercream and the sides with roasted, flaked almonds. Cut into the required number of portions, decoration was completed with a simple scroll of similar cream, segments of glacé pineapple, walnut halves and a pinch of green almond nibs.

Pear Torte

The torte illustrated in Illustration 5.9 utilised crystallised pears, produced as glacé pineapple, with, in this instance, pink colour added to the first sugar boiling. It should be explained that these were ordinary tinned pears, seven boilings being required to bring the fruit to the correct condition.

A plain buttersponge base was used, the pale pink buttercream filling being flavoured with the pear syrup and some of the chopped fruit included. The coloured and flavoured buttercream was used for masking, the sides being covered with a mixture of roasted flake almonds and grated chocolate, prepared with the aid of the coarse section of a household nutmeg grater. After cutting the gateau into segments, decoration was completed with simple scrolls, crystallised pear and angelica.

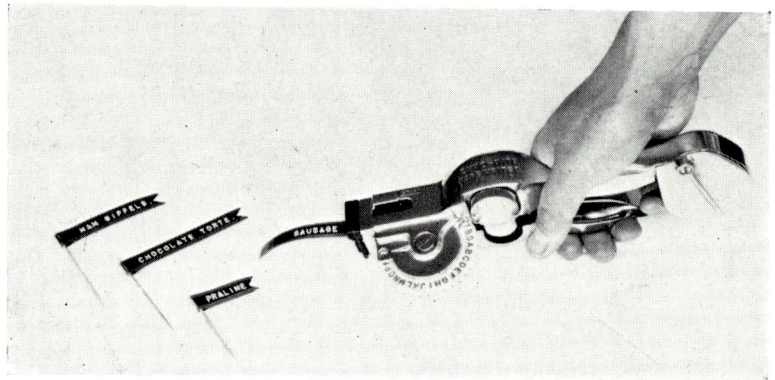

5.11. *The use of a hand embossing machine to produce buffet flags.*

Coffee Torte

The coffee torte (Fig. 5.10) comprised a coffee buttersponge base, a filling of praline- and rum-flavoured buttercream, masking in similar medium, with sides covered with chocolate corallettes. After dividing into segments, with an "S" scroll piped between chocolate and cake edge, a whole roasted hazelnut was placed at the joint between chocolate and cream, and the whole of the centre portion was covered with grated coffee chocolate. Final decoration was a motif, which had been piped in coffee chocolate on to wax paper, allowed to set, lifted with a palette knife and placed in position.

Amongst many items mentioned have been buffet flags.

These may be obtained from the sundries man or wholesale paper merchants, the flag itself being a type of paper, which necessitates a neat writer to give a good effect. The drawback to these is that they may generally be used once only, sufficiently neat hand writers are at a premium and are often not available at the moment required. These points added together make this type of flag quite expensive.

The hand-embossing machines (Illustration 5.11) are, I find, ideal for the job. The rolls of plastic can be obtained in various colours, and, personally, the black, gold edged, appeals to me for its classical simplicity. The tape, when the backing is removed, is self-adhesive and may be fastened round a cocktail stick. A "V" cut may be made at the end of the flag for added gaiety, and the flag may be used many times, just changing the cocktail stick regularly.

Whilst the embossing machine may be considered to be expensive initially, many other uses will be found for it, and here is one small item of equipment that can be thoroughly recommended.

CHAPTER 6

Cocktail Parties and other functions

Comprehensive information on buffets of various sizes and prices having been given, the reader should now be able to use these menus and, by compiling different variations of the items detailed and adding some specialities of his own, will be in a position to accept any buffet order and bring it to a successful conclusion.

Occasionally the confectioner is called upon to cater for cocktail parties, but in the majority of cases the order for a set quantity of the various types of goods is given, the customer often supplying her own service. Or, again, the confectioner may be requested to set out the goods and return later to collect the empties, again supplying no actual service other than this. Should the reader be called upon to perform this service, then it can be done in the manner already described, treating the function as a buffet.

The quantities required will vary considerably with the price per head the customer desires to pay. It may be helpful, however, if a list of goods suitable is given, the reader, in co-operation with the customer, then arranging the menu, or list, required to suit individual needs and tastes.

It should be remembered that a cocktail party is in no way a meal and that the refreshments are generally partaken standing. Therefore, all items should be small and dainty, much thought being given to neatness of finish, and presentation.

Goods Suitable for Cocktail Parties
SAVOURY

Cocktail savouries
Roasted salted whole almonds
Bridge pies
*Cocktail vol-au-vent
*Cocktail sausage rolls
Cheese straws

Ham crescents
Cheese éclairs
Vienna sausage
Cocktail ham and tongue rolls
Cheese mirroars

* The customer should be informed that these articles are only to be recommended if facilities exist where they can be served warm.

SWEET

Petits fours glacés, including
   othellos
Cocktail chocolate éclairs
Swans
Petits choux

Caramel fruits
Marrons glacés
Almond dessert
Small puff mince tarts in season

All the items presented should be small and dainty, but because this is so, the confectioner should not fall into the trap of selling his goods cheaply. Indeed, the saving of actual raw material is infini-

6.1. *Vienna sausages, nicely glazed and ready for display.*

tesimal, but the time taken to produce them is the same as for normal-sized articles—in fact, sometimes greater—in order to ensure the neatness necessary. Costings should, therefore, be gone into very carefully before quoting.

Dealing first with the savouries, an item not previously covered is vienna sausage. These may be purchased already cooked and solid-packed in jelly, the tins varying in size from the "baby", containing 8 to 10 sausages, up to quite large sizes. Hence it is possible to accept quite small orders without undue waste. To prepare, open and re-move from the tin, separating and removing any surplus jelly adher-ing. Spear with a cocktail stick in the centre and immerse in aspic jelly, slightly above setting point, placing the sausage on a wire standing over a suitable tray to collect the drippings. After a few minutes in normal conditions, the jelly will set, when the procedure should be repeated.

The aim should be to achieve a good glaze, yet keeping the amount of jelly to a reasonable thickness.

Set in small chocolate glacine paper cases for despatch and display.

Cocktail Savouries

Whilst many caterers use a variety of bases for these goods, it is all too easy to make the production of them rather a test of endurance. Many times does one see minute bases, heavily over-decorated, often completed with great numbers of spots of piped butter. Set out in a haphazard fashion, they look anything but tempting. Croûte biscuits, produced by the confectioner himself, cut out with several different shapes of cutters, all part of a set, are, I feel, the prerequisite to a set of cocktail savouries that should look very clean, bright, neat, and eminently edible. Whilst one may argue that only one type of base leads to lack of variety, the answer surely lies in the fact that the variety comes from the flavours of the materials placed on the biscuits.

When an order is being produced, it is policy to decide beforehand how many, and in what variety they are to be made. Carefully worked out in this fashion, those produced may be set out in rows upon a tray, as illustrated, ready to be placed directly upon the buffet table.

Croûte Biscuits

These are basically produced from a good quality pie pastry to which a little baking powder has been added, to ease any slight toughening caused during mixing and working off.

The recipe is:

2 lb. flour	$\frac{1}{2}$ oz. baking powder
14 oz. shortening	10 oz. cold water ($\frac{1}{2}$ pint)
$\frac{1}{2}$ oz. salt	

Produce by the rubbing in method.

After mixing, roll out the pastry to about $\frac{1}{16}$–$\frac{1}{8}$ in. thick, dock well with the roller docker, and cut with the appropriate cutter.

Transfer the shapes carefully to a sheet tin covered with greaseproof paper, and allow a period of rest to prevent shrinkage. It is quite often a good plan to produce these the day before they are required, allowing them to stand overnight on the prepared sheet tin. Bake at 450°F and allow to go quite cold before finishing.

In finishing, they are rather like the open sandwiches dealt with previously, for all are buttered lightly. Divide them into the four varieties of meat, fish, cheese, and salad, spreading the meat with

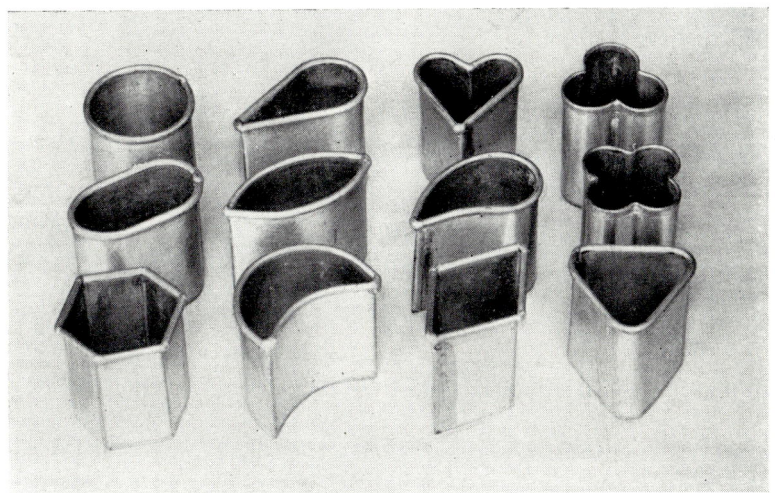

6.2. A set of cutters suitable for croûte biscuits and some types of genoese fancies.

meat paste, fish with fish paste, cheese with cream cheese, and salad left plain.

Whilst only a limited number of varieties may be dealt with here, a short study of the illustrations, in conjunction with the brief explanation, will be sufficient to encourage the reader to create others for himself and further stamp his individuality upon the business.

Oval biscuit

A slice of tongue, not too thinly cut, is cut out by the same oval cutter and placed upon the biscuit. Place two half slices of hard-boiled egg at either end.

Round

Place a $\frac{1}{4}$-in.-thick slice of tomato on the croûte biscuit, together with a small amount of cream cheese. Garnish with a caper.

Oval

Place two whole shrimps on the croûte biscuit, thicker parts to the ends. Complete by piping on a star of mashed potato, previously sieved to pipe smoothly, topping with a very small cube of mashed potato and pinch of clean, fresh parsley.

Oval

Cut out a piece of smoked salmon with an oval cutter the size of the biscuit and place it on the biscuit. Pipe a line of mashed potato along the middle, garnishing with a single garden pea.

Round

Cut a disc of salami with the same size cutter, placing this upon the biscuit. Garnish with a half silverskin onion, and two small sprigs of parsley on either side.

Round

Spread a biscuit liberally with liver sausage, decorate with pieces of lightly fried mushrooms, garnishing with a pinch of parsley.

6.3. Cocktail savouries.

Cheese

Pile grated cheese on to a round biscuit, topping with a reasonable slice of gherkin.

Mushroom

Divide lightly fried, medium sized mushrooms into quarters and place into position on the perimeter of a round biscuit. In the centre place a disc of cooked carrot.

Asparagus

Cut an asparagus tip to the same length as an oval biscuit. Split the asparagus down the centre, placing one portion along the middle of the biscuit. Split, by cutting the remaining asparagus, placing a piece on either side of the centre, garnishing with a slice of tomato, placed over the asparagus "belt" fashion.

6.4. Ready for setting out on the buffet.

Ham

Cut out a circle of ham with the round cutter, placing this upon a round, prepared biscuit. Upon this place a disc of hard-boiled egg, followed by a roasted split almond.

Liver sausage

Spread an oval croûte biscuit with previously sieved liver sausage, bringing this up to pyramid shape. Along the top, using a star tube, pipe liver sausage in a crinkling motion, completing with a sprig of parsley.

6.5. A further range of cocktail savouries.

Completing the Savouries

As each variety is completed, place them upon a draining wire, inserting cocktail sticks in each at an angle of 45 deg. Place the wire upon a four-sided tray and cover each savoury thoroughly with aspic jelly that is almost at setting point. This may be accomplished by using a funnel, a ladle or spoon or, by far the best way I have tried and indeed the quickest, by use of a spray. Before using this, it is advisable to sieve the jelly, but the use of this small item of equipment ensures thorough, yet very thin, glazing.

When all the savouries have been glazed, place them into the refrigerator to set, then re-jelly to ensure that the glaze does, indeed, cover the savoury and to give the necessary sparkle. Even so, it should not leave the goods coated with a thick jelly, which would be unpleasant to eat.

To set them on trays ready for the function, cover each tray with white doilies, or tray papers if these are used, then cover this with a piece of transparent cellulose, cut to the exact size of the tray. Placing the savouries upon this ensures that each may be lifted off cleanly, with no sticking to the tray paper, which would most certainly otherwise occur.

A last word about the jelly. Whilst it is not particularly difficult to produce one's own aspic jelly, it is very very doubtful whether this

6.6. A novel way of presenting cheese and biscuits, especially suitable for a cocktail party. Cut grapefruit in halves, placing two of these, flat side down, on to a papered silver flat tray. Using several varieties of cheese, with cocktail sticks spear cubes of cheese with an assortment of maraschino cherries, segments of pineapple, silverskin onions, pieces of gherkin, etc., arranging for the best effect of colour and flavour. Place into the grapefruit halves, porcupine fashion, until the whole is covered. Into the vacant spaces on the tray arrange suitable biscuits in variety.

is a commercial proposition today, when one can, so easily, purchase the powder, which only requires the addition of water. If this is not available, then a very nicely seasoned pie jelly, provided that it is clear, is quite acceptable.

Roasted Salted Almonds

There are two successful methods to do this, the first being to take the blanched whole, or split almonds and to fry in hot fat or oil, at a temperature of 360°F, to an attractive golden brown. Allow a few moments to drain, dredge with fine dairy salt and rub through the hands to ensure even distribution of salt.

The above method is very satisfactory if one does not have to heat up the pan of fat or oil specially. As an alternative, place the blanched almonds on to a clean marble slab, pour over them a small quantity of fresh egg whites, rubbing through the hands to ensure that all the nuts are coated. Dredge with fine dairy salt, again rub through the hands, and place on to a sheet tin covered with silicone or grease-proof paper. Roast in an oven of 380–400°F to the golden shade that assists in making them so popular, remembering to turn them at intervals to ensure that they neither stick nor take on too much colour.

Caramel Fruits

Here again is a fine opportunity for the confectioner to produce something that is different.

Sugar is boiled in the usual way, taking the normal precautions to prevent graining, to the hard crack, 312°F. Add 1 teaspoonful of glucose at 225°F. Great care must be exercised that the temperature is correct, otherwise instead of the "crack" when consumed, the sugar will be "chewy", thus spoiling the whole effect and, perhaps, causing annoyance to the consumer.

In preparing the sugar, $\frac{1}{2}$ pt of water and 2 lb. sugar is sufficient at any one time. Stand the pan in a bowl of cold water for 10 sec. to prevent the temperature increasing by the latent heat of the pan, dipping as quickly as possible.

Oranges

These should be sound, seedless, and easily peeled, the most satisfactory being mandarins, as this variety is of a suitable size. Peel, separate into segments and remove odd pieces of pith without actually piercing the inner skin. If desired, a "bloom" of carmine colour may be added to one side by using a fine camel-haired brush. Whether or not this latter is done, allow the segments to stand in a dry atmosphere for a few hours.

Prepare the sugar as detailed, remove from the gas and immerse each segment completely in the pan, lift out with a dipping fork and place upright immediately on to a clean marble slab which has been previously rubbed over with beeswax. Should this not be available, treating the slab with pastry margarine or fat will be found quite satisfactory. The dipping fork should not be drawn over the edge of the pan for fear of graining the mass.

Grapes

These may be black or green, or a combination of both. If large, only one is required, but if small, two, joined together by the stalk, should constitute one unit. Leave approximately $\frac{1}{2}$ in. of the stalk in, and immerse in the syrup, leaving a small perimeter round the stalk not coated; afterwards stand immediately on the treated slab. The fruit chosen must, of course, be sound, free from blemish and carefully wiped with a clean, soft cloth.

Strawberries

Choose good, sound fruit of good shape and colour; on no account must the stalk be removed, otherwise the juice of the fruit will very soon have an adverse effect on the caramel. Dry thoroughly with a clean, soft cloth and, holding the stalk with a pair of nippers, immerse in the sugar, leaving the perimeter around the stalk. Set on the slab and allow to cool.

Cherries

Once again, good, clean, sound fruit should be chosen, if possible joined pairs, with stalks left in position. Immerse for a few hours in liqueur brandy, then lay on a clean cloth and place in a warm cupboard for a few hours to dry, before dipping as for grapes.

Prunes

Remove the stones by splitting the fruit lengthwise. Fill the cavity with white marzipan, moulded to the shape of the stone, and press the edges of the fruit together so that the marzipan is clearly visible. Insert a cocktail stick in one end at an angle of 45 deg., immerse in the sugar and stand on the slab until set.

Dates

Using the boxed, dessert variety, the finish here is as given for prunes, in this case using pale green, maraschino-flavoured green marzipan.

6.7. *Grapes and oranges.*

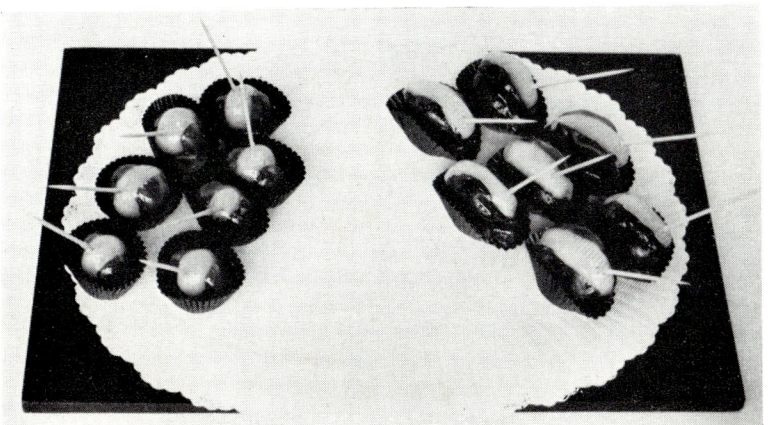

6.8. *Glacé cherries and prunes.*

6.9. *Dates and walnuts.*

6.10. Caramel fruits set out ready for the buffet.

Walnuts

Pair sufficient walnut halves, choosing each individually for size, colour and shape. Taking a piece of marzipan, coloured either neutral, pale green or pink, and, using a piece slightly larger in size than a cherry, mould it round and place it between the two walnut halves, pressing each together to adhere until the marzipan is pressed to the size of the nuts. Insert a cocktail stick into the marzipan at the correct angle, immerse in the sugar, and set on to the prepared slab to cool.

Glacé Cherries

Using glacé cherry halves, the method of finish is similar to that given for walnuts. Use neutral-coloured marzipan, well flavoured with kirsch, and in this case the marzipan should be larger than the cherries, flattened slightly on the bottom to allow the finished article to set, without rolling, after dipping.

After the goods are complete, set them in small chocolate glacine paper cases, packing in varieties in rows on a board, separating each row with tissue paper to prevent rolling during transit.

Marrons Glacés

These are, of course, crystallised chestnuts, and although they may be satisfactorily prepared by "rule of thumb" and experience, the use of a saccharometer is to be recommended.

The first rule for success is to restrict the boilings to fairly small

6.11. *Marrons glacé, which would be placed into chocolate glacine paper cases before display.*

numbers. Remove the outer skin of the nuts without cutting the kernel, and cook gently in water until reasonably soft, but do not overcook or they will break up and become useless for this particular purpose. When cooked as indicated, remove from the water, strain, and cover with fresh boiling water. Remove a few nuts at a time from the water and, while still hot, lift away the second skin, using a small knife.

Prepare a pan of hot sugar syrup to give a saccharometer reading of 16 deg., drop in the nuts and allow to simmer very gently for 15 min., adding one or two vanilla beans to the syrup. Remove the syrup from the gas, and, after cooling, lift out the nuts, placing them on to a

6.12. *Pulled-sugar basket, the ideal centre piece for sweets.*

F

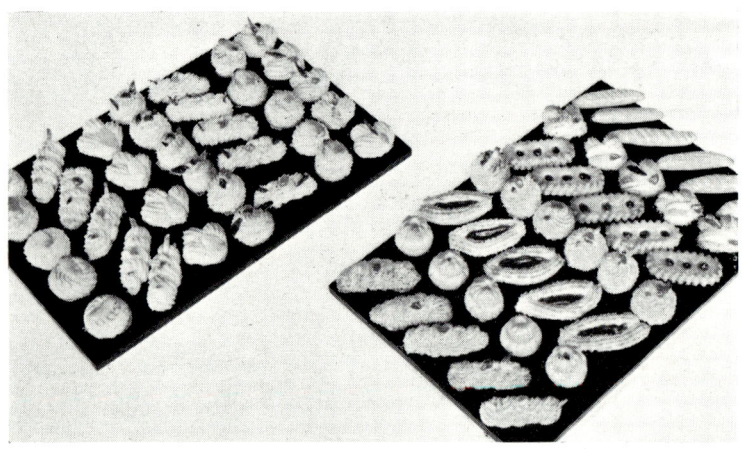

6.13. *Parisian rout biscuits, ever popular in an assortment of almond dessert.*

draining wire until next day; reboil in the syrup for four of five consecutive days, or until the saccharometer gives a reading of 36 deg., removing from the syrup to a draining wire after each boiling. Stored in air-tight jars, the nuts will keep indefinitely, whilst any that have become broken during the process may be crushed up and used as a flavouring for buttercream.

To prepare for the table, boil up a clear syrup containing a vanilla bean to 235°F. Grain by rubbing a little of the sugar on the side of the pan with the spatula, scrape into the syrup and stir. Drop in a few nuts at a time, lift clear and lay on to draining wires. Stand at the mouth of a drying oven for a few minutes, when the nuts should be coated with a clear, dry sugar. Set in small chocolate glacine paper cases, the goods are ready to take their place on the table.

The process may appear long and complicated. This is not the case, for in reality all these things are, with ordinary care, simple to do. The goods readily command a good price, lift a business clear of competitors, and give that individuality which alone will bring in more custom.

Almond Dessert

This term can be used to describe quite a large variety of small almond biscuits such as Dutch macaroons and Parisian rout biscuits, etc., which are always popular at a cocktail party. Whilst they command a good price at any time, it is perhaps for functions of this type that these goods really come into their own.

Parisian Rout Biscuits

1 lb. ground almonds	7½ oz. egg whites
1 lb. castor sugar	Egg colour and vanilla essence

Mix the dry ingredients, afterwards adding the remainder to produce a fairly stiff paste but one which can be piped reasonably from an ordinary large star tube No. 15. Fit this into a plain savoy tube, in a savoy bag and pipe the paste on to a greased and lightly-floured sheet tin, or wafer paper.

These biscuits may take a variety of shapes such as scrolls, fleurs-de-lis, whirls, stars, etc., and may be of very small size or, alternatively, if for use at a cocktail party, piped rather larger to the size of a half-penny, when the shapes may take various animal forms, using both star and plain tube.

Decorate the biscuits with split, strip and nib almonds, small pieces of walnut, cherries, angelica, and, if animals are produced, currants to represent the eyes. Allow to stand overnight in the bakery rack in order to take on a dry skin, when the biscuits are ready to flash in an oven of 500°F, the sheet tin being placed on wires or upturned sheet tins to prevent undue bottom heat. Immediately on withdrawal from the oven, brush over with a gum-arabic solution.

Buffet Afternoon Tea

One other type of cold-meal catering that the confectioner may be called upon to cater for is the buffet afternoon tea, these orders usually coming from women's organisations, who often like to round off a meeting with afternoon tea.

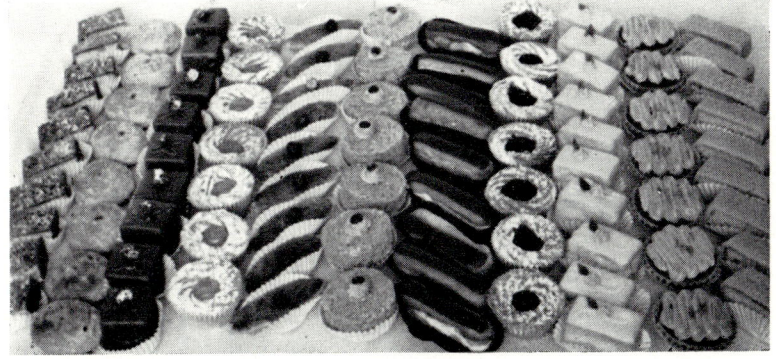

6.14. *An assortment of fancies with a wide range of flavours, suitable for afternoon tea.*

Generally the caterer is only called upon to deliver the goods, the women supplying their own service, but the beverage itself may have to be delivered ready to serve. In this case, it is a simple matter to make this in the bakery in an urn, remove the infuser at the required strength, and supply the milk and sugar separately, for adding as required.

Alternatively, the tea may be supplied in the dry state for the women to produce when required. As in the case of the cocktail party, no hard and fast rules can be laid down as regards menus, so a list of goods suitable is given; the caterer then, in consultation with the customer, is able to devise a menu to satisfy particular requirements.

Brown and white bread and butter
Various filled finger rolls
Continental ham gipfels
Cheese mirroars
Bridge pork pies
Plain and currant tea scones, buttered
Cherry scones, buttered

Sweet pikelets, buttered
Sweet cakes
Fancies
Cream sandwiches—cut
Victoria sandwiches—cut
Gateaux—various
Individual sherry trifles
Tea

Let us turn for a moment to a variety of savoury rolls suitable for buffets, evening refreshments or, in some cases, afternoon tea or children's parties.

It has always been the author's experience that, in any type of catering, the unusual article is the one which, if correctly made and properly presented, brings forth favourable comment and further orders. Hence careful thought should be given to the type of bread used. As the production of sandwiches is within everyone's possibility, I would immediately discard the idea of normal sandwich bread as being too ordinary, and decide upon either:

(a) Finger or bread rolls;
(b) Croissants, baked straight instead of crescent-shaped;
(c) Brioche, baked finger-shaped.

It will be assumed that in all cases the reader will cut and butter the rolls chosen in the normal way, taking every care to remove any butter smears with either cloth or tissue paper before serving.

Smoked salmon.—The fish should be sliced very thinly and cut into the shape of the roll.

Fresh or tinned salmon.—Fish in either of these two forms may be used as follows: remove any skin or bones and mash, together with a small amount of mayonnaise. Season very carefully with a small amount of cayenne pepper and pass through a fine sieve. If many are to be produced and time is an important factor, sufficient creamed butter can be added, thus saving the task of buttering the rolls.

Potted lobster.—Remove all sinews from the required amount of fish. Mash to a smooth paste and add a pinch of nutmeg, cayenne pepper, a little anchovy essence and 6 oz. creamed butter to 1¼ lb. fish. Mix all well and pass through a fine sieve. If not for immediate use, level off in suitable dishes and spread a thin layer of creamed butter on the top to prevent crusting. Store in suitable conditions.

Potted beef.—Using steak or beef of reasonable quality, remove all fat and gristle, dice, and place into a suitable pan. Cover with cold water, add a little salt and pepper, allowing to simmer until thoroughly cooked, by which time the liquid should be reduced to a small quantity, though sufficient should remain to moisten the finished product.

Add a pinch of mace and nutmeg, a spot of pink colour and a little blackjack to give a rich brown colour. Pass twice through a mincer fitted with the smallest plate. After the second time, add a little of the gravy as required until the mixture is quite soft, adjust seasoning as necessary and fill into shallow dishes. When cold, layer very thinly with creamed butter or margarine, using a suitable knife, and store until required in a refrigerator.

If desired, this may be cheapened by the addition of a small amount of fine rusk, added when the meat is cooked. To ensure that this does not sour, the mixture should be left on a low light and stirred constantly until it returns to the boil. If this commodity is exposed for retail sale and the latter course adopted, then care should be taken that the amount of filler does not infringe any of the pure food laws.

Potted veal and ham.—Though a little expensive, this is worth the trouble involved. Using two parts of veal to one part gammon, dice and place into a suitable pan with sufficient stock to cover, add a very small amount of butter and a pinch of mace, allowing to simmer gently until tender.

Drain off the liquor and pass twice through the mincer, again using the fine plate. Next add a small amount of melted butter, a little of the stock as required, seasoning as necessary, and a pinch of nutmeg, proceeding then as for potted beef.

The remarks concerning filler also apply here.

Shrimp.—Mash the required number of shrimps to a smooth paste with a little cayenne pepper, a spot of anchovy essence and a small amount of butter, colouring a pale pink. If desired, a sprinkling of mustard and cress may be added.

Sardine.—Prepare the butter for the rolls by adding to it a little chopped parsley, a little finely chopped onion and a spot of lemon juice. Complete with either whole or mashed sardines and, if desired, a sprinkling of mustard and cress may be added.

Chicken.—Three methods are possible here. The first is the normal one whereby the chicken is placed between the roll, and spread thinly with stuffing.

The second method is to prepare the filling by chopping the chicken and adding it to cooked, chopped mushrooms. Coat the whole with a thick white sauce, and use when cold. It should, perhaps, be stressed that a minimum of white sauce be used, otherwise it will tend to turn the roll soggy.

The final method is to chop the chicken again, and mix with finely chopped gherkins, seasoning as necessary.

Anchovy.—As the flavour of this fish is not welcomed by all palates, it is perhaps wiser to use the potted anchovy. To this should be added a filling of mustard and cress.

Potted foie gras.—Remove from the container, add a little butter, blend well together and season to taste.

Tongue.—Mix a little mustard with the butter used for spreading, slice the tongue and cut to the shape of the roll.

Beef.—To the butter used for spreading, once again add mustard and a little washed and finely grated horse-radish. Slice the beef thinly, and cut to the shape of the roll.

Cucumber.—Peel and slice thinly the amount required, place in a suitable dish, add a sprinkling of salt and pepper, and allow to stand for an hour or so. Drain well, and use on the buttered rolls, having first added a little lemon juice to the butter prior to spreading.

Mustard and cress.—Wash, pick and dry the mustard and cress, then add to the prepared rolls. On the top of the cress add a sprinkling of finely chopped, seasoned, hard-boiled egg.

Tomato.—Add a little chopped parsley to the butter, and prepare sufficient sound tomatoes by removing the stalks and steeping the fruit in boiling water for a few minutes. Skin with a knife, and slice thinly, afterwards laying the slices in a dish with a few slices of onion, seasoning, and a little vinegar. Leave for half an hour or so, drain and use.

To these varieties may be added ham gipfels.

Outdoor Functions

The final type of cold-meal catering to mention is that of the outdoor function, such as agricultural shows, garden fêtes, carnivals, etc., where the caterer is expected to recoup his costs on the spot.

For the caterer in a smaller way of business, I would most strongly advise him to reject such an approach without hesitation, for the dice are far too heavily loaded against him.

To start with, the vagaries of an English summer are only too well known to mention. It is possible, I know, to take out an insurance policy against this contingency, but the premiums required are generally sufficiently high to prove an obstacle, for, even if given good weather, they would take too large a slice from the net profit.

There is the matter of quantities to be considered and the question of selling points, usually quite numerous, each of which would require a thoroughly honest, competent and reliable person to deal with the cash taken. As, generally, the smaller caterer has not sufficient people of this calibre within his orbit, this can be a real headache.

Finally, there is the matter of the equipment to be considered, of which much would probably have to be hired, with the consequent loss by breakage and pilfering.

This type of catering is much better left to the larger firm, the smaller man sticking to functions where he is given a definite number on which to base his charge; where he can show his craftsmanship by producing the "different" article, and where there is every prospect of him showing a credit balance at the end.

CHAPTER 7

Hot Meals and Dinner-Dances

This type of catering calls for very much more care in timing than that for cold meals, for the food has to be placed before the guest hot and in prime condition. We have all experienced tepid meals, supposedly "hot", and that is sufficient in itself to lose further orders for a caterer. Again, whilst it may be excusable for the guests to be late, the caterer must always be punctual, so a degree of elasticity must always exist in the organisation to allow for such an occurrence.

As with cold meals, the caterer will be called upon to cater at a variety of venues, many of which will be quite unsuitable for the whole production of the meal. Therefore, many of the menus published in this section will bear that fact in mind, using, for instance, cold sweets in some that may be wholly produced in the bakery and thus ready for serving without further attention.

Now to equipment: before quoting and submitting specimen menus, it is advisable that the confectioner should visit the venue and inspect personally the facilities offered. By "inspect" is meant to probe into everything, light oven gases, test gas and electric burners, etc., to ensure that everything really does work, rather than merely rely upon the caretaker's opinion, who, quite often, has no conception of what is required.

This latter point can be well illustrated by a personal experience of the writer who was on one occasion called upon to cater for a hot meal at a hall possessing six very large and efficient-looking gas stoves. Another person had been assured that these were "wonderful," but on the night of the function with work commencing, it was discovered that many of the top burners were useless. By dint of improvisation, the meal was served to time and brought to a successful conclusion, but it is not an experience that the writer would like repeated.

For regular catering for hot meals, such items of equipment as hot cupboards and portable ovens may be purchased, but for one just taking up this work the hire of these is to be recommended when, as trade justifies the outlay, they may be purchased later. Again,

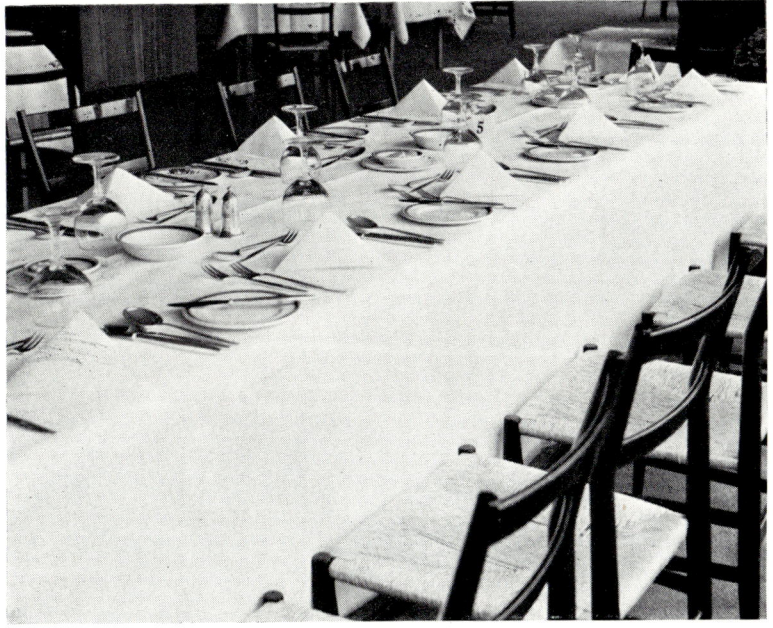

7.1. *The tables set, awaiting floral decorations.*

experience will soon show what types and size of equipment are most needed and in what order they should be purchased.

In deciding sizes, it should be borne in mind that these have to be transported, and, in many instances, have to be carried up several or, quite often, a flight of stairs.

If the equipment is hired, then the reader should ensure that the necessary gas or power points, with correct fittings or plugs, are available. These details may seem elementary to mention, but they are easily overlooked and can make a vast difference to the smooth running of the organisation.

More crockery, cutlery and general utensils are required than with cold meals, and the confectioner should decide if the main courses are to be plate or tureen service. In either case, for a function of any size, plate hoops will be required to allow the plates to be stacked during the serving and thus assist in keeping the food hot. Provision will, of course, be made to ensure that the plates are really piping hot before serving begins.

The actual laying of the tables and floral arrangements may be done as described in the "Cold Meals" chapter, although no food apart from bread or rolls and the first course, if cold, will be set, whilst the actual layout of the tables should be done with an eye to cutting the distance, as far as possible, between the kitchen and tables.

In computing costs, any hire charges should be taken into consideration when quoting: it should be borne in mind that quite often more transport is required—an expensive item.

In some instances it may be that the venue is sufficiently close to the bakery for the entire cooking to be done there, using the special Thermos containers for transporting it, whilst soup, for instance, may be made and transferred to a preheated urn. If, after use, this is well scalded and washed out thoroughly with a good detergent, finally rinsing well, no after taste will be apparent.

Hygiene is an aspect that needs very careful watching, for an outbreak of food poisoning following a function can be disastrous. If the meat, for instance, is precooked and refrigerated to allow ease of carving, later to be reheated in gravy for serving hot, then the most stringent precautions must be taken to ensure that a sufficiently high temperature is reached and maintained for long enough to kill any bacteria.

No hard-and-fast rules can be laid down, for every venue will differ in layout and facilities offered, but if properly organised by the person in charge and staff responding to good leadership, there is no reason why every job tackled should not be a resounding success. One caterer I know, a week before every hot meals function, sits down quietly and draws up a time-table, together with a van loading list, of the day each particular job is to be done. This is an idea I can wholeheartedly commend.

As with cold meals, the caterer should be given a guaranteed number two or three days beforehand, and the menu, previously arranged, set and permitting of no alternatives during the meal.

MENU 1

Tomato soup	Petits pois
Spring chicken	Carrots
Bread sauce and stuffing	Vacherin
Pommes croquette	Cheese and biscuits
Pommes à la maison	Coffee

TOMATO SOUP

Allow 6 oz. per guest. Using medium-sized vegetables, take three each of onions, carrots and turnips, slice, and with a little chopped ham place in a suitable pan with 3 oz. of butter and a few sprigs of parsley. Place the pan on a medium gas, stir for approximately 10 min., then adding 3 qt of good stock and 15 ripe tomatoes of average size. Allow the whole to boil gently for approximately 2 hr, afterwards passing through a fine sieve. Return to the pan, season, adding if desired a little pink colour and very small amount of castor sugar, thickening with a little roux if required.

Bread, in the form of fancy-shaped dinner cobs, should be served, allowing 10 per cent extra for those guests requesting a second one.

SPRING CHICKEN

If of the normal small plump variety, they should be nicely roasted to a golden brown, with one chicken between two guests, served on the bone.

BREAD SAUCE

Allow 1 oz. per guest. To 1 qt of fresh milk add a small, whole onion and bring to the boil. Add 4 to 6 oz. of bread crumbs, depending upon the consistency required, and allow to simmer gently for 10 minutes. Remove the onion, add 2 oz. butter, stirring well in and season to taste.

STUFFING

Again allow 1 oz. of stuffing per head.

1 lb. 8 oz. chopped onions; boil until tender, strain, and add to
2 lb. 4 oz. breadcrumbs
1 oz. powdered sage ⎫
1 oz. rubbed thyme ⎬ or to taste
8 oz. egg
10 oz. ($\frac{1}{2}$ pt) milk (approx.)
8 oz shredded suet
$\frac{1}{2}$ oz. baking powder
Season to taste

Mix all well together, using some of the onion water also if required, place into a suitable tin containing a little hot dripping, afterwards baking at 400°F until the top is crisp and brown.

POTATOES

It will be noticed that two varieties are featured in this menu, but a total allowance of 10 oz. per guest, unpeeled, should be made, which should allow approximately 8 oz. cooked per head. They should then be divided equally for the two varieties.

POMMES CROQUETTE

For these, the potatoes should be boiled with seasoning in the normal way, care being exercised that they are not allowed to fall.

Strain very thoroughly, replace on the gas for a few moments without lid to dry, place in a machine bowl fitted with beater, and beat well to mash smoothly, afterwards allowing to go cold.

To make up, add a little melted butter and milk or cream, with sufficient egg to bind, again beating smooth. Mould to a rope of 1-in. thickness, cut into $2\frac{1}{2}$-in. lengths, wash with egg and roll in either breadcrumbs or fine rusk, finally frying in fat or cooking oil at 360°F as for doughnuts. Serve hot, either dry or with brown gravy. For outside catering, all the initial preparation may, of course, be carried out in the bakery, transporting on greaseproof-papered boards, the frying being done at the venue.

POMMES A LA MAISON

Again, boil in the normal way with seasoning, taking care that the potatoes do not fall. Strain, replace on the gas without lid for a few moments to dry. Transfer to a well-warmed machine bowl and beater, add butter and cream, with a little baking powder to lighten, and beat well, adding further seasoning if required. Serve with an automatic ice cream spoon.

PETITS POIS

Quite a wide choice exists here, using fresh, tinned, dried or frozen peas, all of which are suitable if correctly handled.

Put the prepared peas into a pan with sufficient boiling water to cover. Add sprigs of mint and parsley, one small onion, a little salt, sugar and butter. Allow only to simmer until cooked, for, if allowed to boil, the peas will "shell". When cooked, strain off the liquid and add a little melted butter to glaze, allowing $1\frac{1}{2}$ to 2 oz. per guest.

CARROTS

Allow $2\frac{1}{2}$ oz., unpeeled, per head. Peel, cut into even size, and boil until tender, with sufficient salt and a little sugar. When cooked, chop slightly, once again using a little melted butter to glaze.

VACHERIN

One of 12 in. diameter should yield 20 servings.

Quantities for cheese and biscuits and coffee were fully dealt with in the Cold Meals Chapter.

STAFF

What of staff for serving this menu? Depending upon the facilities available, one waitress would be required for each 8 to 10 guests, with one person to assist in the kitchen for each 30 guests, once again depending upon facilities available, and the amount of cooking being done upon the premises.

Thus for a function serving 100 people, a minimum of 13 people, excluding the person in charge, would be required. These figures should be taken as a maximum, for quite often a small, well-trained staff can perform wonders, but guests should not be kept waiting unduly between courses. Neither should any hint of rush and bustle behind the scenes be apparent.

The waitresses would first serve the soup, and as each finished her particular section of the table, would withdraw to the kitchen to assist in setting out the main course, leaving one on duty to attend to any unforeseen circumstance.

The setting out of the main course on to the hot plates should be on the basis of one person, one job, with each plate being filled in a clean manner, keeping the different foods separate. Then, using plate hoops, they may be stacked on the hotplate to await service. On a signal from the waitress on duty, the soup plates should be collected by a few of the waitresses, leaving the remainder to set out as long as possible, so that, by the time the soup plates have been removed, the setting out of the main course is practically completed.

With the main course served, then, a short breathing space is found to prepare the sweet, cheese, biscuits, and coffee ready for serving.

Autumn is the time of the year when enquiries are received for hot meals to be served prior to, and after, Christmas. These functions mainly take the form of annual dinner-dances, and an organisation having received previous satisfaction may be expected to return to the caterer they know.

It has been my experience that on occasions an organisation, whilst having been satisfied previously, will, on account of price, accept a lower tender. An occurrence such as this, however, should not unduly disturb the caterer provided he is happy in the knowledge that the service and food he has provided are second to none, and that no competitor can give greater value for money than he does.

Then, such an occurrence can prove a blessing in disguise, for all too often does the competitor fail to measure up to your previous high standard. Thus, in retrospect, does the previous function at which you catered take on a new and greatly enhanced prestige, with the consequence that, when the matter of a further order is under discussion, the decision on who shall have the order is unanimous. Provided the caterer is giving the utmost possible value in service and food, yet bearing in mind that a function should be profitable to himself, he can be assured of annual repeat orders.

For enquiries during this season a number of menus can be submitted for consideration. There should not be any hesitation in

7.2. *Ideas for very simple Christmas table decoration. This particular one, illustrated in stages, is produced from cork bark, modelling paste, flower light candles, ribbon, and fresh or imitation holly. Extra effect may be obtained by the careful use of clear gum and glitter.*

including one of reasonable proportions, presenting a festive appearance. With the function being in the nature of an annual affair, and each guest being responsible for buying his own ticket, it is usually found that purse strings are slightly loosened, for, unlike a wedding reception, the account does not have to be met out of one pocket. Again, the type of meal visualised by many of the guests will be as may be served at a good-class hotel.

Whilst the facilities for the caterer may not always exist to come up to this standard, it should always be his aim to match it. With alert minds and sharp eyes to improvisation, a really good team, all pulling together, can perform miracles and thus give satisfaction all round.

Careful thought should be given to table decoration, remembering full well that Christmas is a time of gaiety. Therefore, no detail should be neglected that will give a warm, bright and cheerful welcome to the guests. Holly and mistletoe may be utilised as table decorations, and, so far as expense will permit, a profusion of candles, with red satin, helps to create the necessary atmosphere.

Indeed, the writer well remembers one such occasion when the Christmas puddings were carried into the hall in procession by the waitresses, each pudding "fired" with spirits provided by the organisers, the only light being that from the candles provided as table decoration.

This touch was one talked about for long afterwards by the guests, and brought much favourable publicity.

7.3. This one utilises bark, candles, live holly, pine cones and crackers.

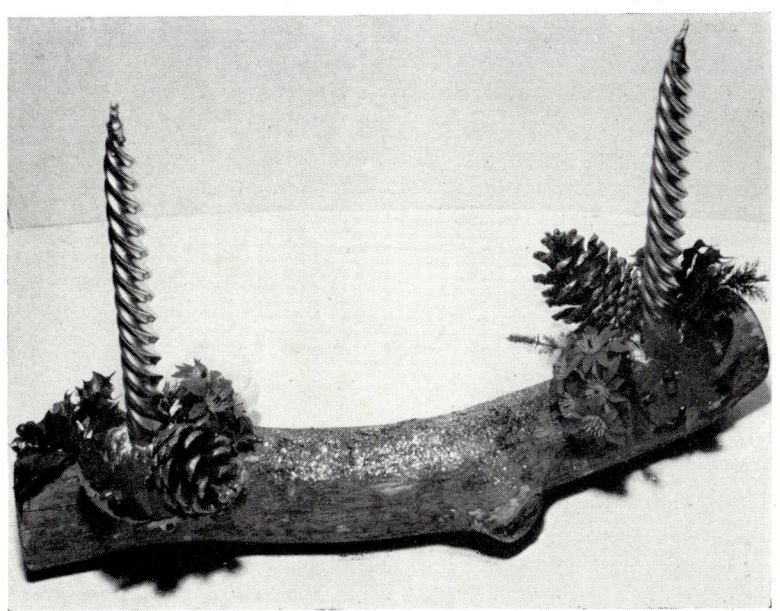

7.4. A larger Christmas table decoration that could also be used as a centre piece for a small buffet.

MENU 2

Hors-d'oeuvre	Pommes à la maison
Soup (fancy-shaped dinner	Carrots
cobs—110 per cent)	Sprouts
Turkey, sage and onion	Plum pudding
stuffing	Rum sauce
Pork and apple sauce	Cheese, biscuits, and celery
Roast potatoes	Coffee

At first sight, this menu may appear formidable to tackle in outside catering, but let us break it down, course by course, and see how the preparation and cooking of it may be accomplished.

The first course of hors-d'oeuvre may be entirely prepared in the bakery, transporting these in suitable containers to the venue, there to be set out on the dishes.

Similarly may the soup be made "at home", transporting this in a pre-heated urn, as described previously.

The poultry and meat may be pre-cooked, along with the stuffing and apple sauce, whilst the mashed potatoes may be cooked in the bakery and transported in the special, pre-heated containers. This may also apply to the carrots and sprouts, though, preferably, these latter should be cooked at the venue to prevent the sogginess which does become apparent if they are confined in steam for any length of time.

The roast potatoes may be part boiled, strained well and roasted at the venue, for these, if not fresh from the oven, do soon become soggy, which is something to avoid. If, however, the venue is within reasonable travelling distance of the bakery and a hot cupboard is available, they can be cooked, the fat strained off, and the potatoes immediately transported to the venue and, ultimately, to the hot cupboard.

The rum sauce, again, can be transported in the special containers, whilst the puddings may be subjected to the final boilings in the afternoon, removed from the water in the bakery and taken, while still hot, to have the boiling completed in the preparation room, which will not occupy valuable gas and heating rings for very long.

Similarly may two urns be employed, one for coffee and one for milk. Working on these lines a minimum of cooking utensils is needed at the hall, and as every caterer will readily agree, these tasks are much more easily accomplished in the familiar surroundings of the "home" bakery, where utensils are to hand and any improvisation needed is easier to accomplish.

However such a menu is tackled, it should be borne in mind that the battle to get the food to the guest piping hot and in prime condition is a never-ending one; if the caterer can accomplish it he is well on the road to success. Should this battle be lost, then all his efforts have been in vain.

Hors-d'oeuvre

These comprise a variety of savouries, a very small amount of any particular one only being served, as they are intended to whet the appetite. They are usually served on a small plate to the guest's choice from the hors-d'oeuvre dish.

This latter may be round or oval and segmented, although many caterers have now dispensed with this and use instead a 14-in. or 16-in. round dish, using sticks of celery to separate the varieties. I much prefer the conventional segmented dish as being neater of appearance and more appropriate, the other idea savouring rather too much of "make do and mend".

Alternatively, they may be displayed in plastic dishes and transported to the guests via trolley.

VIENNA SAUSAGE

Empty sufficient vienna sausage from tins and slice into $\frac{1}{4}$-in. discs. Prepare aspic jelly at double strength and, just prior to setting point, pour over the prepared sausage, making certain that each segment is thoroughly coated. Set out in one section of the dish, garnish with a little chopped parsley, and allow three segments to each guest.

SMOKED SALMON

Slice smoked salmon very thinly and place on thin oval croûte biscuits, previously buttered. Lay upon clean, fresh, dry lettuce leaves on the dish and allow one per guest.

TOMATO WITH ANCHOVY

Slice small, round tomatoes $\frac{1}{4}$-in. thick. Lay in a dish and sprinkle with salad oil, vinegar, salt and pepper. Allow to stand for half-an-hour or so before placing each disc upon a round, buttered croûte biscuit. Place a rolled fillet of anchovy on the top and garnish with grated hard-boiled egg, allowing one per guest.

CHICKEN

Spread buttered, oval-shaped croûte biscuits with finely chopped chicken in tartare sauce, garnishing with a strip of tomato and half a stuffed olive. To make tartare sauce, place the raw yolks of three eggs in a basin with a little pepper, salt and mustard. Stir quickly with a

G

wooden spatula or whisk, adding a few drops of salad oil at a time at first until the mixture begins to thicken, then it can be added in larger quantities.

When the desired consistency has been reached, add a little vinegar and lemon juice, finally adjusting the seasoning as required. Allow one per guest.

SARDINE

Lay a sardine on to a small piece of buttered toast cut to the same size and shape, allowing one each.

BEANS

These are simply baked beans in tomato sauce to which a little chopped ham and parsley have been added. Allow one teaspoonful per guest.

STUFFED OLIVES

Butter round croute biscuits, afterwards spreading with anchovy paste. Place on the top stuffed olives and garnish with grated hard-boiled whole egg.

PRAWNS

Chop lettuce very finely and add some salad cress. Mix with mayonnaise and heap on to a buttered oval croute biscuit. Place two prawns on top and decorate with diced beetroot and cucumber. Allow one for each guest.

POTATO SALAD

The method of producing this is given in Chapter 2. Add to it a little chopped parsley and allow one teaspoonful for each guest.

SILVERSKIN ONIONS

Allow one per guest.

SALAMI

Small squares of thinly sliced salami are served with finely chopped pickled gherkin.

CELERY

Lay sufficient discs of celery hearts on to the dishes, pipe on a whirl of mashed, sieved potato, garnished with a pinch of parsley and a green pea.

Although a dozen varieties of hors-d'oeuvre are mentioned, very many more are possible, and working on the lines given it should be possible for the reader to produce his own varieties and, if these often feature in his menus, prevent choice from becoming stereotyped. Using such items as liver pâté with truffles, tongue sausage, liver sausage, Lyons and German sausage, with a variety of pickles, chutneys, vegetables and salads he can produce endless variety.

For any menu a variety of eight or nine should be sufficient, each waitress being equipped with the various types of servers required, whilst knives and forks are, of course, necessary for the guests.

The quantities of soup are as previously detailed, and this may be tomato or green-pea soup.

Put 8 lb. of well-soaked green peas, half a dozen sprigs of fresh or 2 oz. dried mint, a large bunch of well-chopped parsley and 2 lb. chopped onions into $10\frac{1}{2}$ pt of boiling stock and allow to simmer. When the peas are cooked, strain, place the strainings into a machine bowl and beat together, afterwards returning to the stock, stirring constantly.

When thoroughly mixed, pass through a fine sieve, heat, season to taste and add $\frac{3}{4}$ pt fresh cream. If the colour is not as required, add a little green colour. Care should be taken with the types of bone used in the preparation of the stock. Ham bones, for instance, are often extremely salt and can easily spoil the soup.

TURKEY

Much will, of course, depend on the type available, but as a general guide an allowance of 5 to 6 oz. dressed, uncooked weight per guest should suffice to allow approximately 2 oz. meat per head. The turkey should be well washed and dried, a little butter, lard or dripping rubbed in, rashers of fat bacon placed on top and roasted until tender, the usual 20 min. per pound plus 20 min. over in an oven of 370 to 400°F, depending on the size of the birds, generally being a good guide.

If being cooked the day before the function, allow to cool before placing in the refrigerator. Carve as previously described for chicken and when required lay in slices in a suitable dish, cover with a cold, fairly thin gravy or stock and, when reheating, observe most stringently the rules to prevent the development of bacteria and, in consequence, possible food poisoning.

PORK

The above remarks apply particularly to this commodity. Loin is usually leaner than leg, but rather more difficult to carve. Leg, therefore, is preferred, and this should be boned by the butcher, stringing if necessary and tucking the "tail" well in before cooking. An allowance of 2 to $2\frac{1}{2}$ oz. raw meat per head should be made, which, after allowing one-third loss in cooking and a loss in carving, should give each guest 1 to $1\frac{1}{4}$ oz.

To cook, place the legs in suitable tins or bowls, salt the scored rind to crisp, place a little fat on the top and cook for the first half-hour at 500 to 520°F to crisp and seal.

Turn down the heat and allow the oven temperature to drop gradually to 320°F, allowing again 20 min. to the pound, plus 20 min. extra on the total, but testing with a fork at the end of the period to make certain that it is thoroughly cooked and tender.

Remove from the oven and pour the fat into a bowl, allowing this to set. The dripping can then be lifted off and used, in part, to produce pie pastry, etc., whilst the jelly remaining can be used towards the stock or making gravy.

POTATOES

Once again, allow 10 oz., unpeeled, per head, dividing these equally into two and preparing the *pommes à la maison* as previously described.

The roast potatoes may, as mentioned, be part-boiled before roasting, but whether this method is adopted or not they should be placed in a suitable roasting tin containing a little hot fat, which may take the form of lard, dripping or compound. Salt lightly and place in an oven of 380 to 430°F, the lower temperature being necessary if the potatoes have not been part boiled. Roast to an appetising golden brown, turning half-way during the cooking.

Carrots have also been previously dealth with.

Allow 2 to 3 oz. sprouts, as purchased, for each guest, depending upon the waste that may be expected. Trim off outer leaves, wash thoroughly and boil in the usual manner, straining well and drying off before serving.

Allow 1 oz. each of stuffing and apple sauce per guest.

Christmas Pudding

A fine opportunity for advertisement occurs here for the confectioner who still produces these for retail sale. They are, alas, a dying commodity in confectioners' shops, many probably having ceased production through competition from the factory-produced article. There is no reason, however, why these should not again be introduced to assist in Christmas shop sales.

By serving his own product at a dinner the confectioner/caterer can be assured that all the guests present will be well aware of the quality sold, and thus can be built up valuable retail goodwill. These can, of course, be produced during a quiet season and infinitely improved by lengthy storage under correct conditions.

2 lb. 8 oz. weak flour	7 lb. breadcrumbs
7 lb. brown sugar	7 lb. suet
5 lb. mixed peel	3 oz. nutmeg
8 lb. currants	$3\frac{1}{2}$ oz. salt
8 lb. sultanas	Juice and zest of 18 lemons
7 lb. seedless raisins	Juice and zest of 7 oranges
$2\frac{1}{2}$ oz. baking powder	$\frac{1}{2}$ pt rum
1 lb. 8 oz. grated carrots	$1\frac{3}{4}$ pt old ale or beer
$6\frac{1}{2}$ oz. mixed spice	$3\frac{1}{2}$ pt eggs

3 oz. black jack

Mix all the ingredients thoroughly together, and scale off into well-greased basins, ensuring that they are filled. Place a greaseproof paper circle on the top, followed by a pudding cloth securely tied in such a way that it will remain firmly in position during cooking. When all have been so treated, place in boiling water and for $1\frac{1}{2}$-lb. size boil for 6 hr, giving 1 hr extra for $2\frac{1}{2}$-lb. size. It should be stressed that at no time should the water be allowed to go off the boil and if, during this period, more water has to be added, then only boiling water should be used. Alternatively, a steamer may be used.

When the cooking time has elapsed, the puddings should be lifted from the water, still vigorously boiling, one by one, using for this a pot-hook screwed into a piece of brushtail. Cloths must be removed immediately and the puddings allowed to go thoroughly cold before wrapping in greaseproof paper for storage. For retail sale, the basin should be wiped clean, and a disc of greaseproof paper, followed by a disc of transparent cellulose may be tied round.

To prepare for serving, replace the pudding cloth and re-boil for 2 to $2\frac{1}{2}$ hr to ensure that they are hot right through, observing the boiling rules mentioned above. An allowance of 3 to 4 oz. per guest should be made.

RUM SAUCE

A choice exists here of a normal white sauce or a clear sauce. For the former use 1 qt milk, $1\frac{1}{2}$ oz. butter, 4 oz. sugar, and 3 oz. cornflour, produced in a similar manner to vanilla, adding, after cooking, sufficient good-quality rum to give a pronounced flavour.

For the alternative, place 1 qt simple stock syrup into a suitable pan, the juice and zest of 4 lemons, a pinch of cinnamon and 6 oz. ground almonds. Bring to the boil and add 1 qt water into which has been mixed 8 tablespoonfuls of arrowroot. Allow to simmer for a few minutes, remove from the gas and strain, adding, again, sufficient rum to flavour. Whichever variety is decided upon, 2 to $2\frac{1}{2}$ oz. per guest will be sufficient.

What of the staff for serving such a menu? Once again, much will depend upon the facilities that are available, but, as a guide, one waitress for each eight guests, with one person in the preparation room for each 25 guests, should be ample.

If much cooking is being done at the bakery, with food to be transported ready cooked, then it is advisable that the staff is divided into two, with one section, in the charge of the head-waitress, to set out the tables and ensure that all plates are clean and warming, and that everything is prepared as far as possible.

The remaining staff will be employed in preparing the food, and in such a case it would be reasonable to assume that several van trips would be necessary. After the hors-d'oeuvre, the soup would be next to go, followed by the next course and so on, in the order that the food would be served. As the staff in the bakery can be spared, so should the number be reduced and thus increased at the venue where their services would next be required. Worked this way, should any unforeseen circumstance occur in the bakery to delay proceedings, the staff at the venue are in a position to commence serving when instructed and can adjust affairs accordingly.

Now consider a menu with a fish course as an entrée.

Grapefruit	Pommes croquette
Soup	Sprouts
Sole au gratin	Charlotte royale
Turkey, sage and onion stuffing	Cheese, biscuits, and celery
Pommes à la maison	Coffee

The quantities for grapefruit having been dealt with previously, I would like here to include a recipe for a consommé, or clear, soup. Whilst the favourites in my experience are tomato and green pea, the recipes of which have already been given, and I shall dwell at greater length on soups later, I realise that the caterer, when quoting, often desires to give the customer a wide choice. Thus is included here the recipe for consommé, which is the basis of a wide variety.

Consommé

Put 7 lb. diced stewing beef into a stockpot, including any suitable bones and chicken carcasses, cover with 10 qt water, place on the gas and bring to the boil. Using 3 oz. butter, braise a further 3 lb. diced stewing beef to a nice brown colour, and add to the stockpot, which should by now be almost at boiling point. Skim carefully when commencing to boil, then add $\frac{3}{4}$ pt cold water, which will have the effect of bringing any further scum to the surface, allowing to boil for a few minutes to ensure that all scum has been successfully removed. Turn the gas very low and allow to simmer gently for 5 hr; if prolonged vigorous boiling is allowed, it will tend to cloud the soup.

After this period has elapsed, dice and add three carrots, one turnip and two onions, all of average size, and include also a celery top, a pinch of mace and mixed spice, thyme and seasoning to taste, allowing the whole to simmer gently for $1\frac{1}{2}$ hr. Strain, adjust the seasoning as required—in this respect a little celery salt will immeasurably assist.

This, then, is the basis of consommé which, with various additions, can give a wide variety of soups.

Cheese Choux

One which readily finds favour is to serve the above, nicely seasoned, along with small cheese choux. For these, prepare chou paste in the normal way, take out sufficient for requirements and add to this a little celery salt and sufficient baker's or grated parmesan cheese to ensure a good flavour. Pipe out in very small balls, about the size of marbles, on to greased sheets, baking off at 430°F to a golden brown, ensuring that the little balls are thoroughly dried out.

These may be added to the soup at the last moment before serving, for, if left in too long, they will become sodden. Preferably, however, they should be thoroughly warmed at the venue and served hot in separate dishes.

The amount of soup is as previously mentioned and, as soon as it is set before the guest, a sprinkle of cheese, either baker's or grated parmesan, should be added. Once again, allow 110 per cent dinner cobs.

Soles au Gratin

Allow approximately 4 to 5 oz. cleaned and prepared fish per guest, and place in buttered dishes. If costs allow moisten with a little wine, season with salt and pepper and cook in an oven of 370°F. When almost cooked, pour over a thin layer of brown Italian sauce; sprinkle the fish with either fine rusk or bread crumbs, previously coloured with a spot of egg colour, rubbed between the hands and dried out in a cool oven. Return the fish to the oven to complete cooking.

To make Italian sauce take 2 qt of stock and pour on to a little sliced ham, some chopped parsley, and one each of medium-sized onions, carrots and turnip previously braised in a little butter. Add a little tomato purée and allow to boil gently for $\frac{1}{2}$ hr. Thicken with a brown roux rather more than will be required, thus allowing for further ingredients to be added later. Simmer gently, skimming off all the fat, afterwards straining and adding a little black jack to colour if required. For the above quantity, chop and cook in a little butter four medium-sized onions, 8 oz. mushrooms and a little rubbed thyme, adding to the brown sauce and simmering gently for 20 min., afterwards skimming, straining and adjusting seasoning as necessary.

The sole should be served with a garnish of clean, fresh parsley.

An allowance of 5 to 6 oz. dressed, uncooked weight of turkey per guest should be made, with the remainder of the main course as previously detailed.

Full details for the production of charlotte royale are to be found elsewhere in this book. One of 12-in. diameter should yield 20 portions.

Again, the reader may consider this an ambitious menu for the outside caterer to tackle, but I am certain that if he will break it down in the manner described previously he will agree that, with careful planning and an eye to detail, it can be successfully accomplished. The staff required is as previously detailed.

Another Festive Menu

The following menu is, again, one that will require a similar number of staff and is suitable for the festive season, but here the facilities required at the venue will need to be reasonably good, for the second and sweet courses are such that a good oven will be required right up to the time of serving.

Chicken soup	Pommes à la maison
Vol-au-vent	Green peas
Roast chicken and bread sauce	Omelette surprise
Roast potatoes	Cheese, biscuits, and celery
Coffee	

Chicken soup would not normally preface a chicken main course, but is included here as an illustration.

For this prepare as for the consommé, but include in it small quenelles produced from two chickens, the bones of which have been used with the stock and reduced until a good chicken flavour has been produced. Strain, and add to the soup small cubes of carrot, turnip and green peas, allowing to simmer until these are cooked.

The second course of vol-au-vent must be served hot, the filling of the cases being done just prior to serving. They may be individual in size, or take the form of large ones to be served at the table, but whichever is decided upon there are pros and cons. The small, for instance, take longer, both to produce and to fill, but are served much more quickly, whilst the reverse is true of the larger size. Personally I would choose the smaller, individual size, and here would suggest a 3-in. cutter as being appropriate. The filling will, of course, depend upon customers' choice and the price to be obtained, but for this menu a mushroom filling would be acceptable.

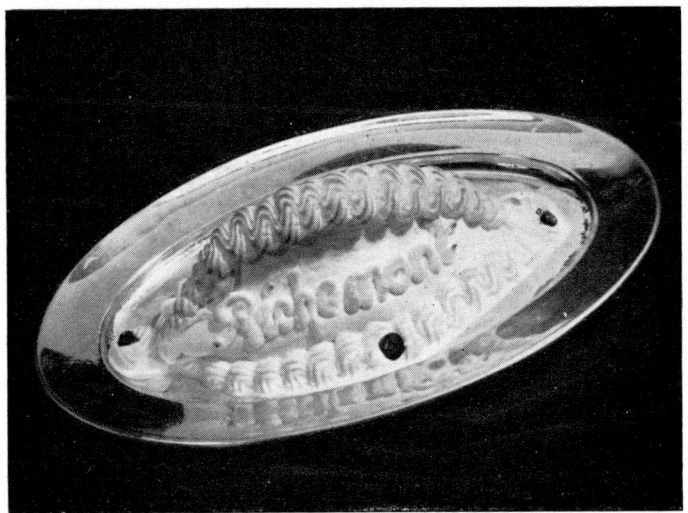

7.5. Omelette Surprise, a very popular hot sweet.

Omelette Surprise

The only other item not previously dealt with is the omelette surprise, and wherever served it has evoked many expressions of both pleasure and surprise, for this latter nomenclature is evoked by the fact that this sweet comprises cold ice cream and hot meringue.

Using a silver dish, place an oblong of unrolled sponge roll in position, previously spread with a good-quality raspberry jam, with the jam uppermost, followed by a layer of fruit salad. Upon this place a block of solidly frozen vanilla ice cream, allowing 2 oz. per serving. Mask entirely with a cold meringue and, if possible, pipe on the name of the organisation holding the dinner, using a savoy bag and small, plain tube; dredge with castor sugar. Flash in an oven of 500°F and serve immediately. Careful timing is, of course, necessary to ensure that it is in reality "omelette surprise", although, if a deep freeze is available, the sweet may be prepared beforehand and stored until required for flashing.

Lower Priced Menu

We have, so far, considered menus which, of necessity, would be fairly high priced, and it may be advantageous if one were included of lower price. The following, while still suitable for the festive season, may be found satisfactory, viewed from this angle:

Sliced melon	Sprouts
Roast pork and apple sauce	Continental charlotte russe
Roast potatoes	Cheese and biscuits
Pommes à la maison	Coffee

The melon should be cut into conveniently sized segments, seeds removed, and served with a cocktail cherry, speared by a cocktail stick, in the centre. Melon is, of course, eaten with a small knife and fork, and bowls or dredgers of castor sugar should be provided, one between each six guests, together with ground ginger.

A novel idea, when serving this, is to use the stick as a "mast", with the segment of melon to represent a boat, and produce "sails" from suitable paper, speared top and bottom by the cocktail stick, upon the "sail" being neatly printed the guest's name, thus serving the dual purpose of place card and course.

As only one type of meat is served in this menu, it would be advisable to increase this to $3\frac{1}{2}$ oz. raw meat per head, to ensure that, after loss in cooking and carving, each guest receives approximately 2 oz.

All other items having been previously dealt with, suffice to say that a charlotte russe of 12-in diameter should, again, yield 20 portions.

It will be obvious to the reader that much of this menu can be previously prepared, and a staff of one waitress to each 10 guests, plus one person in the preparation room to each 30 guests, should provide for a good service.

The next menu suitable for this season is again one that can be quoted at a reasonable figure.

Soup	Creamed carrots
Roast beef and horse-radish sauce	Sprouts
Pommes à la maison	Gateaux, various
Roast potatoes	Cheese and biscuits
	Coffee

Any of the soups previously mentioned will be satisfactory, although tomato or clear soup would be more acceptable.

The beef may take the form of sirloin or fillet. If the former, trim and skewer the flap underneath. Place in a suitable roasting dish, lard well, and place a piece of beef fat on the top. Commence roasting at approximately 420°F, and after the first 20 min. reduce the heat, allowing the oven to fall to approximately 350°F, basting at intervals as necessary. Shortly before cooking is completed, remove the fat and dredge lightly with salt. If fillet of beef is used, allow this to stand for 2½ hr or so in a dish containing some salad oil, a little salt and pepper, turning occasionally, then roasting as detailed. Allow 3½ oz. raw meat per head.

Roast beef is, by tradition, usually undercooked, but it has been my experience that this is not acceptable to the majority of people. However, this is a matter for the caterer, and should he decide upon this menu he can, of course, enquire as to the degree of cooking the customer prefers. If tradition is to be followed, then 15 min. to the pound, plus 15 min. over, should suffice, whilst, if the alternative is required, an extra 5 min. should be added to each of these times.

To make the horse-radish sauce, produce a normal white sauce, using two-thirds milk and one-third water, thickened with a white roux and adding a small knob of butter. Season nicely with salt, cayenne pepper and a little vinegar, finally adding sufficient grated horse-radish. Allow a dessertspoonful to each guest.

One other traditional trimming served with beef is Yorkshire pudding, but this has not been included in the menu for, unless properly made and served immediately, the result can all too often be just a square of nondescript, leathery material. Again, very few venues offer the necessary good facilities to enable this to be produced in the quantities required to allow it to be served as it should be. However, for the happy reader to whom the above does not apply, the following should prove very satisfactory.

Sieve 12 oz. flour, ½ oz. baking powder, and a pinch of salt into a suitable bowl; make a bay and into this crack two fresh eggs. Commence whisking these, and from ¾ pt fresh milk add a little at a time, whisking constantly until the whole assumes the smooth consistency of a thick cream. Allow to stand for at least 2 hr, then pour into a suitable roasting tin containing a little really hot fat, pouring in only sufficient to coat thinly the bottom of the tin. Cook immediately in an oven of approximately 400°F, serving as soon as removed from the oven. Again, traditionally, the Yorkshire way of serving is with hot gravy immediately prior to the main course.

The reasons for the many failures when producing this are:
(1) Insufficient rest after mixing;
(2) mixture too stiff;
(3) fat not hot enough;
(4) pouring too large a quantity into the tin;
(5) cooking too slowly.

The remainder of this course, with quantities, is as detailed previously.

The type of gateaux visualised are those of Continental origin, i.e., kirsch, rum, or Black Forest, or, alternatively, the type of torte that conforms to the description of unusual, with the accent on flavour. Of the first three mentioned, a gateau of 10 in. dia. should yield 18 portions, whilst the torte, of course, cut in the usual manner, will provide its own answer to the question of quantity.

The staff required for this menu will be approximately one waitress to each 8 to 10 guests, depending upon facilities, with one person in the preparation room for each 30 guests.

Cheaper Menu

In such a book as this, it is so fatally easy to dwell upon the higher class and priced trade, and completely to ignore the cheaper and more ordinary type of menu and goods. As the practical reader will agree, by far the larger proportion of his shop customers are those who spend comparatively small amounts, but who are, nevertheless, good customers in that they return week in and week out, and upon whom he generally relies for a living. Similarly in catering not every enquiry comes in for a four or five-course meal.

I have in mind now such enquiries that emanate from Rugby and soccer football clubs, requiring an end-of-season celebration, choirs, and similar types of organisation, who require a hot meal in free-and-easy fashion, not too expensive, yet good of its type, and where a pleasant "get together" is envisaged with a minimum of formality. Indeed, on some occasions, the only requirement is that the caterer shall supply the food, ready to serve, at a pre-arranged time, the particular organisation then supplying their own service both to keep down the costs and ensure privacy with absence of formality. In some cases he is requested to supply crockery and cutlery, and in others absolutely nothing but the food is required. Should the former be the case, the caterer should state at the outset what the hire charge will be, together with replacement charge for any breakages. It has always been the author's experience that, when this course has been adopted, all utensils have been ready for collection the next day, washed and packed in generally good condition, but if a hire charge is not made, then the caterer may stand to work at a loss, having to purchase replacements for breakages.

Although the price per head may not be high, the caterer should, as always, strive to give quality and value for money; for well does the author remember attending a hot-pot supper given by a local football club. The hot pot itself, well enclosed in a thick brown gravy, certainly looked, smelled and tasted good, but odd pieces of bacon rind, found first by one member of the party, then by another, and so on, only gave rise to the most grave suspicions as to what had been used to contribute to the bulk.

So, in quoting, the caterer should bear in mind the fact that, although the price per head is to be on the low side, he should only quote at a figure that will allow him to do himself justice, maintain a high standard and show a profit commensurate with his effort.

The first of these menus might take the form of:

No. 1
   Steak and kidney pie
   Mashed potatoes
   Peas
   Apple tart and cream

This is the basic menu but cheese, biscuits, and coffee could be included if desired.

For the steak and kidney pie, allow 4 oz. steak and 2 oz. kidney per head. Cube the meat coarsely—for to do so finely would only result in its disintegration during cooking—removing all fat and gristle in the process. Place in a suitable pan, cover with water, season, and allow to simmer until cooked. When this point has been reached, thicken as required, using cornflour or, preferably, a mixture of cornflour and potato powder, with a little gravy salt, then return to the gas, stirring constantly to prevent burning, until the mixture returns to the boil. Adjust seasoning as required, and add a little black jack to produce a rich colour.

From this point on the caterer is very much on his own, for a great deal of how the pie will be presented depends very much on the numbers attending, who is to provide the service, and what facilities are offered.

For instance, if the number to be catered for is small, then the pies may be made in shallow-sided tins, similar in size to a slab tin; or they may be produced on four-sided sheet tins and served as a "slice"; or served from the bulk with the pastry baked separately; or, finally, in oval dishes of a size to permit two servings to one pie, using foil cases. Whichever course is adopted a first-class pie paste will be required and, if the lid is to be of puff-paste, then a full puff, rolled thinly, should be used. A quantity of good gravy should also be supplied.

Once again allow 10 oz. unpeeled potatoes per head, and peas as previously detailed. Enquiry should be made as to whether bread in one form or another will be required.

The sweet is, of course, quite straightforward, and here again the caterer has the choice of producing this on a sheet tin and cutting into squares, or, alternatively, producing sufficient plate tarts and cutting into the necessary portions, adding the whipped and sweetened fresh cream just prior to serving.

Of the two methods the author much prefers the second as being the more workmanlike type of job, even though it may be a little more trouble.

7.6. *Apple pie, portioned, with cream and ready to serve. This work can be done in the bakery prior to transportation.*

No. 2

Meat and potato pie

In preparation, this is very similar to the steak and kidney pie.

Allow 4 oz. cubed cooked steak per head, removing all fat and gristle, and again 10 oz. diced potatoes, taking care not to have the latter too small. Place in a suitable pan or bowl, season, add 2 oz. chopped onions per guest, cover with water and allow to simmer gently until cooked. Thicken as previously detailed, colouring as necessary. The pie can be produced in any of the forms mentioned. Some caterers do add a small amount of carrot to this, but this is much better omitted.

Traditionally, red pickled cabbage and beetroot are served with meat and potato pie, and one addition I have found to be most welcome is sliced raw onion, very lightly salted, and served in dishes containing a very small amount of a mixture comprising approximately equal quantities of vinegar and water, with just a pinch of castor sugar to relieve any sharpness. The sliced onion is placed in the dishes and the vinegar applied by means of a bottle fitted with a spot cork, the whole being allowed to stand for an hour or so prior to serving.

No. 3

Hot pot

Originally very much a local speciality of Lancashire, there is no reason why this should not become popular in all areas. Indeed, at the present time many church choirs in that county still hold their annual "hot-pot supper", which is very much looked forward to as the traditional winter treat. On many occasions this is produced by some kindly soul connected with the church, but there is no reason why the caterer should not produce this. In restaurants this dish is one that conveniently disposes of various types of odds and ends of meat, but this is not to be commended.

It is traditionally produced in round, fire-proof dishes, and consists of alternate layers of meat and onion and sliced potatoes, allowing the same proportions as for the meat and potato pie, seasoning carefully with salt and pepper as the layering proceeds. The top layer should be of sliced potato, a little water added, and the whole cooked in a medium oven, depending upon the size of the dish, approximately 2 hr being required. Traditionally, red pickled cabbage and beetroot are again served with this.

The meat, before cooking, should have all fat and gristle trimmed off and be nicely cubed, otherwise it will be necessary to skim off the grease. Again, some caterers prefer to add a little liver to the meat content, in order to give flavour and add a little "body" to the gravy produced, but it is, perhaps, better not included.

CHAPTER 8

A Miscellany of Dishes

HAVING dealt comprehensively with menus for any type of function for which the confectioner is likely to be asked to cater, it will be of assistance if recipes and methods of production of various dishes suitable for different types of functions, which have not, so far, figured on any of the menus, are given. These, together with his own specialities, should place the reader in the position of having a wide variety of choice for the potential customer, and enable him to compile his own menus.

Clear Oxtail Soup

On the basis of two oxtails to each 6 qt consommé, divide the oxtails into reasonably small pieces, blanch, add to the consommé and allow to simmer until almost cooked, skimming at intervals as necessary to remove the grease. Add small, diced, carrots and turnips as required, and continue to simmer until cooked. Finally, re-skim and adjust the seasoning as required.

Cauliflower Soup

For each 6 qt of consommé, take four turnips and four carrots of medium size, peel, dice small and add. Using two good, medium-sized cauliflowers, divide the heads into small flowerettes, wash, and then blanch for a few minutes in boiling water, afterwards adding to the stock and allowing to simmer for half an hour. Add a small amount of the white leaves of lettuce, finely chopped, and allow to simmer until cooked. Adjust seasoning as required and serve.

Clear Vermicelli Soup

Using 1 oz. vermicelli to each quart of stock, break as required, place into a pan of boiling water, allow to boil for approximately 5 min., remove from the pan and place into cold water. Strain, add to the consommé and allow to simmer gently until cooked, removing froth as required. Adjust the seasoning and serve with grated parmesan cheese.

Clear Macaroni Soup

Very similar to the above—the macaroni should be flavoured with salt and pepper, adding a little butter during the initial cooking. This, again, should be served with cheese, and will take somewhere between $\frac{1}{2}$–$\frac{3}{4}$ hr to cook.

Thick Soups—Chestnut Soup

For each quart of white stock take one onion, four cloves and 1 lb. chestnuts.

The skins of the chestnuts should be slit; heat in a medium oven until the shells and skins split, when they can easily be peeled whilst hot. Chop the kernels roughly and add to the stock, along with seasoning and the onions, which are peeled and stuck with the cloves, allowing the whole to simmer gently until the nuts are tender. Remove the onion, rubbing the remainder through a fine sieve and returning to the gas, thickening with a white roux as required. Finally, colour a very pale pink and adjust seasoning as necessary.

If desired, a pinch of nutmeg may be added, along with 5 oz. cream to the quantity given, but if this latter course is adopted, the soup should not be allowed to boil, though it must, of course, be served hot.

Oxtail Soup

For 6 qt of stock, three oxtails, cut into convenient-sized pieces, should be braised along with four each of medium-sized onions, carrots, turnips, two celery heads, a little thyme and parsley, and a slice of ham weighing about 8 oz.

Add all to the stock and allow to simmer until the ham is cooked, after which it should be removed. Thicken with sufficient brown roux, allow to simmer for a further $\frac{1}{2}$ hr, then strain through a crumb sieve. Allow to stand for a short time, remove all the fat, add the pieces of tail, reheat, adjust seasoning as necessary, and the soup is ready.

Asparagus Soup

Three bundles of asparagus are required to each 6 qt of veal stock. Wash and cut up the vegetable, afterwards adding to the boiling stock. Allow to simmer gently until cooked, strain, season and add a little green colour as required.

Croûtons of fried bread are normally served with this soup.

H

Roux

This is produced from equal quantities of butter and flour, the colour (white, fawn or brown) depending upon the degree of cooking, and is used for thickening soups and sauces.

Melt the butter over a low light, add the flour and stir constantly until the required colour is obtained. Too rapid cooking will scorch the flour and give an unpleasant, strong and burned flavour. Usually, 2 oz. of roux is sufficient to thicken 1 pt liquid. When of the correct colour, add the stock and continue to stir, raising the gas until the liquid reaches boiling point, to prevent lumps forming.

A word now about the cost of soup. Many catering confectioners rely on the purchased varieties, with or without additions. Naturally, each tackles any particular job from his own viewpoint, but I feel that, by purchasing, ready-made, this course, he is incurring needless expense. Except under very abnormal conditions, he would never consider purchasing confectionery, so why purchase a course that he can just as well produce himself? Admittedly, simmering, etc., takes a little time, but once the gas is correctly adjusted the soup will cook itself, the remainder of the preparation taking but very little time. I am convinced that, if he will produce his own soup once or twice, and then sit down with paper and pencil and cost both, he will fully agree that to produce his own will either make his catering more profitable or allow him to price his functions more competitively.

For any of the soups given, 6 to 8 oz. per guest should provide for a good, average quantity.

Hors d'oeuvre

In addition to the varieties previously suggested, the following are also suitable:

Celery: Dice fairly small, and dress with mayonnaise.

Chicken: This should be chopped, though not too finely, and coated thoroughly with mayonnaise.

Egg: Hard-boil the number required and quarter lengthwise. Coat the quarters in aspic jelly at slightly above setting point, and to which a small amount of chopped parsley has been added. Allow one quarter egg to each guest.

To hard-boil the eggs correctly, and prevent the "black line" between yolk and white, place them in a suitable pan, cover with cold water and bring to the boil, then immediately reducing the gas, allow them barely to simmer for 20 min. When this time has elapsed, pour off the water and stand under running cold water for 15 min., prior to shelling.

Crab: Remove all sinews, etc., and mix with an equal quantity, by weight, of chopped olives.

Tomato: Slice and dress with mayonnaise to which a small amount of aspic jelly, almost at setting point, has been added.

When setting out the hors d'oeuvre, and in deciding the types to be produced, colour should be borne in mind, and the varieties set out in the dishes to give maximum effect. Remember that eye-appeal comes first, and to this end the different colours and as wide a variety as possible of flavours should be arranged attractively and tidily. Food, when it is arranged in a haphazard, tossed-about fashion, loses easily 75 per cent of its possible eye-appeal. A neatly arranged, well set-out selection immediately, if only subconsciously, puts the guests in a happy frame of mind to enjoy the meal.

Fruit Cups

So far, the only fruit cups mentioned have been grapefruit and sliced melon. Whilst these are often popular in the less inclement weather, it is always to the caterer's credit if he can suggest several variations to the enquiring customer. These can include:

Diced melon with seedless green grapes.
Grapefruit with seedless grapes.

In each case use equal quantities of the named fruits and allow a total of 4 oz., including any syrup if using tinned grapefruit. Castor sugar would, of course, be necessary, and to this end one sugar basin should be allowed to each six guests.

Orange Salad

To prepare this unusual fruit cup, obtain good, sound fruit and allow a half, medium-sized orange for each guest. Remove the rind by segmenting the skin only with a sharp knife, divide the orange into segments and remove any pips and as much of the pith as possible. Place in a suitable dish or bowl and cover with a simple stock syrup to which sufficient orange curaçao has been added to give a definite flavour, allowing to stand for an hour or so before serving.

This can, ideally, be prepared in the bakery beforehand and transported in a suitable container in bulk, setting out in the individual dishes just prior to the guests entering.

Fruit Juice Cocktails

These are becoming increasingly popular, and may be served in addition to, or in place of, hors d'oeuvre or a fruit cup. A plentiful variety is now obtainable in tinned form, and so the caterer can, in this instance, offer a choice at the table, for no waste need be incurred. The waitress may offer a choice from three varieties, the tins being opened as required. If at all possible, they should be well chilled and served in pony glasses, allowing approximately 3 oz. per guest.

Besides the ever-popular tomato juice, we have the choice of apple, orange, pineapple, grapefruit, and lime juice.

Meats

In writing this book it was not the author's intention to write a comprehensive series of recipes on cookery, but only to include those dishes that the outside catering confectioner

(a) is likely to be called upon to produce, and

(b) can successfully tackle, bearing in mind the difficulties with which he quite often has to contend, such as facilities offered at a particular venue, and the necessity of transporting equipment, etc.

Many of the meats, then, that he is called upon to serve have been dealt with previously under the various menus. The following serve to supplement that list.

ROAST HAM

It is preferable that this be boned and strung before roasting to make for easier carving. Place into a suitable roasting tin or bowl, add approximately 1 qt water, and roast in an oven of 330 to 350°F. The largest of hams should cook for 15 min. to the pound, plus 15 min. extra, whilst small hams will probably take around 20 min. in each case, with medium sizes in between these times.

Test with a carving fork before removing to ensure thorough cooking, pour off all the liquid and allow the ham to go thoroughly cold before removing string and rind, partially defatting and rolling into either bread crumbs or fine rusk, which has been coloured yellow with egg colour, rubbed through the hands and dried in a very slow oven.

Of the liquid, when cold, the dripping may be lifted and used for roasting, pie pastry, etc., whilst the jelly remaining can, if used with care, be used in stock, gravies, etc., but, as this is normally salty only a small proportion should be used, and further seasoning only added afterwards.

VEAL

This meat requires long, slow cooking for approximately 25 to 30 min. per lb. in an oven of 300 to 320°F.

LAMB

Either leg or shoulder should be roasted for 25 to 30 min. per lb. at 325–350°F, meat thermometer 175–180°F.

Vegetables

NEW POTATOES WITH CREAM

Allow 5 oz. raw, scraped potato per guest. Cut into $\frac{1}{4}$-in. slices and cook in the usual way. When cooked, drain well, add a small amount of fresh cream, a little lemon juice and a pinch of nutmeg. Toss, without breaking the potatoes, and dress with a small amount of clean, chopped parsley.

POMMES A LA MAÎTRE D'HOTEL

Prepare the potatoes as above, and when cooked put them into a saucepan containing a little white sauce, butter, salt and pepper, and a small amount of lemon juice. Toss, again without breaking, to coat the potatoes thoroughly and sprinkle with chopped parsley. These are normally served with small croûtons placed around. Again, allow 5 oz., uncooked, per guest.

CHIPPED POTATOES

It will, perhaps, be noticed that no menu including these has been given. The reason for this is that the serving of them is rather too risky from all viewpoints, for, unless served hot immediately they are cooked, the meal is spoiled. Again, very few venues offer the facilities necessary to enable the caterer to produce these successfully in the quantities required in the time allowed. Again, should the starting time for the meal be delayed by the guests for some reason—which quite often happens—another headache arises as to how these shall be kept hot.

No, the serving of chipped potatoes is best left alone, for the caterer only stands to lose a good name. Should an enquirer suggest these, it is as well to point out the snags and show the very good reasons as to why it is felt that these are not a practical proposition.

VEGETABLE MARROW

The choice of two methods exists here. The first is to peel the marrow, cut into conveniently sized pieces, boil in water containing sufficient seasoning, strain, and serve with a white sauce.

The second method is to place the prepared marrow into a sauté pan, add a little butter, seasoning and a fractional amount of castor sugar. Add to this a little white stock and allow to simmer gently for approximately 15 min., then turning up the gas and boiling briskly until the liquor is reduced to a glaze. Now add a little brown sauce containing lemon juice to the glaze. Toss well together without breaking the marrow unduly and serve.

Whichever method is used, allow 3 oz., as purchased, per guest.

ASPARAGUS

Allow 4 oz., as purchased, per head. Prepare by scraping and washing clean, afterwards, keeping the heads all one way, tying into conveniently sized bundles. Place into a pan of hot water, containing salt to season, and boil for approximately 20 min. Strain on to a cloth without breaking, remove string and, if serving by tureen, serve on toasted bread with hot, clarified butter or white sauce.

BROAD BEANS

All too often are these served merely boiled, with the vegetable tending to eat rather dry. Although the alternative is a little more trouble, it is trouble well spent.

Choose young beans, and boil in water containing salt, a little parsley and onion. When cooked, drain and return them to a pan containing a little fresh butter, chopped parsley, salt, pepper, and grated nutmeg. Toss, and add a little white sauce immediately prior to serving.

Allow approximately 6 oz., fresh as purchased, per guest, to permit a serving of 2 oz.

CAULIFLOWER

Using only good, sound vegetables with a close flower of good colour, allow 6 oz. per guest, as purchased, to provide for a cooked portion of approximately $2\frac{1}{2}$ oz. Remove the outer stalks and soak in salt water for 1 hr. Wash well and boil in water to which a little salt has been added, and, when tender, drain well and serve with a little white sauce. Whilst boiling, it is advisable to remove the scum as it rises to the surface.

An alternative to white sauce is to serve cauliflower with a cheese sauce.

FRENCH BEANS

Allow 3 oz. per head, as purchased, and if of reasonable quality this should provide for a 2-oz. cooked portion per guest.

String the beans and shred into small pieces. Wash well, drain and add to a pan of boiling water to which a little salt has been added, boiling quite vigorously until tender. Strain, and then they may be served thus, or, alternatively, be dressed with a white sauce to which a little butter, chopped parsley, and lemon juice have been added.

Forcemeat Stuffing

2 lb. breadcrumbs or fine rusk	1 oz. rubbed thyme
8 oz. chopped suet	Grated rind of three lemons
2 oz. chopped parsley	Salt and pepper
4 oz. finely chopped bacon	

The whole should be bound together with egg, and may be stuffed into the crop or body of the bird, or roasted *en masse* with a little hot dripping. Alternatively, and to speed serving, it may be moulded into 1½-oz. balls, the quantity per guest, and roasted as indicated until crisp and nicely browned.

Chestnut and Sausage Stuffing

This is normally stuffed into the crop of the bird, and, again, an allowance of 1½ oz. per guest should be made.

Wash 2 lb. chestnuts, slit the skins, place into a pan of cold water, bring to the boil and allow to simmer for 10 min. Strain, remove the skins and replace in the pan, just covering the nuts with fresh water and allowing to simmer until tender with all the water absorbed.

Mash well, add 1 lb. sausage meat, 6 oz. breadcrumbs or fine rusk, 4 oz. melted margarine and sufficient salt and pepper to season.

Cranberry Sauce

Undoubtedly fresh cranberries are the ideal, but if these are not obtainable the tinned fruit, or cranberry jelly from a jar, may be utilised.

Wash and pick 1 lb. cranberries, put into a saucepan with just sufficient cold water to cover, allowing to simmer until tender. Rub through a sieve, return to the pan and add 5 oz. castor sugar and 1 oz. butter, reheating until the sugar has dissolved.

The sauce may be served hot or cold, and once again the allowance per guest should be 1½ oz.

Apple Sauce

This is usually served with pork, duck or goose. If served cold, an unusual addition, and one which quite often finds favour, is to incorporate the flesh of orange, cut small, and a little finely chopped celery. If desired, a clove could be added, but as this is not a universally popular addition, it is, perhaps, better omitted. To 3 lb. chopped apples add 12 oz. castor sugar and simmer until apples "fall".

Caper Sauce

This is, of course, served with boiled mutton. For the liquor use half milk and half mutton stock, thickening at the rate of 2 oz. white roux to each pint of liquid. Season with salt and pepper, add chopped or whole capers as required and ¾ oz. caper vinegar to each pint of liquid used. If desired, a small amount of fresh cream may be added, whilst an allowance of 1½ oz. sauce per guest should be made.

Mint Sauce

This is served with either hot or cold lamb, but all too often spoiled by the use of too much vinegar.

Dissolve 1½ oz. castor sugar in ¼ pt hot water, allow to cool, and add ¼ pt vinegar. Now chop very finely approximately 2 oz. washed mint leaves with a small amount of sugar and add to the liquid, stirring well.

Roast Veal Sauce

In stock, boil for 10 min. or so one sprig of thyme to each pint of meat stock required. Strain, add a small quantity of lemon juice, chopped parsley as required, and ¼ pt brown sauce. Season with salt and cayenne pepper and allow a portion of 1½ oz. per guest.

Gravy

Great care should be exercised that this is not greasy, for it can ruin an otherwise excellent meal.

For clear gravy remove the meat from the roasting tin, pour off the fat and allow approximately $1\frac{1}{2}$ oz. juices to 1 pt stock or vegetable water or combination of both. Add this latter to the juices, bring to the boil, adjust seasoning as required, strain, and should any grease be present remove by skimming with a piece of folded greaseproof paper. Allow $1\frac{1}{2}$ oz. per guest.

For thick gravy, produce a roux by adding 1 oz. flour to the meat juices, otherwise proceeding as detailed. Allow 2 oz. per guest.

White Sauce

A wide variety of sauces may be produced from a basic sauce by the addition of small quantities of flavouring ingredients. The usual recipe for the sauce is:

2 lb. 8 oz. milk (1 qt)	Seasoning
4 oz. butter or margarine	One medium-sized onion
4 oz. flour	

Place the butter or margarine into a suitable pan, preferably copper, and melt. Add the flour and mix in, cooking for a few minutes over a medium gas, yet taking care that the roux does not take on colour.

Now add the warmed milk gradually, stirring constantly to produce a smooth sauce.

The onion should now be added which, if desired, has been studded with a clove, allowing to simmer for about half-an-hour. Remove the onion, strain, and, to prevent a skin from forming, add a small knob of butter, which will form a film on the surface.

Cheese Sauce

Add to the above 4 oz. baker's cheese and two egg yolks.

Parsley Sauce

To the quantity given above add two tablespoonfuls washed, chopped parsley. Allow 2 oz. per guest.

Anchovy Sauce

Add two tablespoonfuls of anchovy essence.

Onion Sauce

To this quantity of white sauce, add 8 oz. chopped, boiled onions.
Served hot or cold with roast mutton, allow 2 oz. per portion.
In all cases, check that the seasoning has been adjusted as required.

Vol-au-Vent Fillings

Whilst the white sauce given above will be satisfactory as a base for
these fillings, the following is an alternative.

2 lb. 8 oz. milk (1 qt)   2 oz. butter
4 oz. cornflour   seasoning as required

Use a small amount of cold milk in which to dissolve the cornflour,
boiling the remaining milk along with the butter. As soon as the milk
has boiled, combine with the cornflour paste and return to the gas,
stirring constantly and cooking to ensure that the cornflour has
gelatinised. To this may now be added:

1. Diced chicken.
2. Chopped ham or other meats.
3. Mushrooms, having been lightly fried in butter previously.
4. Baker's cheese. 5 oz. will be required to the above quantity,
   seasoning with celery salt.
5. Fish, such as lobster, crab, salmon, shrimps, etc.

When producing the latter, it is as well to use half fish stock and
milk, adding a minute spot of pink colour to give the sauce a shell-
pink tint, together with a little vinegar to taste.

In all cases, finally and very carefully adjust seasoning, remembering that it will be necessary for the flavour to be predominant over
the vol-au-vent into which it will be placed.

Prawn Cocktail

Allow 1–1½ oz. prawns per portion, previously peeled, washed and,
if large, cut into reasonably sized pieces.

For each eight guests allow one lettuce, which should be washed,
dried and shredded fairly finely, before dividing between the requisite number of glasses or, as they are frequently termed, Paris
Goblets. The lettuce should be about 1 in. deep. Now add the prepared fish and coat well with shellfish cocktail sauce.

There are two methods of producing this.

The first is to add tomato juice to mayonnaise in the ratio of one part tomato juice to two parts mayonnaise.

Alternatively, add two parts tomato juice to three parts lightly whipped fresh cream, a few drops of lemon juice, and season with salt and pepper.

Whichever method is used, allow $1\frac{1}{2}$ oz. per portion.

Decoration on the edge of the glass can consist of a lemon segment and/or a whole prawn, whilst often segments of peeled sliced tomato are included.

As an alternative to prawns, diced lobster, the shredded white meat of crab, or peeled and washed shrimps may be used.

Flavoured Butters

In the production of rolls and savouries of similar type, the use of flavoured butter can greatly assist in giving the "different" flavour so desirable. Cream up 8 oz. butter to the consistency and colour of whipped cream, add a spot of lemon juice and any of the following:

CHEESE BUTTER

4 oz. baker's cheese, adding celery salt for flavour.

ANCHOVY BUTTER

3 tablespoonfuls anchovy essence, $1\frac{1}{2}$ teaspoonfuls lemon juice, a sprinkle of paprika, and, if desired, a small quantity onion juice.

CHUTNEY BUTTER

3 tablespoonfuls finely chopped chutney.

GARLIC BUTTER

3 teaspoonfuls finely chopped garlic.

TOMATO BUTTER

4 oz. tomato ketchup, added slowly.

CHIVES BUTTER

2 teaspoonfuls lemon juice and 3 oz. finely chopped chives.

MINT BUTTER

$1\frac{1}{2}$ teaspoonfuls lemon juice, 3 tablespoonfuls finely chopped mint, spot of pistachio green colour.

HORSERADISH BUTTER

1½ teaspoonfuls lemon juice and 3 tablespoonfuls grated horse-radish.

ONION BUTTER

3 tablespoonfuls finely chopped onion or young onion tops.

SALMON BUTTER

4 oz. salmon paste, 2 teaspoonfuls lemon juice, cayenne pepper to taste.

SARDINE BUTTER

4 oz. mashed sardines, 1 teaspoonful lemon juice and tomato ketchup.

SHRIMP BUTTER

5 oz. finely chopped cooked shrimps, 2 dessertspoonfuls lemon juice and paprika.

PARSLEY BUTTER

2 dessertspoonfuls parsley, finely chopped, 1 dessertspoonful lemon juice, salt and cayenne pepper.

WATERCRESS BUTTER

4 tablespoonfuls finely chopped watercress, 1 dessertspoonful lemon juice, 2 dessertspoonfuls Worcestershire sauce.

CHAPTER 9

A Miscellany of Recipes

Finger Rolls

Soft and tender, with an excellent glaze, baked in a really sharp oven, these items will be found useful in all forms of catering.

QUICK PROCESS

5 lb. flour (strong)	2½ oz. milk powder
1½ oz. salt	2 lb. 13 oz. water (2¼ pt)
1 oz. sugar	10 oz. shortening
5 oz. yeast	

Produce straight dough with finished dough temperature of 80°F. Allow a bulk fermentation of 30 min., knocking back after 20 min.

It is advantageous to add the shortening after the dough has been made.

LONGER PROCESS

5 lb. strong flour	2½ oz. milk powder
1¾ oz. salt	3 lb. water
1 oz. sugar	10 oz. shortening
2½ oz. yeast	

Produce a straight dough with a finished dough temperature of 78°F, once again adding the shortening at the end of the mixing period, clearing well. Allow bulk fermentation of 1½ hr, knocking back after 1 hr.

The size of the rolls will, of course, depend upon the purpose for which they are required. For children's parties and buffet work generally ¾ oz. per roll will be found to be large enough. Scale the dough at a size suitable for cutting on the dough divider available, mould the pieces round, then into finger shape.

Needless to say, the dough should be light and lively to the touch, with no trace of stickiness at all.

Place the fingers on to a greased and slightly warmed sheet tin, and here again a decision should be made as to whether the fingers should touch or not. If they do, then the rolls will have soft, virtually crustless sides, and will certainly be different from those that are kept separate. In either case, egg wash with a solution that includes a fair proportion of yolks, then place in a prover. This should be only just warm, with merely a trace of steam—provers like a Turkish bath ruin the goods.

When almost ready for the oven, place the sheet tins containing the rolls into a cold place, so that the dough pieces will set. This will enable a second egg wash to be applied, and so produce that beautiful golden glaze that will enhance any buffet upon which these goods are to form a part. Bake at 500°F, giving some bottom protection in the form of a biscuit wire or upturned sheet tin.

General Purpose Cake Mixing

It is always useful to have a recipe that will be suitable for many different types of cake, and this one can be used for queen cakes, gateau and torten bases, cream shells and victoria sandwiches, these latter being scaled at 10 oz. into a 7-in. greased and floured tin. The very simple finish of splitting and filling with jam or lemon cheese, finishing by dredging with castor or icing sugar, makes them eminently suitable for afternoon teas, picnic catering, and the like.

This particular recipe is one of medium quality, yet, properly made and presented, is popular and extremely pleasant to eat.

2 lb. castor sugar	2 lb. 14 oz. weak flour
1 lb. margarine	1 lb. 4 oz. milk (1 pt)
4 oz. golden shortening	$2\frac{1}{4}$ oz. baking powder
$1\frac{1}{2}$ oz. glycerine	colour
1 lb. 4 oz. egg (1 pt)	flavour

Produce by the sugar-batter method, creaming the fats very lightly together, warming if, and as necessary. Add the eggs in four or five quantities, scraping down bowl and beater at intervals. Add half the milk and break in, add the sieved flour and baking powder, partially clear, add the remainder of the milk and beat well. The glycerine may be added at any stage, whilst the colour and essence can be added along with the milk. As far as possible, use natural flavours, such as lemon, orange, lime and tangerine pastes that give the confectionery a really good flavour. Many of the complaints of "shop" cake really stem from the use of too much—and often too cheap a quality, of essence. Always measure or weigh this, so that the flavour is standard.

Small Buns

Using a savoy bag and large plain tube, pipe the batter into small custard or bun tins that have previously been papered with grease-proof paper cases, two-thirds full or, by weight, approximately $1\frac{1}{4}$ oz. Some may be decorated before baking with a sprinkle of currants, flaked almonds, pieces of cherry, etc., whilst others to be decorated after baking may be left plain. Bake at 410°F, allowing them to cool thoroughly before decorating.

9.1. *An assortment of buns produced from the general purpose mix and finished suitably for children's parties.*

All of the buns to be iced should be brushed over with boiled apricot jam before decorating. Some varieties of finish are:

White fondant and a half cherry.

White fondant, dipped immediately in white coconut.

Lemon or orange fondant, with a segment of lemon or orange jelly slice as appropriate.

Pineapple coloured fondant, which has also been flavoured with the addition of the syrup in which the pineapple was crystallised.

Chocolate fondant with a half walnut.

Coffee fondant, with a roasted whole hazelnut.

Whichever finish is employed, the aim should be to keep it as neat as is humanly possible. Cakes that have been coated with fondant that was obviously too soft so that the cake shows through, or with too soft fondant dribbling down the side of the cake, do nothing to enhance a caterer's reputation.

Fresh Cream or Vanilla Custard

Allow the bun to cool thoroughly before removing the centre with the point of a sharp knife, afterwards reversing this on to the bench. Using a small plain cutter of appropriate size, cut the centres neatly, afterwards piping into the depression of the bun sufficient whipped fresh cream. For this, a savoy bag and star tube is desirable.

For the vanilla custard, use a savoy bag and plain tube.

After replacing the tops, dredge liberally with icing sugar.

Cream Shells

Shell tins are obtainable singly, or in trays of four or six, similar to the housewife's patty tin. Clean and grease the tins carefully before piping in about $\frac{3}{4}$ oz. of the batter. Bake at 410°F. When baked, remove from the tins at once, leaving on a cloth or clean sack to cool.

When cold, split horizontally with a sharp knife about two-thirds up from the base and pipe in a good whirl of fresh cream.

Replace the top and dredge with icing sugar.

Currant Lunch Buns

Clean and grease sufficient oval-shaped bun tins, sprinkling a few currants on the bottom. Pipe approximately $1\frac{1}{4}$ oz. of mixing into the tin, or two-thirds full, and bake at 410°F. When baked, remove from the tins and leave reversed side uppermost.

This type of line is, of course, quite good for the picnic basket.

Bakewell-type Tarts

Line plain or fluted 6-in. tart tins with sweetpaste, piping in the bottom a liberal amount of jam—strawberry is very popular. Scale or pipe in 4–5 oz. of the batter, spreading level with the back of the hand moistened with water. Bake at 400°F and, when cold, mask with apricot purée, and ice with white fondant. Complete with a half cherry, and you have completed another line suitable for afternoon tea or the picnic basket.

Cream Sandwiches

Scale at 7 oz. for a well-greased sandwich tin of the normal 6-in. size. Spread level and bake at 390–400°F. After baking, leave on a cloth to cool.

To finish, split, mask the base with a nice layer of seedless raspberry jam, followed by a good layer of whipped fresh dairy cream. For meals service, it is a good plan to segment the top before service. Not only will this give better portion control, but it can be set on the table and, as it is served, it does not look too untidy.

Victoria Sandwiches

The reader looking for one of better quality may like to try the following.

1 lb. 12 oz. butter	1 oz. lemon paste
12 oz. golden shortening	3 lb. 4 oz. weak flour
2 lb. 6 oz. castor sugar	1 oz. baking powder
3 lb. 2 oz. eggs (2½ pt)	egg colour
3 oz. glycerine	

Produce by the sugar-batter method, clearing the flour well by hand in the last stage. Scale at the desired weight into greased and floured sandwich tins, baking at 380–400°F, depending on size. After thorough cooling, split, spread with jam, replace the top and dredge with either castor or icing sugar.

Sweetpaste

Sweetpaste is used in a wide variety of goods, and perhaps the simplest is to use the paste as it is, for the production of animal biscuits. Upon these a child's name may be piped, using them as place names as dealt with in an earlier chapter.

As with many other lines, a number of recipes are available, all of which, if properly handled, give good results.

The first is the usual and perhaps the most popular.

SWEETPASTE No. 1

4 lb. weak flour	1 lb. castor sugar
2 lb. butter or margarine	8 oz. egg

Produce by the rubbing in method, make a bay, place eggs and sugar into this, dissolve the sugar in the eggs and mix together to produce a smooth paste.

SWEETPASTE No. 2

Without doubt, this is a considerably cheaper recipe, relying on the creaming method breaking down the gluten of the flour in the first stage to prevent toughness.

1 lb. 4 oz. margarine	1 lb. 4 oz. shortening
2 lb. 8 oz. flour	

Place into the machine bowl fitted with beater and cream together very lightly, using the beater and warming as necessary. Any scrap may be added at this stage, but it must be well creamed in! Now add:

3 lb. weak flour	½ oz. baking powder

and mix in on slow speed to the consistency of ground almonds.

I

Then add:

6 oz. egg	$\frac{3}{4}$ oz. salt
6 oz. milk	egg colour

and clear until the paste leaves the sides of the machine bowl cleanly.

The pastes made by either method are suitable for hand working or machine blocking.

Biscuits

Care should be taken when rolling out the paste to ensure even thickness, and here a marble slab will be found ideal. Coupled with this, two sticks of the required thickness upon which the ends of the rolling pin will rest can be very useful. When the desired thickness has been achieved, roll over with a marzipan roller to give added interest, and cut out with animal cutters. Using a palette knife, transfer the shapes carefully to a sheet tin previously lined with greaseproof paper, baking at 410°F.

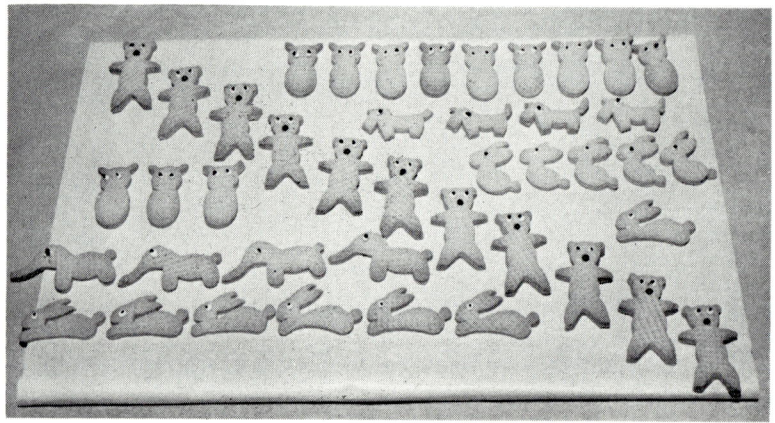

9.2. Sweet-paste animal biscuits, which are quickly turned into place "cards" by piping on the children's names.

When cold and baked, pipe in the representation of the eye, using a bold bulb of royal icing, followed by the pupil—a spot of chocolate coloured royal icing. Notice the variety of expressions obtained by a very slight alteration in the position of this. Finally, pipe on the name, again using chocolate royal icing, very simply, so that the child may easily recognise it.

Langues De Chat Biscuits

These small delicious biscuits are invaluable for many decorative jobs; most noteworthy are they useful for decorating trifles and torten.

Made by the sugar-batter method, they are very similar, in recipe only, to the madeira cake, the difference being that a reduced quantity of egg is used, and this takes the form of whites only.

As the yield is very high, and they are not used in great quantities, only a small recipe need be given.

8 oz. butter or margarine	9 oz. weak flour
8 oz. castor sugar	vanilla essence
5 oz. egg whites ($\frac{1}{4}$ pt)	

Having produced the mixing by the sugar-batter method, pipe out, using savoy bag fitted with $\frac{1}{4}$-in. tube, into finger shapes of about $1\frac{1}{2}$ in. long, or small bulbs the size of a shilling, on to cleaned, greased baking sheets.

As the biscuits flow during baking, allow space for this. The centre should be quite white, with edges a golden, very crisp, brown. A baking time that is too long, or an oven that is too cool, will produce biscuits that have taken on too much colour, thus detracting from their appearance.

When cold, store until required in an airtight biscuit tin to maintain the quality.

Othellos

It is, perhaps, unfortunate that these goods are not more widely produced, for they offer a fine opportunity for the individual craftsman to shine by providing a variety of differently flavoured fillings, and thus a further outlet for him to express his personality and at the same time to produce the "different" type of goods so necessary to keep and expand his trade.

The bases for othellos are dry in character and insipid to the taste, thus providing the ideal vehicle for a wide variety of fillings and finishes. To assist production, they may be stored in a dry place for a considerable time.

RECIPE FOR OTHELLO BASES

42 fresh eggs	1 lb. 10 oz. soft flour
1 lb. 9 oz. castor sugar	1 lb. cornflour

The usual strict grease-free precautions must be taken before commencing mixing.

The eggs, by number instead of the more usual weight, refer to standard size, and adjustment will have to be made should these be of the small or large variety.

Separate the eggs, place the whites into a suitable machine bowl along with 1 lb. 2 oz. of the sugar, and commence whisking to full peak on top speed.

Meanwhile, commence whisking the yolks and the remaining sugar in a hand bowl sufficiently to break these down and to dissolve the sugar. It is not necessary to whisk them to a sponge.

When the meringue has reached full peak, put the machine on bottom speed, add the yolks and sugar, allow to amalgamate and then remove from the machine. Knock out the whisk, blending in the previously sieved flour and cornflour gently by hand. When all is thoroughly blended, pipe out in round bulbs, of approximately 1-in. diameter, and oval bulbs of a size in keeping. Dust lightly with flour, and bake at 360°F, with damper or oven door open to ensure a thorough, steam-free drying out.

When baked, allow to become cold before preparing for finishing. This consists of pairing each bulb, cutting the rounded top of one to produce a flat base on which to stand without rolling, and making a hollow in the flat base of each to enclose the filling. When filled, the halves of the othello should fit flush, and none of the filling should be apparent to the customer.

The ideal medium for the filling is well-beaten, cold vanilla custard with flavourings added, using true liqueurs where applicable. This, after being enclosed for a short time, will soften the biscuit and, if flavoured correctly, will give an article second to none in palate appeal. Fresh cream, in varying quantities, may be added to the vanilla custard to lighten.

VANILLA CREAM OTHELLOS

Use equal quantities of vanilla custard and whipped and sweetened fresh cream. Fill the biscuits and when complete brush the tops with boiled apricot purée.

Dip in white fondant, brought to normal dipping temperature and consistency, to cover completely the joint between the two biscuits, and complete with a whirl of white piping fondant and a small piece of cherry.

KIRSCH OTHELLOS

Flavour sufficient of the custard with kirsch and fill as already indicated. Brush the tops with the boiled apricot purée, mask with

9.3. *Othellos and Petits Fours Glacés, as detailed in this chapter. Note the effect obtained by the method of setting out as would be done for a buffet.*

pale pink fondant, and complete with a whirl of the same coloured fondant and a small piece of cherry.

COFFEE OTHELLOS

Rum-flavoured vanilla custard is used as the filling, with the othello masked in coffee-coloured and flavoured fondant.

Complete with a whirl of the same medium and a roasted hazelnut.

CHOCOLATE OTHELLOS

Soften sufficient praline paste to a smooth cream, and add the required amount of vanilla custard, a little at a time, to produce a smooth filling for the bases. Mask with apricot purée, dip in chocolate-coloured and flavoured fondant, completing with a whirl surmounted by a silver dragée.

PINEAPPLE OTHELLOS

For this variety, flavour the vanilla custard with glacé pineapple syrup and small pieces of chopped tinned pineapple. Fill the othellos, brush the tops with apricot purée and dip in pineapple-coloured fondant, reduced by adding pineapple syrup in place of water or stock syrup, to flavour.

Complete with a whirl of the same coloured fondant and a small piece of well-drained glacé pineapple.

APPLES

For these flavour the custard with maraschino, fill the biscuits, and mask with apricot purée.

Roll out sufficient natural-coloured marzipan and cut with a 3-in. cutter. Wrap the othellos neatly, bringing the edges of the marzipan to hide the joint, and place them in rows along the bench. Using a suitable brush dipped in apple green colour and stamped on a sheet of paper until almost dry, brush along one side of the row of othellos. Wash and dry the brush, then using pink colour, repeat the process along the other side. Complete by pressing a small currant in the top centre to represent the core of the apple. A spray gun may be used for colouring if available.

PEACHES

Using plain vanilla custard as the filling, proceed as for apples, using in this case the pink colour on both sides to represent the "blush" of the peach. Mark in the "crack" with a modelling tool or the back of a knife. Complete with artificial leaf.

POTATOES

Oval biscuits are used for this variety, with the praline-vanilla custard filling. Proceed as for the peaches, using natural-coloured marzipan rolled out thinly. When all are covered, wash with a slightly water-dampened brush, and dust lightly with a mixture comprising two-thirds cocoa powder and one-third icing sugar. Brush off the surplus dust and make one or two cuts in each to represent the eyes.

PREPARATION FOR SALE

With all the above lines, of course, the othellos are placed in paper cases before being set out on trays.

It should, perhaps, be made clear that the shelf life of these goods is strictly limited. Again, they should be finished as soon as possible after being filled, for, if left any length of time, it will be found that the vanilla has softened the biscuit to the extent of making enrobing very difficult.

In any Continental variety of petits fours glacés, othellos similar to these described are extremely popular and, for cocktail parties, if produced approximately two-thirds the normal size, they enjoy great popularity.

Puff Paste

A word regarding the ingredients. Flour should be of fair strength. Some recipes call for the addition of cream of tartar or cream powder to strengthen the gluten, but I find that as the optimum is so fine and as it is so simple for an operative to add "about" the right amount rather than weigh it, a more regular puff is produced without its addition, for too much will toughen the paste, making it "wild" during baking, even after giving the necessary resting periods. A small amount of salt is added to give the necessary flavour.

The butter must be of a good, tough character and the choice of pastry margarines and fats, now very wide, can produce a very good article. However, for superior eating quality a proportion of the fat should be butter, for the use of pastry margarine alone can, if the goods are eaten cold, leave, in some opinions, an unpleasant "suety" after-taste, due to the high melting point of the fat.

For producing the paste, it is very convenient to make up the total required for a week in units of 3 lb. flour, which, after turning, is placed in large slab tins lined with greaseproof paper. Two such pieces of paste separated and placed in polythene bags fit comfortably in one tin, and, if kept in a refrigerator, will not skin and are always on hand. Made regularly on the slack day each week, it is a simple matter, when required, to take out the amount required and work off, rather than produce daily.

UNIT RECIPE

The unit recipe, then, is:

3 lb. flour	5 egg yolks ($\frac{1}{4}$ pt)
6 oz. butter or cake margarine	$\frac{3}{4}$ oz. salt
1 lb. 9 oz. water ($1\frac{1}{4}$ pt)	2 lb. 10 oz. butter/pastry margarine

Place the flour, salt, and a small amount of butter in the machine bowl fitted with a dough hook and start the machine on slow speed. Add the water and egg yolks—or egg colour if replacing the yolks with water—and mix to a smooth dough. Remove from the machine and replace with the butter and pastry margarine, running the machine on slow speed until a smooth plasticity is obtained.

If more than the above unit is being produced, scale the dough at 5 lb. 4 oz. and mould round. Scale off the butter/pastry margarine at 2 lb. 10 oz. and form into a cube shape, using a small amount of dusting flour as required.

Reverse the dough, and with a french knife cut a cross half-way through and open out to form a cross with a thick centre portion and thin edges. Place the cube of butter in the centre and fold over the edges, envelope fashion, to enclose totally. Roll to a rectangle of approximately 18×12 in., cover with polythene and allow a short period—$\frac{1}{2}$ hr is ideal—to rest.

After this period has elapsed, roll out the dough to a large rectangle and fold each end to meet in the centre, making certain that the corners in all cases are square, otherwise uneven lift in the various articles to be produced will result. Now fold the right-hand half over to cover the left-hand half. Roll out the pastry again to a large rectangle and fold as already indicated, afterwards leaving in a cool position, covered with the cloths, for a period of at least 1 hr. The pastry will now have had what we may call one full book turn, each individual roll and fold being known as one half-turn. Dusting flour will, of course, be necessary during rolling, but this should be well brushed off before folding.

STORING THE PASTE

After the period of rest, the pastry should be given one more full turn, and, if the idea mentioned of producing sufficient to last the week is adopted, then the paste should be placed in the large, lined, slab tins, separated and covered by polythene until required.

When this time comes during the busy part of the week, it is a simple matter to take as many pieces as required, give one further half-turn, a rest of 1 hr, and the paste is then ready for working off.

The method just described is merely one way of making puff paste, and is the one I prefer simply because it does save a little time in that it needs only five half-turns to the six half-turns required by the methods now to be described. Whilst the time saved may appear to be infinitesimal, all these odd minutes throughout the day do count, and where the results are exactly similar, then I feel that preference must be given to the quicker method, even if the saving of time is quite small.

ENGLISH METHOD

Using the recipe already given, produce the dough as detailed, afterwards scaling at the unit weight, moulding round and allowing a period to recover: meanwhile working down the butter/margarine to a smooth plasticity.

Roll out the dough to an oblong, ensuring that the corners are square, and place the butter over two-thirds of the surface in "dabs". Fold the untreated third over half the treated two-thirds and fold over again so that now there are three layers of dough enclosing two layers of butter. Pin out to a large rectangle, brush away surplus dusting flour and fold into three in the manner previously described, repeating the procedure so that one full turn has now been given.

Allow a resting period of at least 1 hr in a cool position, covering to prevent skinning. Give one further full turn, followed by the resting period, again give a further full turn, and allow at least another hour's rest before working off.

FRENCH OR CONTINENTAL METHOD

Proceed as already detailed to mix, scale and mould the dough, and work the butter to a smooth plasticity, afterwards moulding to a cube as for the first method. Now, take the dough and pin out to a cross, once again with a thick centre and thin edges, placing the cube in the centre and totally enclosing, envelope fashion.

Proceed as detailed for the English method, to give three full turns, together with the necessary resting periods.

SCOTCH METHOD

Place flour, salt and total fats (previously cubed) in the machine bowl fitted with the hook, and allow the cubes of fat to become coated with flour. Add the liquid and produce a rough dough, afterwards stopping the machine. Mould to a ball, allow a short rest, and then pin out as detailed for the English method until three full turns have been given. Allow the usual period of rest before working off.

FURTHER POINTS

Any of the methods which are adopted will produce consistently good results but, apart from the correct choice of ingredients, attention to the small details such as brushing away surplus dusting flour, ensuring that at all times the corners are correctly squared, is necessary. Again, with the rolling, the pastry must be rolled quite thinly, otherwise some of the butter will remain in too thick a layer, thus causing uneven rising.

Finally, strict attention must be paid to the resting periods.

SMALL VOL-AU-VENT OR PATTY CASES

Correctly made and served warm with a tasty savoury filling, these are always acceptable, although, perhaps, the production of really good patty cases with even lift is the greatest test of any puff paste variety. For use as a cocktail savoury the cases must be small and in keeping with the size of the remainder of the savouries, but if intended as a course in a meal then they will be needed correspondingly larger.

Take a piece of virgin puff and, to assist even lift, trim off the edges and pin out to slightly less than ⅛ in., ensuring even thickness of the paste, and afterwards cutting with the appropriately sized cutter, which, for these lines, should be fluted. Pick up the discs carefully so as not to disturb the shape, reverse, and set out on a clean sheet tin previously covered with a sheet of greaseproof paper.

For the tops, roll out another piece of paste to the same thickness and cut with the same sized, fluted cutter. afterwards removing the centre with a smaller sized, plain cutter, The sizes recommended are 1¾ in. for the outer and 1 in. for removing the centre.

Here, and as an aid to speedy production, I would recommend that two cutters of the appropriate size be soldered together so that the cutting of the tops can be accomplished in one operation. The price of cutters is very cheap, and it is a simple matter to solder across the two a strip of metal, so that the time taken is reduced by half. It is possible now to purchase a tool to do this job.

Egg-wash the discs which are to form the bottoms, and carefully place in position the tops, the fluted edges on the former corresponding with those on the latter. The practice of using egg-wash to join the halves together may seem unusual, and indeed wrong, for the line of egg-wash may be visible in the finished case. However, the reason for the use of this will be apparent later.

As stated previously, it is possible to produce goods to be ready first thing in the morning, hence the reason for setting out the patty cases on greaseproof paper, for, if cut out in the afternoon, they can be left overnight in a refrigerator or similar cool place, and thus have a sufficient period of rest before baking in the morning. The grease-proof paper is necessary to prevent any discoloration of the bottoms, which often occurs through the contact with the metal of the sheet tin.

When required for baking off, egg-wash the tops very carefully, ensuring that no egg-wash runs down either inside or outside, for if this occurs it will hold down that part of the puff and thus cause uneven lift.

Bake off carefully at 420–440°F, depending on size, until thoroughly baked, but do not allow the cases to take on too much colour, for the goods generally have to be warmed again.

It is sometimes necessary to hurry along the production of patty cases, and bake off before sufficient rest has been given. In these cases it will be found a help if, after the final egg-wash, three or four holes are made by inserting the blunt end of a cocktail stick through the two pieces comprising the patty case. These form what we may term a

9.4. Vol-au-vent ready for serving.

"lock", and thus assist even rise of the puff. The small holes thus made reseal during baking, and become invisible.

The typically English method of finishing is to produce a lid from puff paste, using a cutter somewhere between the inner and outer sizes, and then decorating with a small puff paste leaf, but I must express preference for the Continental method, accepting that the filling is the whole point of the case, and consequently the latter should be as thin as possible.

When cold, then, the centre of the patty case should be removed with a small, sharp knife, and this portion used as a lid—the reason for egg-washing the top to the bottom now becoming apparent.

Now for the filling. If to be consumed on the premises the cases may be warmed and the filling added, afterwards setting the goods out on silver dishes and garnishing with parsley, cut tomato, etc. If purchased for use later, the filling should be made, put into a jar, and instructions given to the customer to immerse the jar in hot water for approximately half an hour or so, before filling the already warmed cases.

Ham Crescents

Here is a further variety which is always popular as a cocktail savoury.

Pin out sufficient virgin puff to slightly less than $\frac{1}{10}$ in. and, using the seven-wheel cutter, cut into horizontal strips $2\frac{1}{2}$ in. wide.

Cut the strips into triangles having a base of 3 in. and in the centre of the base place a small amount of lean, cooked, chopped ham. Moisten the paste with water, roll and make into a crescent shape, place on a clean sheet tin, with the apex of the triangle now underneath.

Egg-wash, rest for a period of 1 hr, egg-wash again and bake at 430°F.

Chou Paste

Many recipes exist for producing the basic paste and the majority of them, in capable hands, produce excellent articles, but whatever recipe is used some degree of craftsmanship is necessary, for the stumbling blocks causing the most trouble are obtaining the correct consistency of the paste and correct baking.

With regard to the former, the amount of egg required will depend on the strength of the flour and degree of cooking, but, generally speaking, the more eggs absorbed the lighter and more acceptable will be the finished product. The paste, when mixed, should be just stiff enough to retain its shape when piped out, but, in the case of cream buns, should be slightly softer yet still just retain the shape of the star tube used.

Baking should be carried out at the temperatures stated, preferably with a little steam introduced in the early stages, but all varieties should be quite crisp and thoroughly baked before being removed from the oven, when they are immediately slid on to a wire to cool.

The recommended recipe is:

1 lb. 9 oz. water (1¼ pt.)	1 lb. 4 oz. flour
8 oz. butter or margarine	1 lb. 14 oz. eggs (1½ pt)

Place the water and butter or margarine in a suitable bowl or pan on to the gas and bring to the boil, meanwhile sieving the flour on to a sheet of paper. When the water and butter are boiling vigorously, add the flour and stir well with a wooden spatula, while still subjecting to heat, for approximately 1½ min., when the mixture will be thoroughly cooked and leave the sides of the bowl or pan cleanly.

Remove from the gas, and transfer the paste to a suitably sized machine bowl fitted with the cake beater. Start the machine on second speed and commence adding the egg in small portions until the correct consistency has been obtained, scraping down bowl and beater at intervals to ensure thorough amalgamation of the eggs.

PASTE FOR CREAM BUNS

It was the practice in former years to make up a separate paste for cream buns, but this, with increased labour costs and the fact that a good article can be produced from the foregoing recipe with the addition of a small quantity of egg and carbonate of ammonia (vol), makes the production of a separate paste unnecessary. To the recipe given, if required for cream buns, add sufficient egg—probably in the region of 4–6 oz.—and a quarter teaspoonful of vol, dissolved in the last of the egg and beaten well in, care being taken to ensure thorough amalgamation. In normal production, the paste required for éclairs and other varieties would first be removed, then the extra egg and vol in proportion to weight of remaining paste added.

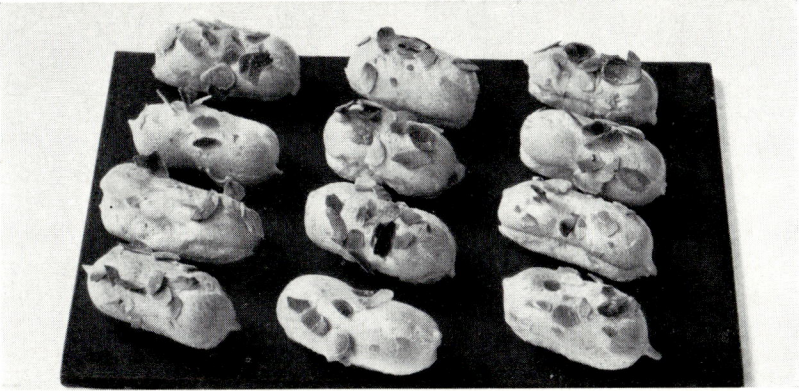

9.5. *Cheese éclairs.*

Cheese Éclairs

Using a $\frac{1}{4}$-in. plain savoy tube, pipe out on a lightly greased sheet tin small éclairs approximately $1\frac{1}{2}$–2 in. long, but certainly of a size in keeping with the remainder of the savouries. To prevent the éclair having a tail, after piping the correct length stop pressure, lift the tube slightly upwards and, in the same motion, take the tube forwards and off, thus leaving a clean finish. Only a small point, but one that counts in neatness of the finished article.

Having piped out a sufficient number in neat rows, scatter liberally with slightly-chopped flake almonds. Any falling between the rows can be collected after baking and used for finishing various other articles. Bake at 430°F, ensuring thorough baking, otherwise the cases will soften and tend to eat tough and leathery.

When thoroughly cold, slit carefully and fill with a white sauce/cheese filling.

9.6. *The ever-popular chocolate éclair.*

Chocolate Éclairs

Using a $\frac{1}{2}$-in. plain savoy tube, pipe out the paste in lengths of approximately 3 in. on to lightly greased sheet tins, using the method previously described to preserve a neat finish. Bake at 430°F.

After thorough baking and allowing sufficient time to cool, split the cases open by using a sharp knife, making the cut rather higher than half-way up the side of the case, afterwards piping in a liberal amount of whipped and sweetened vanilla-flavoured fresh or synthetic cream.

Now prepare sufficient chocolate fondant by warming white fondant to 100°F, reducing with stock syrup or water to normal dipping consistency, afterwards adding approximately 25 per cent melted, unsweetened block cocoa or bakers' chocolate, stirring well in and reheating slightly or adding further stock syrup or water as required to restore to normal dipping consistency and temperature.

Finish the éclairs neatly by icing the flat side, i.e. the part previously in contact with the sheet tin, using a small palette knife or the finger to remove any surplus. This latter is a job that calls for considerable care, for, neatly done, the finished article has a greatly enhanced appearance: we have all seen displayed for sale really messy-looking éclairs that must have repercussions.

After a short time to allow the fondant to dry, place in the long paper cases, when they are ready for display and sale.

FURTHER VARIETIES

In my experience, the public remain true to the chocolate éclair, but I have no doubt that in some districts—and especially when catering for parties and dances, etc.—further varieties would be quite popular.

These consist of filling the baked case with a differently coloured and flavoured whipped and sweetened cream, e.g. coffee, raspberry, strawberry, etc., and finishing by icing with appropriately coloured and flavoured fondant. The icing may be applied with flattened ½-in. savoy tube and savoy bag.

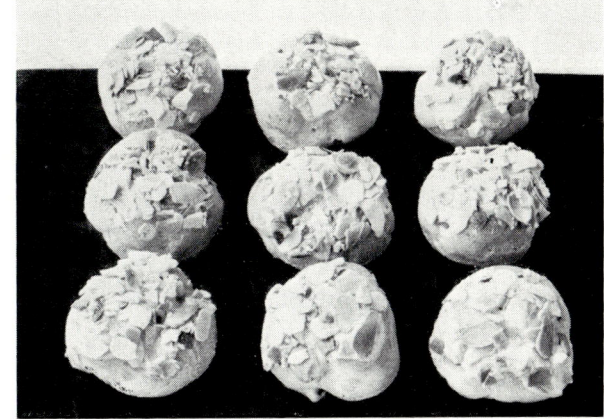

9.7. *Rognons.*

Rognons

Using the same paste as for éclairs, pipe out in kidney shape, keeping the size fairly small, whilst using a ½-in. plain tube, otherwise the finished article will be apt to look clumsy.

Bake thoroughly at 420°F and, when cold, slit open the cases, piping round the shape whipped, sweetened and vanilla-flavoured cream with a savoy bag and star tube.

When all the cases have been so prepared reduce coffee-coloured and flavoured fondant to the usual consistency and temperature and, holding the case in the left hand, immerse the top, removing the surplus with a small palette knife or fingers of the right hand. Dip immediately into finely roasted flake almonds, and the rognons are complete.

Cream Buns

Prepare the chou paste as previously detailed, adding the extra egg and moistened vol until the required piping consistency is obtained.

If the special deep-lidded cream bun tins are available, pipe out the paste, using a large star tube, in bulbs of approximately 1¼ in. diameter, ensuring that all are of the same size and that sufficient space

9.8. *Not the most dainty confection to consume but, nevertheless, cream buns are very popular.*

is allowed for the great expansion that will take place. Should these tins not be available, pipe bulbs out on to a lightly greased sheet tin, covering each as piped with a 1-lb. bread tin to ensure correct spacing.

As stated previously, one of the greatest difficulties in producing these goods is in the baking, for if the lids covering the buns are lifted and steam allowed to escape before the goods are properly baked, the buns will collapse, and thus prove useless. How, then, can this be surmounted?

When all the buns are piped out and covered with either the deep lid or 1-lb. bread tins, pipe a $\frac{1}{2}$-in. bulb in the centre of the lid, or on top of one of the bread tins in the centre of the sheet. This bulb then gives an indication of what stage the baking of the bulbs has reached, and when this "pilot" bulb has taken on a dark brown, almost burnt appearance, then the goods can be safely removed from the oven, the lids removed, and the buns placed on a wire to cool. The baking temperature should be 430°F and the buns will take approximately 30 min. to bake.

Completion takes the form of piping in each bun a liberal amount of fresh whipped and sweetened cream. Split with sharp knife, afterwards piping in the necessary amount of cream, or insert finger into side of the bun and pipe in the cream through the hole thus formed. When all the buns are so treated, complete by dredging lightly with icing sugar.

Petits Choux

Using a very slightly softer paste than for éclairs, yet without using vol, pipe out small bulbs on to a lightly greased sheet tin, afterwards baking at 420°F without covers.

After baking and thoroughly cooling, slit carefully and fill with a variety of whipped, sweetened, coloured and flavoured fresh or synthetic cream, e.g. vanilla, raspberry, strawberry, coffee, etc. Afterwards complete by dipping the tops of the petits choux in appropriately coloured and flavoured fondant—chocolate for vanilla cream, pale pink for raspberry, and so on.

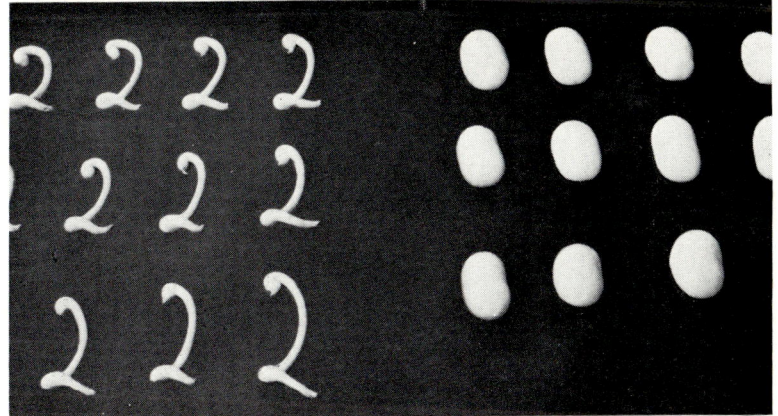

9.9. *Necks and bodies for swans. Note that these must be baked on separate sheet tins.*

Swans

Not by any means a new line, this is, nevertheless, very attractive and commands attention if properly made.

Prepare sufficient bases for the number required by piping small bulbs of chou paste on to a lightly greased sheet tin, using a ½-in. plain tube, in a similar manner to petits choux, but in this case the bulbs will be very slightly smaller, and oval in shape.

The heads and necks are prepared by using a ¼-in. plain savoy tube and piping out the required number in the form of a figure 2, piping carefully to get as near as possible to the graceful arch of the swan's neck. A small flaked almond is inserted to represent the beak. These will, owing to the difference in baking time, be piped separately on a greased sheet tin, afterwards being baked at 420°F.

To finish, split the bases crosswise slightly above the half-way mark, remove the top portion and cut into two. Now pipe in the base

K

9.10. *The swans completed.*

sufficient fresh cream, spiral fashion, and insert the head and neck portion by putting the "foot" of the figure 2 well into the piped cream.

Complete by turning the cut portions of the top to an angle of 45 degrees and placing in position to represent the wings. Lightly dredge with icing sugar.

Coffee Creams

All the lines described so far consist solely of chou paste, but used in conjunction with puff or sweet pastry, the range can be further extended.

For this particular line, roll out virgin puff pastry quite thinly or, alternatively, sweet or german paste to $\frac{1}{8}$ in. thick. Cut with a 2-in. plain cutter and place the discs on a clean sheet tin, allowing a resting period of 1 hr. Using a $\frac{1}{4}$-in. plain tube, pipe rings of éclair paste round the edge of each disc, ensuring that each joint is neatly made. Bake at 420°F.

When cold, complete by dipping each chou ring in coffee-coloured and flavoured fondant, and piping in the hollow a whirl of fresh cream, surmounted with a small piece of cherry and pinch of green almond nibs.

Gâteau Saint-Honoré

This may, of course, be made to a size to suit the customer and occasion but, generally, a size of 7 or 8 in. diameter is acceptable.

Roll out sufficient virgin puff very thinly or sweet paste to $\frac{1}{8}$ in. thick and transfer the disc carefully to a clean sheet tin, care being taken to ensure that the shape is not disturbed. Dock heavily and allow a rest of at least 1 hr.

Moisten the edges of the paste with egg, and pipe in a ring of chou paste just inside the edge, using a ½-in. plain tube. Using the same paste and tube, pipe on to a separate sheet tin sufficient small bulbs to cover the ring of chou paste when baked, together with one extra, which will go in the centre of the finished gâteau. Egg-wash the ring carefully and bake all at 410°F until thoroughly dry.

When baked and cool, mask the base and outer ring edges with boiled apricot purée and cover with roasted flake almonds. The centre of the ring may now be partially filled with cubes of sponge, genoese, or swiss roll, afterwards soaking carefully with a little stock syrup well flavoured with sherry or a liqueur. Follow this by a layer of cold, beaten vanilla cream, with fruit salad if desired.

Make an aperture in the side of each cream bun and fill with whipped cream. Have ready a small pile each of washed and chopped cherries, roasted flake almonds, green almond nibs and silver dragées.

Now, observing the normal sugar boiling rules, boil a small quantity of sugar and water to 285°F. On attaining that degree immerse the base of the pan in cold water for a few seconds to prevent a further rise in temperature. Dip the tops of the buns first in the prepared sugar and then into the decorative materials prepared, ensuring that sufficient of each are produced to go alternately round the side of the gâteau. When all are completed, attach the buns to the ring of chou by first dipping the base into the sugar, and then placing in position, following in sequence until this part of the decoration is completed. Just one bun—the one dipped into silver dragées, should be left, and will be placed in the centre after fresh cream has been piped over the vanilla, when the gâteau is completed.

Further adornment may be added in the form of spun sugar, which certainly greatly enhances the appearance of the gâteau, but such is our atmosphere that it is very questionable if this added touch is worth the time spent on it, for all too soon does it disappear.

Almond Goods

Whilst the various allied trader firms specialising in almond goods have covered this field extensively by use of different publications and demonstrations, it is my intention here to give details for two quite popular lines and concentrate rather more on the ever-popular frangipane fancy.

As the reader will be aware, the high price of almonds in recent years has severely curtailed their use; hence the introduction of persipans, containing for the most part ground apricot kernels as the nut constituent. Use is made of this material for the first line.

PERSIPAN MACAROONS

3 lb. 12 oz. persipan	1 lb. 14 oz. egg whites or
5 lb. castor sugar	albumen (variable)
egg colour	vanilla essence

Using grease-free utensils, place the persipan and sugar into the machine bowl, fitted with beater, and run the machine on slow speed until a crumb appearance is obtained. Commence adding the whites in small quantities and, when approximately half have been incorporated, stop the machine, scrape down bowl and beater, and recommence beating on top speed. Add the remainder of the whites, until soft piping consistency is obtained, then add the colour and essence, again scraping down and beating.

The mixing may be used immediately, although a better "crack" is obtained if it is allowed to stand overnight in a cool place, warmed in a water bath to blood heat, and then given a further 10 min. beating on top speed.

To work off: using a $\frac{3}{8}$-in. plain tube fitted to a savoy bag, pipe on to greaseproof-papered sheet tins, placed upside down, buttons of approximately 1 in. diameter. Bake at 350°F with steam damper and door slightly open.

The most popular finish is perhaps to join two biscuits together with fresh cream. Also the flavour of the biscuit itself lends itself well to various finishes using ganache.

Alternatively, it may be piped out in very small buttons and used in place of ratafia biscuits for the decoration of large trifles and other after-dinner sweets.

DUTCH MACAROON CREAM FINGERS

6 lb. icing sugar	1 lb. 14 oz. whites (approx.)
3 lb. ground almonds	

Mix the sieved icing sugar and ground almonds together and add the whites gradually to form a smooth, semi-liquid paste.

For the fingers, using a $\frac{1}{2}$-in. tube, pipe out to $2\frac{1}{2}$ in. long on sheet tins previously covered with greaseproof paper. Allow to stand in a rack in a warm place until quite a thick skin has formed, cut along the centre of each finger with a sharp knife, and bake at 350°F.

If properly made, during baking the centre will rise through the knife cut, while the biscuit at each side will take on a shiny appearance.

9.11. *Filled with fresh cream.*

9.12. *Ganache.*

9.13. *Praline buttercream, ginger crush, spun chocolate.*

When the centre portion has dried out thoroughly, the biscuits are baked and, after allowing to cool, are reversed on the bench. Brush the papers with warm water, allow a few moments for the moisture to soak through, then peel the paper away.

The biscuits can be stored in tins ready to be finished with fresh cream, simply joining together in pairs.

DUTCH MACAROONS

Using the recipe and method already detailed, pipe out ovals approximately 1 in. long. Dry, cut, and bake and, when removed from the paper, join together in pairs, using baker's chocolate or couverture.

Frangipane Fancies

In former, less hurried times, it was acknowledged that frangipane fancies were of different shapes, thus paving the way for a wider variety of finishes. Time and costs taking their toll, however, have demanded a speed-up of production. Hence, the greater majority are now round, facilitating quick and easy blocking of the paste by hand or automatic blocking machine; even the hand blocker of smaller bakeries is infinitely quicker than pinning out the paste by hand.

When blocked, a reasonable amount of raspberry or apricot jam is piped into the case, and the filling piped in until two-thirds full.

Here again, changes have taken place, for the original frangipane filling was:

1 lb. castor sugar	1 lb. ground almonds
1 lb. margarine	1 oz. flour
1 lb. egg	

Made by the sugar-batter method, and baked at 360°F.

Costs, however, have necessitated substituting part of the ground almonds for sponge crumbs, with the addition of a spot of essence to restore some flavour, which, really, is to be deplored.

The nearest in flavour to the original used by the writer is:

3 lb. 2 oz. persipan	10 oz. flour
2 lb. 6 oz. castor sugar	$12\frac{1}{2}$ oz. milk
2 lb. 8 oz. margarine	vanilla essence
1 lb. 9 oz. egg ($1\frac{1}{4}$ pt)	egg colour

Produce by the sugar-batter method, beating in the persipan along with the sugar and margarine. Baked at 350°F, this mixing gives the moist-eating flavour of the original recipe. The batter should not be beaten too lightly.

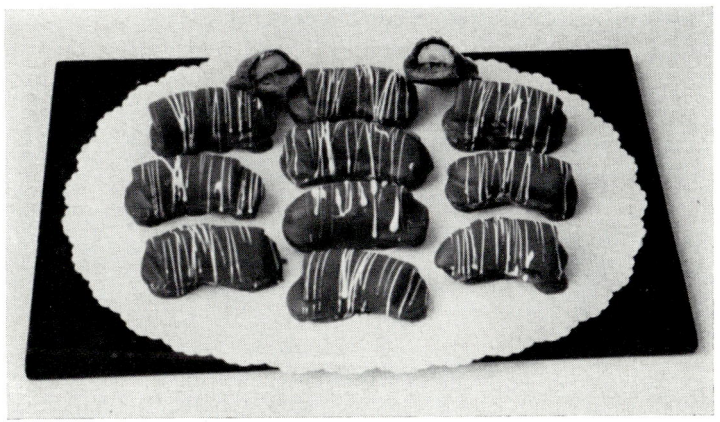

9.14. *Bananas. For this unusual fancy, the macaroon is piped out to banana shape and baked. To finish, mask the flat side of the biscuit liberally with pineapple jam. On to this place a piece of banana, cut to shape, and enrobe with baker's chocolate. Complete by "scribbling" with white cake coating. Shelf life about three days.*

Some Types of Finish

KOPJE

Remove the centre of the frangipane with a 1-in. plain cutter, and place the centres thus produced carefully on one side. Place all the prepared bases close together and dredge with icing sugar. Into the hollow pipe a whirl of white, vanilla-flavoured buttercream. Return-

9.15. *Three half-finger biscuits are joined together with praline cream, with the bases dipped into chocolate. Pipe a whirl of the cream on the top and complete with a chocolate button.*

ing now to the centre plugs, lightly coat the top of each with red piping jelly, mask with green almond nibs, and replace on to the buttercream.

NOUGAT

Spread the top of the frangipane with praline buttercream, mask with crushed praline nougat nibs (see below) placing the fancies as finished in neat rows. Place a stick along each row, the stick being somewhere in the region of $\frac{1}{2}$ in. wide, and dust with icing sugar. Carefully remove the stick: the full effect can be well observed in the illustration.

Praline Nougat—To make the praline nougat, place 1 lb. sugar and the juice of 1 lemon into a saucepan. Using direct heat and stirring constantly, warm until the sugar turns to a golden-coloured liquid. Meanwhile, $\frac{3}{4}$ lb. nib almonds should be warmed to dry out thoroughly, taking on a very pale fawn colour. Now add to the liquid sugar, and cook for a few moments, still stirring constantly, to ensure that the nibs are thoroughly coated with sugar. Turn out on to an oiled slab and pin thinly with a well-oiled rolling-pin.

When cold, the nougat should be crushed with a rolling-pin to approximately coarse nib nut size. Sieve—the dust passing through can be used to flavour buttercream, whilst that remaining can be used as indicated.

OYSTERS

Split the top horizontally half-way across and, holding the frangipane in the left hand, with the fingers keeping wide the incision, pipe in white, vanilla-flavoured buttercream, using a small star tube. To complete, dust with icing sugar.

9.16. *A variety of frangipane fancies, finished to the instructions in this chapter.*

9.17. More frangipane fancies.

CHERRIES No. 1

Mould three small pieces of marzipan round, and fix in the centre with a spot of apricot jam. Warm raspberry piping jelly to a liquid, immerse them, and mask the edges with roasted nib almonds. Complete with a small upright angelica diamond in the centre.

CHERRIES No. 2

In order to provide as wide a range of finishes as possible, the tops for this line are masked with fudge, made basically from proprietary high-ratio shortening. Two half glacé cherries are placed in position and stalks piped on with piping chocolate.

PINEAPPLE

Ideally, the jam baked within the case is, instead of raspberry or apricot, pineapple. Mask the tops of the frangipane with well-boiled apricot purée, and pipe a ring of pineapple-coloured buttercream round the edge, flavoured by the addition of syrup from glacé pineapple. Flavour the fondant with the same medium, colour with egg colour, warm as usual, afterwards filling in the centres, using a paper bag.

Complete with a segment of well-drained pineapple.

CHOCOLATE

Chocolate-coloured and flavoured buttercream is piped on to the top of the fancy; a segment of cut chocolate and a sprinkling of green nib almonds at the apex completes.

COFFEE

This is finished in a similar manner to the pineapple, using, of course, coffee-coloured and flavoured buttercream and fondant, and a piece of walnut to complete.

PRALINE

Praline buttercream is piped, "end-to-end" fashion, across the fancy, using a star tube. Piping chocolate is piped across at right angles; two roasted hazelnuts and a piece of angelica complete.

ORANGE

Orange-coloured marzipan is rolled thinly, the basket roller applied, and discs, the size of the top of the fancy, cut with a fluted cutter.

Pipe orange-coloured and flavoured buttercream along half the circumference and place the marzipan disc in position.

ALMOND

Roll natural marzipan thinly and cut, with a fluted cutter, just slightly smaller than the top of the fancy. Remove the centre with a 1-in. fluted cutter. Place the disc in position—fix with apricot if desired—pipe a whirl of almond-flavoured buttercream in the centre and replace the disc.

ALMOND CHERRY

Brush the centre of the fancy with apricot, and place in position a whole cherry. Pin out green marzipan thinly, apply the basket roller and cut with an appropriately-sized cutter.

With a sharp pointed knife, cut a cross in the centre of each disc and place in position, the cross now opening to display the cherry.

I feel that with the varieties detailed, the reader will agree that the range is endless, so wide a variety of raw materials being at hand to assist in finishing.

Apart from the small fancies, larger varieties may be produced, using a thin water icing finish, while still greater variety can be achieved by baking the frangipane on a sheet tin, cutting various shapes and using various finishes.

Butter Sponge Bases

Each of the following recipes will produce two bases, each baked in a greased 10-in. hoop, standing on a greaseproof-papered sheet tin.

Whisk up the eggs and sugar to a full sponge in a well scalded machine bowl, meanwhile sieving together the flour and cornflour, bringing the butter to a warm, not hot, oil.

Having reached full sponge, add any colour and flavour, allowing the machine to take it in. Remove bowl from the machine, knock out the whisk, add the flour and commence mixing very gently.

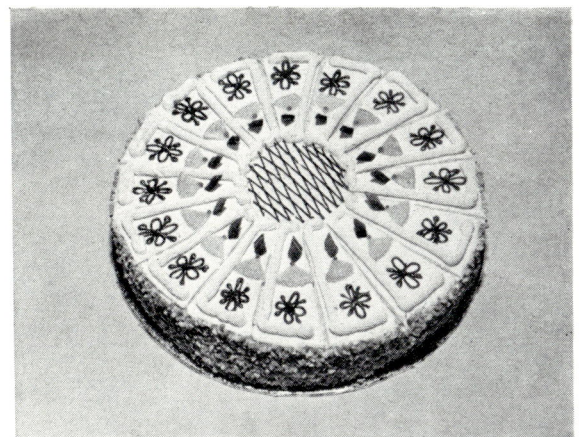

A VARIETY OF
FINISHES FOR
TORTEN

9.18. (*Left*)
Lemon.
9.19. (*Below*)
Chocolate.

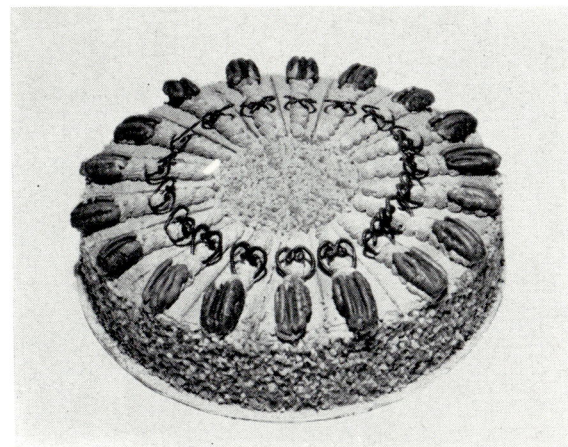

9.20. (*Right*)
Lime.

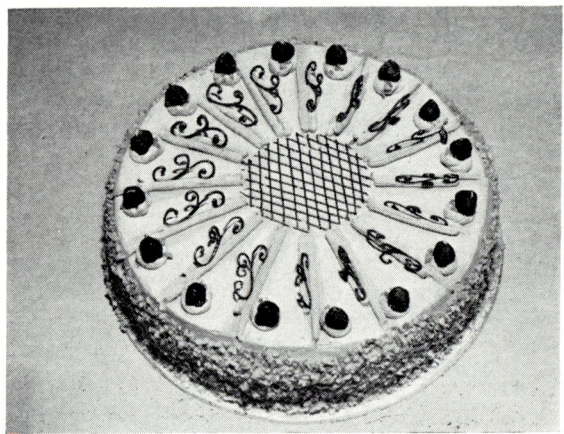

9.21. *Praline torte.*

When half cleared, add the oil and clear very gently, so that the sponge does not collapse. Divide between the prepared hoops, baking at once at 360°F, approximately 35 min. being required.

Chocolate Torte

1 lb. egg	4 oz. melted butter or margarine
11 oz. castor sugar	pink colour
5 oz. soft flour	chocolate colour and
1½ oz. cornflour	flavour compound
2 oz. chocolate powder	

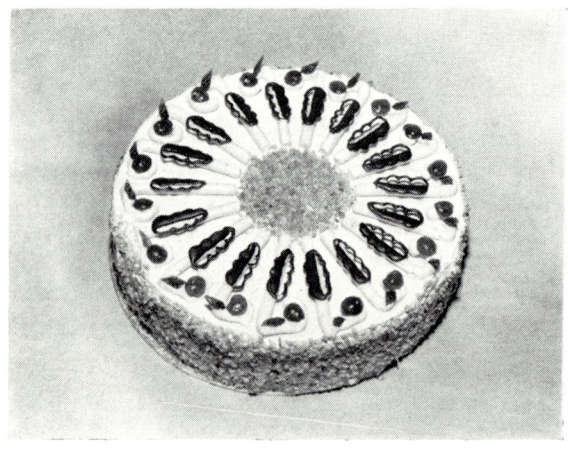

9.22. *Mara-schino torte.*

9.23, 24 and 25. The three stages of stencilling the hazelnut jap tops for Kirsch gâteaux, the stencils illustrated being made from plastic.

Lemon Torte

1 lb. liquid egg	4 oz. melted butter or margarine
10½ oz. castor sugar	Zest and juice of 1 lemon
5 oz. soft flour	*or* lemon essence *or* oil
3½ oz. cornflour	*or* ½ oz. lemon paste

CARDBOARD TEMPLATES

Jap discs are necessary in the production of kirsch or rum gâteau.

From a sheet of stout, clean cardboard, cut out a template of the required size; place in position on to a heavily greased, lightly floured sheet tin, add sufficient jap mixing, spread level and remove the surplus, afterwards lifting the template clear and continuing until sufficient have been produced, allowing two jap discs for each gâteau. Figures 9.23–25. More permanent templates may be produced using plastics, etc.

Hazelnut Jap Tops

Group 1	*Group* 2
1 lb. 4 oz. egg whites	1 lb. roasted hazelnuts
1 lb. castor sugar	8 oz. castor sugar
1 oz. cornflour	4 oz. cornflour

This mixing is produced as detailed and is balanced for use by stencil, using the rubber stencil mat, cardboard templates, or simply spreading on to sheet tins.

Produce a meringue from the materials of Group 1, meanwhile sieving together the materials of Group 2. When the meringue is ready, add the cornflour and allow to mix in on a slow speed. Remove from the machine, knock out the whisk, add and blend in the materials of Group 2.

Work off as detailed above.

Kirsch Gâteau

The base for this gâteau is a good quality butter sponge.

Spread the top of the sponge thinly with pale pink, kirsch-flavoured buttercream, place on a disc of hazelnut jap, top downwards, press lightly in position and reverse, trimming the jap as necessary with scissors to conform to the exact size of the sponge. Now soak what was formerly the base of the sponge with kirsch syrup, produced from 2 lb. sugar boiled with 1 pt water. When cool, add sufficient kirsch liqueur to give a pronounced flavour.

The syrup is perhaps better applied by a bottle fitted with dropper cork, rather than using a spoon, but whichever method is adopted sufficient should be added to moisten the sponge thoroughly.

A further thin layer of kirsch buttercream is now spread on to the sponge, and the second jap disc added, again top downwards, trimming as necessary.

Now spread the top and sides thinly with kirsch buttercream, and mask the sides with either sieved jap crumbs or roasted flake almonds. Dredge the top heavily with icing sugar. The gâteau may be completed with centre portion marked with a cutter and edges marked with a knife. A cherry tree "branch" is piped in baker's chocolate or couverture, with two cherries and leaves to complete.

Alternatively, and preferably for a smaller gâteau, knife marks forming a diamond pattern may be used.

9.26. *Kirsch gâteau.*

Rum Gâteau

The base for this is a chocolate butter sponge, using a syrup produced as previously mentioned but substituting rum for kirsch. The buttercream used is praline, or well-beaten ganache (see page 146).

The make-up of the gâteau is as detailed for kirsch, but after the praline buttercream has finally been applied to top and sides, the gâteau should be placed in a refrigerator to harden off.

When firm, enrobe the top and sides with baker's chocolate, and after the chocolate has set, place strips of wood or cardboard across and dust with icing sugar, adding a pinch of green almond nibs to complete.

An alternative and attractive finish is to pipe the word "Rum" in bold longhand on to wax or greaseproof paper, using white chocolate. When set, and just before the baker's chocolate covering the gâteau has set, carefully remove the piping from the paper with a palette knife and place in position on the gâteau, nothing else being required.

Chocolate Ganache

Bring to the boil 2 pt fresh cream and add 4 lb. chocolate couverture, previously broken into small pieces. Remove from the gas and stir well until dissolved.

Should this prove rather too expensive, a cheaper ganache may be produced by boiling together 2 pt fresh milk and 4 oz. butter, meanwhile chopping finely 4 lb. chocolate couverture or baker's chocolate

9.27. *Rum gâteau.*

of good flavour. When the milk and butter are boiling, remove from the gas, add the chocolate and stir well until all is dissolved.

In both cases, allow to cool and set. When required for use place the quantity required into a suitable machine bowl fitted with beater, warm slightly and beat to good spreading consistency.

To speed up the process, the chocolate may be previously warmed and added in liquid state.

Sponge Drops and Fingers

1¼ lb. egg (1 pt)   1 lb. sugar   1 lb. soft flour

The quantity to be produced at any one mixing will, of course, depend on the facilities available, but as sponge batters deteriorate rapidly, it has been my experience that 1 qt of egg is the maximum amount that two people can conveniently handle, one person being employed in working off the sponge, the other baking each sheet as it is completed. Production, however, can be speeded up by employing two machines, starting the second as the first sponge is removed. With careful timing, the person employed in working off can be kept supplied with freshly-mixed sponge.

Place the egg and sugar in the machine bowl, fit on the whisk, and commence whisking on second speed. Should the egg be really cold, it will be an advantage to place a gas-ring with a low flame beneath the bowl to bring the sponge to correct condition rather more quickly. When blood-heat has been reached, turn out the gas and change to top speed to complete.

WORKING OFF

While this is proceeding, weigh and sieve the flour on to a sheet of clean paper, place on one side, and prepare the bench for working off the sponge.

Using the above quantity, have before you four sheets of grease-proof of good quality cap paper, cut to the size of the sheet tin, one upon the other. Beyond these, with its edge just underneath the four sheets, place a further sheet, upon which is a sieve containing castor sugar. To the right-hand side place four inverted sheet tins, ready to receive the papers after the savoys have been piped out. These are baked on the underside of the sheet tins to keep bottom heat to a minimum. Finally, fit a $\frac{3}{8}$-in. plain tube into a savoy bag, pushing the end of the bag into the tube to prevent drips, turning down the top of the bag to facilitate holding when filling.

A simple way to discover whether full sponge has been achieved is to stop the machine and count up to six fairly slowly. On reaching "six" the whisk marks should still be visible.

Remove the bowl from the machine and knock out the whisk. Add the sieved flour to the sponge and clear carefully. To do this, keep the fingers of the right hand open, going right to the bottom of the bowl and gently bringing to the surface, moving the fingers all the time in the way that the conductor of an orchestra brings in the various instruments with his left hand. While this action is proceeding, the left hand should be employed in turning the bowl round slowly. As soon as the flour is incorporated, stop mixing and remove the right hand, for any further manipulation will result in partial collapse of the sponge.

Using a cellulose scraper, three-quarters fill the bag and proceed to pipe out bulbs approximately $1\frac{1}{2}$ in. in diameter. When the first paper has been filled, dredge with castor sugar from the prepared sieve.

L

9.28. *The bench prepared for working off sponge fingers and drops.*

9.29. *Piping out the sponge fingers.*

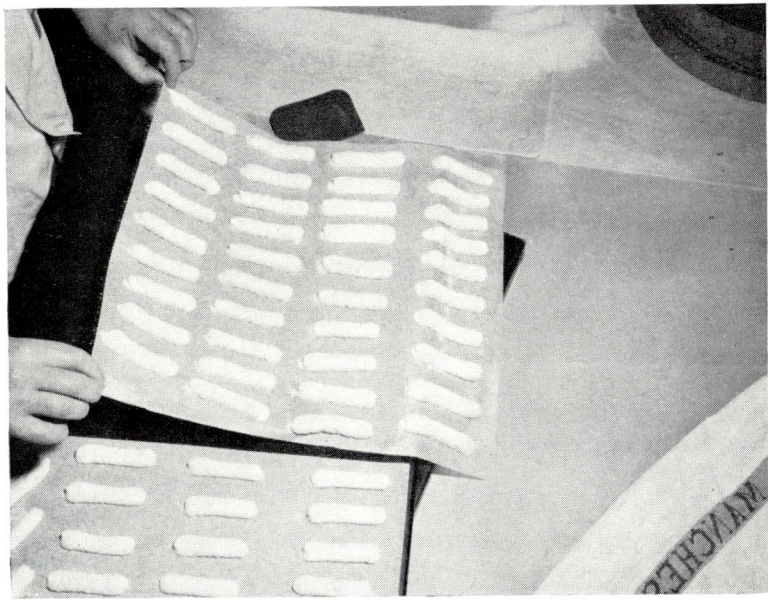

9.30. *The fingers, after dredging with castor sugar, are placed on the sheet tins for immediate baking.*

9.31. *Only a few minutes at 440°F are required.*

Now pick up the paper, using finger and thumb of each hand, at the corners nearest to you, taking the hands upwards and away from you at the same time. This will throw the surplus sugar on to the paper ready to receive it, and then deposit the sheet of drops on to the prepared sheet tins. Bake immediately in a good sound oven of 440°F, only a few minutes being required, the tops of the drops being a nice delicate golden brown, just firm to the touch. Proceed piping out in a similar manner until all the sponge has been used.

FINISHING

When cool, turn upside down on to a clean cloth or sack, and peel the paper very carefully away from the drops. It will generally be found to come away quite easily, but should any difficulty occur, moisten the paper, using a brush and warm water.

Perhaps the most popular finish for these goods is with fresh cream. Lay out the required number, flat side uppermost, and pipe in a spot of good quality raspberry or apricot jam, or lemon cheese, to give a different, attractive flavour. Then pipe on a liberal whirl of the prepared cream, nicely sweetened and flavoured. I say a liberal whirl advisedly, for I do feel that a cream cake is far too often spoiled by confectioners piping in the cream in a very parsimonious manner and this, to my mind, spoils the article and far too often disappoints the customer.

Place on top of the cream another sponge drop, flat side down. Dredge lightly with icing sugar, and place into a paper case to complete.

Savoy Fingers

The recipe is the same as that given for sponge drops. This time, however, the sponge is piped out in rows of neat fingers, care being taken that all are of the same length, approximately 2¼ to 3 in. Sugar and bake in the manner already prescribed for sponge drops.

Plain Roll (for Charlotte Royale)

1¼ lb. egg (1 pt)	10 oz. soft flour
10 oz. castor sugar	

Observing all the normal precautions for grease-free utensils, place the eggs and sugar in the machine bowl and commence whisking. Meanwhile, sieve together the flour and cornflour and place on one side.

9.32. *Sponge drops finished with fresh cream, or,*

9.33. *Buttercream and chocolate.*

Using a sheet tin, 30 in. by 18 in., clean thoroughly, grease and paper, using greaseproof or good quality cap paper, ensuring that the tin is lined to the exclusion of all wrinkles and air.

When half sponge has been reached, remove from the machine and gently blend in the flour, afterwards transferring the sponge to the prepared sheet tin. Very carefully, and with as few strokes as possible, spread level with a trowel palette knife. There is a certain knack to this, but if the knife is kept parallel to, and approximately $\frac{1}{4}$ in. above, the level of the sheet tin, constantly turning the tin round, the knack will soon be acquired. Bake without delay on biscuit wire or double sheet tin in a sound oven of 440°F, for 7 min.

On withdrawal from the oven, turn immediately on to a clean

sugared sack and remove the paper. It will be found that greaseproof paper will leave the sponge quite easily, but cap paper will, in all probability, require moistening with a brush and warm water. Now, leave the roll to cool thoroughly.

To test this, lift one corner of the sponge, and slide the hand between the sponge and sack.

Mincemeat

To the confectioner desiring to produce his own, included here is a recipe which has been well tried and proved satisfactory.

12 lb. currants	$1\frac{1}{2}$ oz. salt
4 lb. 8 oz. seedless raisins	4 oz. mixed spice
5 lb. sultanas	10 oz. rum ($\frac{1}{2}$ pt)
11 lb. apples	10 oz. brandy ($\frac{1}{2}$ pt)
2 lb. 8 oz. mixed peel	5 oz. black treacle
5 lb. 8 oz. Barbados sugar	Zest and juice of
5 lb. 8 oz. suet	10 oranges and
1 lb. 8 oz. glycerine	10 lemons

It is necessary to take all possible precautions to prevent fermentation, and to that end all benches, bowls and utensils should be absolutely free of flour before work commences. Apples should be of the hard, sour variety, carefully inspected for bruises and flaws, well wiped, and afterwards cut into quarters with the cores removed.

Suet should be of good quality as obtained from the butcher, cut into convenient size pieces with all skin, etc., removed. Prepacked suet, usually dusted with rice flour, is not suitable.

Set up the mincing attachment on the machine, fitted with a medium-sized cutter, and start passing the apple, raisins and suet consecutively through until all have been minced. Mix thoroughly with the remainder of the ingredients, the dried fruit having, of course, been previously washed, picked and dried; stir well to amalgamate thoroughly.

The finished mincemeat should then be allowed to stand for at least a week, being occasionally stirred whilst in bulk, before being packed in clean jars or other suitable containers. This will allow the fruit to swell and the flavour to permeate through the bulk. If possible, allow a further four or five weeks to elapse before using, then adding, as necessary, a spot of water to obtain the consistency required.

Small Mince Pies

For the small patty-shaped size mince pies, wipe sufficient tins and divide the requisite amount of paste on the dough divider. Paste up the tins and block, filling afterwards with the mincemeat, the quantity having been pre-determined by careful costing, ensuring, of course, that each pie contains a similar amount.

Pin out sufficient short paste very thinly, using a minimum of dusting flour, and cut with a plain or fluted cutter of a size to fit comfortably the inner circle of the top.

Using a clean piece of cloth folded carefully to fit a cottage pan, pour sufficient cold water into the tin so that the cloth will act as a damp pad. Now touch the underside of the lid on to the pad to moisten it, and place in position on the filled pie. Using the top of a cutter slightly smaller than the lid, press gently to ensure that the lid adheres to the bottom and complete by piercing a small hole in the top with a metal skewer or tip of a french knife to permit the steam to escape. Bake at 430–440°F, dredging with castor sugar to taste.

Meat Patties

These can be produced by using beef or other meats either as they are prepared for pies, or with the addition of a small amount of savoury herbs.

Line sufficient small patty tins with cold meat pie paste, thumb up carefully and add the requisite amount of filling. Roll out sufficient virgin puff paste quite thinly, cut with an appropriately sized fluted cutter, moisten with water, and add the lids. Egg-wash, decorate with a leaf of thin puff paste, allow to rest for 1 hr, re-egg-wash, and insert a small hole with a skewer to allow the steam to escape. Bake at 440°F, ensure that the filling is thoroughly cooked, fill with jelly, and the patty is then ready for sale.

Sweet Pikelets

1½ lb. flour	7½ oz. egg
1½ oz. baking powder	1 lb. 9 oz. milk (1¼ pt)
2½ oz. sugar	2 oz. melted fat

Beat the eggs and sugar together for 2 or 3 min., add the sieved flour and baking powder, three-quarters of the milk, and beat well. Add the remainder of the milk, and again beat well. Now add the melted fat and beat well, the final consistency being very smooth and the batter just flowing to its own level.

Have the hot plate moderately warm and lightly greased. Using the savoy bag and ½-in. plain tube, pipe the batter round approximately 2 in. in diameter, using the forefinger of the left hand to cut off the batter. Look for the "dry top" appearance, when the pikelets will be ready for turning.

Should the pikelets take on too much colour underneath before the top takes on the dry appearance, it is a sign that the plate is too hot, for, if turned over too soon, the resultant pikelet will have a "domed" centre.

Sweet Cakes

These are very similar to Shrewsbury biscuits in character and, delicious as they are, command a ready sale in any season.

1½ lb. flour	¼ oz. salt.
12 oz. margarine	4 oz. currants
12 oz. castor sugar	pinch of nutmeg
½ oz. baking powder	egg colour
3½ oz. egg	

Sieve the flour, nutmeg and baking powder together and rub in the margarine. Make a bay, adding sugar, eggs, and egg colour. Dissolve the sugar, and rub down to a clear shortbread dough, adding the currants when almost clear.

During mixing, the temptation will be strong to add a little more egg, but avoid this.

Roll out the dough to ⅛ in. and cut with a 2-in. fluted cutter, baking on a cool hot plate. When cooked underneath, reverse and, if this is the last article to be produced, the gas may be turned off and cooking completed with the residual heat.

Danish Pastry

Here again a whole new range of lines may be produced by the confectioner using a good basic pastry plus a little imagination. All these lines are quickly produced and generally command attention, but they must be fresh—indeed, they are best enjoyed straight from the oven, and no confectioner should be so foolhardy as to try to foist off day-old Danish pastries as fresh, for there lies the trail of lost business.

One of the secrets here is to produce the pastry in reasonably sized quantities which can be easily handled and quickly worked off.

The recipe for the dough is:

2 lb. 8 oz. flour	5 oz. egg ($\frac{1}{4}$ pt)
1 lb. 4 oz. milk (1 pt)	$\frac{1}{2}$ oz. salt
4 oz. sugar	egg colour
4 oz. yeast	1 lb. pastry margarine
1 oz. compound	1 lb. butter or cake margarine

Sieve the salt and flour together and rub in the small amount of fat. Make a bay, dissolve the yeast and sugar in the cold milk, add the egg and egg colour to give a rich colour and proceed to make into a clear, cold dough in the usual manner. For this work a marble slab will, of course, be ideal to work on. Place the dough on one side and blend the butter and pastry margarine to a smooth plasticity.

Now roll out the dough to a rectangle, using flour for dusting as necessary, and place the plastic fats in the centre, brushing off any surplus flour and folding in the edges of the dough in envelope fashion to totally enclose the fats. Pin out carefully, to ensure that the fat does not strike through the dough, to a fairly large rectangle. Fold into three, puff paste fashion, and again pin out to a rectangle. This time cut the rectangle into two equal pieces and place one cut edge along an uncut edge to assist in dispersing the fat evenly throughout the dough. Again pin out to a rectangle and fold into three, puff paste fashion, and the pastry will then be ready for working off into the desired varieties. A bench brush will, of course, be kept handy to remove all surplus flour during the rolling and folding process.

Several different types of filling will be required to give variety and these should be prepared beforehand so that the working off of the pastry may proceed smoothly and without interruption. Besides the fillings to be made a supply of cut peel and washed and ready-cleaned currants and sultanas should be available.

Fillings
1. VANILLA

2$\frac{1}{2}$ lb. milk (1 qt)	3 oz. butter or margarine
6 oz. sugar	egg colour
4 oz. cornflour	vanilla essence
2 oz. egg	

Mix the cornflour and egg to a smooth paste, using a small amount of cold milk. Boil the remainder of the milk and castor sugar, add the cornflour paste, butter, colour and essence and whisk until stiff.

Only fresh milk should be used for vanilla, but occasionally, perhaps through breakdown in supply or oversight in ordering, it is necessary to use milk powder. In this case the milk powder should be added to the cornflour paste and, should it be necessary to return to the gas for thickening, the bowl or pan should be placed in a water jacket, bain-marie fashion, for, in my experience, no amount of vigilance prevents the vanilla custard from developing that burnt taste when subject to direct heat.

2. ALMOND MIXTURE

2 lb. castor sugar   vanilla and almond essences
12 oz. ground almonds   water to mix to spreading
8 oz. sieved sponge crumbs   consistency

3. BUTTER MIXTURE

8 oz. castor sugar   1 lb. butter or margarine
8 oz. brown Trinidad sugar

GENERAL RULES

A few general rules which apply to all varieties.

All sheet tins to be used should be perfectly clean and no grease is required.

The proving of all Danish pastries requires great care, and the prover itself should be at a temperature of not more than 75°F, only a very small amount of steam being required. Indeed, if the weather is temperate and there is no great hurry for the goods, they will prove quite naturally in the rack without using the prover.

It is a good plan to egg-wash half-way through the proving period because not only do the pastries increase in bulk during this time, but expose portions of the paste previously hidden from view, and a better finish is possible without leaving a "tide mark" of egg-wash.

Generally speaking, a baking temperature of 420–450°F can be utilised, depending upon the size of the goods, but every care should be taken as too hot an oven will, of course, result in the goods taking on too much colour before being properly baked. After baking, all goods are glazed with boiled apricot purée and thin water icing.

Custard Buns

Pin out the prepared pastry to about $\frac{1}{4}$ in. thick and cut into strips approximately $\frac{1}{2}$ in. wide and 12 in. long. Twist the ends into opposite directions and, starting in the centre on the appropriate position of the sheet tin, form into a spiral, afterwards tucking the loose end underneath. Make a depression in the centre with the thumb, prove, egg-wash and, immediately before baking, pipe in a little of the cold, well-beaten vanilla custard, using a savoy bag and plain tube. Bake at 440°F and immediately on withdrawal from the oven glaze, taking care, of course, not to disturb the vanilla during this process.

These, I find, are amongst the most popular of Danish pastry lines and a quicker method may be as follows:

Pin out the prepared pastry to approximately $\frac{1}{2}$ in. thick and cut with a 2$\frac{1}{2}$-in. plain cutter. Prove, egg-wash and, just before baking, make a depression in the centre with the moistened thumb.

Pipe in the vanilla, bake and finish as previously.

Danish Turnover

Pin out a portion of the pastry to $\frac{1}{4}$ in. thick and cut with a 3-in. fluted cutter, brushing over half the surface with water. Place a small amount of either the almond or butter mixture—or a little of each—in the centre and fold over as for making jam puffs. Egg-wash, dip immediately into flaked almonds, prove and bake, afterwards glazing on removal from the oven.

"S" Scroll

Roll out the pastry quite thinly and spread some of the almond mixture over half the surface, using this quite sparingly otherwise it may tend to flow out during baking, thus causing waste.

Cut the paste into two, place the untreated portion on top of the treated and pin lightly to secure. Cut into strips about $\frac{1}{4}$ in. wide and 12 in long. Twist the ends in opposite directions, shape into the "S" scroll, prove, egg-wash, bake, and afterwards glaze.

Fruit Roll

Pin down the pastry to rather less than $\frac{1}{4}$ in. thick and cut into strips of approximately 3$\frac{1}{2}$ in. wide. Along the centre of each strip pipe a rope of the almond mixture and alongside a small amount of the butter or honey mixture. Sprinkle with sultanas, egg-wash the edges and fold over as for sausage rolls, making certain that the edges adhere firmly. Egg-wash, sprinkle with flaked almonds and cut into suitable lengths. Prove, bake and glaze.

Alternatively, roasted flaked almonds may be sprinkled on the rolls after baking and glazing in place of the above method.

Stars

Pin out the paste to $\frac{1}{4}$ in. thick and cut into approximately 3-in. squares. Make a $1\frac{1}{4}$-in. cut towards the centre in each corner, egg-wash the centre portion and fold each alternate corner inwards, pressing well down to secure. Prove and, just before baking, place a sprinkling of sultanas in the centre, followed by a bulb of vanilla, using a savoy bag and plain tube. Bake at 440°F, and finish by brushing over with water icing.

9.34. *Custard buns, Danish rolls, stars and crescents are in this assortment of Danish pastries. For the confectioner with available space, a high-class coffee lounge, serving Danish pastries and coffee in the morning, and light afternoon teas in the afternoon is well worth considering.*

Danish Crescents

Roll out the pastry to approximately $\frac{1}{4}$ in. thick and cut this into 6-in. wide strips and afterwards into triangles. At the base of each pipe in a small amount of the almond mixture and also the butter mixture, afterwards rolling up and placing on the sheet tin in the form of crescents. Egg-wash, prove and bake at 440°F, afterwards glazing and sprinkling with roasted flake almonds.

Tempering Chocolate Couverture

Break up the couverture into small pieces, place in a double-jacketed pan or bain-marie, and place over a low light, stirring occasionally with a spatula, melting at a temperature of 115–120°F; in the case of milk couverture, not exceeding 110°F.

When the temperature indicated is reached, remove pan from the water jacket, wipe underneath carefully to remove all traces of water, and pour half the amount on to a marble slab, working with a palette knife and scotch scraper until amost set, but under no circumstances allowing the couverture to crust. Return the mass to the pan, stir, and bring the temperature to 86°F – 88°F, or, in the case of milk couverture, 84°F–86°F.

If it goes above this temperature, the process must be repeated, for the indicated degree must be reached by an increase, never a decrease, in temperature.

The chocolate is then ready for use.

Baker's Chocolate

The temperatures required for chocolate vary slightly between those from different manufacturers, and upon the purpose for which the chocolate is to be used.

For coating gâteaux, layer cakes, and Swiss rolls, where only a thin covering is required, the chocolate can be worked at a higher temperature than if it is to be used for moulding.

Break the chocolate into small pieces, place into a bain-marie, melt and warm to a temperature between 105–110°F for plain, and for milk, 100–105°F. These are approximately average working temperatures, but each manufacturer will supply exact details and temperatures peculiar to his product.

Cake Coatings—Coloured

These, again, can be considered as baker's chocolate, and are useful not only in decorative work for gâteaux, etc., but also for use in moulded figures, to pick out features.

CUT CHOCOLATE

Using greaseproof or wax paper of suitable size, pour on sufficient chocolate to spread a thin layer with a palette knife over the surface. Pick up the paper at opposite corners and tap gently to remove knife marks.

When setting point is reached, cut as required, using round, plain or fluted cutters, the seven-wheeled cutter for squares, and a sharp-pointed knife for triangles, half circles, etc.

When properly set, these can be packed in boxes for use as required.

ROLLED CHOCOLATE

Ladle a small quantity of chocolate upon a clean, dry, marble slab, and spread to an oblong, back and forth, using a palette knife. After a moment or two, when the chocolate is set, but before it has hardened, holding a scotch scraper or long-bladed knife at an incline, scrape off the chocolate, when it will form itself into thin rolls.

Allow to harden, afterwards packing into boxes for later use.

Moulded Animals and Figures

Moulds for these can be purchased in a clear plastic material, and it was from these that the figures illustrated were produced.

Supplied in halves, with clips as necessary to hold them together, they are ideal for the purpose and, considering their life if properly treated, are reasonable in price.

FILLING THE MOULDS

Clip the halves together and, if desired, apply the coloured chocolate with a small palette knife or, for noses, eyes, etc., a cocktail stick,

9.35. *Although the figures shown are for Christmas, many other moulds are available to suit other seasons. Wrapping in film will prevent finger marking.*

then allow this to set. Fill the moulds with the prepared chocolate, tapping, underneath to remove unwanted air bubbles. Reverse, and tap again to remove the surplus—the ear will soon become attuned to know when sufficient has been removed. Clean off the base with a knife and stand immediately upright on greaseproof or wax paper.

When set, trim the base to leave a clean foot, remove the clips and place in the refrigerator for approximately 30 min.

To remove from the mould, place a knife between the joints and very gently prise apart. One half will immediately come away. Supporting the base, lift the figure carefully away.

METHODS OF PACKING

It is, of course, ideal if these figures can be presented for sale in suitably festive boxes, but the price asked for the number of boxes the small confectioner would require is usually prohibitive, and all too often the price which would have to be charged for them would make the finished article non-competitive. Hence, a method of packing, using fancy ribbons, transparent cellulose both in sheets and bags, that presents the figures attractively and prevents finger marks on the chocolate is to be commended.

Meringues

It is, perhaps, true to say that there is no more profitable range of goods than those produced from meringue, using the term very loosely to embrace japs of various types. The yield is large and, properly made, the varieties command a good price. As to the materials required, fresh or frozen egg white, together with albumen reconstituted at the rate of 3 oz. dried and powdered albumen dissolved in 1 pt lukewarm water, well stirred, will give satisfactory results when the strict rule of absolute cleanliness is observed.

In addition, various proprietary meringue powders are available which, if used to the manufacturer's instructions, give good results. This should, however, be qualified in that these do produce a meringue different in taste from those produced from the natural albumen base. Whilst those made from the latter give a meringue with a "chewy" centre, the former tend to be powdery. As in so many other facets of our trade, no one is qualified to say that either is "correct", the right one obviously being that which appeals to the customers and for which there is a ready sale.

However, for the purpose of this chapter the whites mentioned take the form of fresh or frozen or reconstituted albumen.

The castor sugar used should be of hard grain, dry and free running, whilst great care must be taken to ensure that it is absolutely clean and free from any suggestion of grease in any shape or form.

The various types of meringue are:
1. cold
2. hot
3. boiled or Italian meringue.

The terms "light", "medium" and "heavy" refer to the weight of sugar per pint of whites.

COLD MERINGUE

1 lb. 4 oz. whites (1 pt)   Pinch of cream of tartar
2 lb. 8 oz. castor sugar

Place the whites and cream of tartar into a well-scalded machine bowl, and commence whisking on medium speed, continuing until the character changes from a snow or froth to that of a more solid appearance. At this stage add approximately 2 oz. sugar, continuing whisking and adding at short intervals more sugar until about half has been absorbed. The result should now be a firm meringue. Remove the bowl from the machine, knock out the whisk, add the remaining sugar and stir in carefully, using a wooden spatula.

The meringue is now ready for working off.

SHELLS

The best known, and probably most popular, of any meringue line, shells, should be piped on to a greaseproof-papered sheet tin, using a savoy bag and $\frac{5}{8}$-in. plain tube. Pipe slightly oval in shape and, to obviate "tails", release pressure, taking the tube up, over, and off, at an angle of 45 degrees.

When the sheet is full, dredge with castor sugar and dry off at a temperature of not more than 260°F, with the oven door slightly ajar and steam damper open. When dry, with the meringues leaving the paper quite easily, remove from the oven and, when cool, from the sheet tin, making an indentation in the base of each with the thumb to allow space for eventual creaming. Store, preferably in a drying cupboard, or some other dry place, until required.

For finishing, place the meringues in paper cases in pairs and pipe into the hollows sufficient whipped and sweetened fresh or synthetic cream, completing with a pinch of green nib almonds.

As the shelf life of these is extremely limited, care should be exercised to prevent wastage through over-production.

9.36. *Meringue shells, fresh cream and strawberries for popularity.*

LEMON MERINGUES

For these, empty pastry shells will be required, using sweet or German pastry-lined frangipane tins, baked empty. When cool, release from the tins and set the cases on to a sheet tin lined with greaseproof paper.

Using sufficient of the prepared meringue, add lemon cheese of top quality until the meringue takes on a pale yellow colour, which should also give a definite, piquant flavour. Using a palette knife, fill the pastry cases and spread level with the top of the case.

When all have been so treated, fill a savoy bag fitted with large star tube, and pipe on to the top of each a whirl of ordinary meringue. Dredge lightly with castor sugar, add a sprinkle of fine, flaked almonds, and dry at 300°F, in a steam-free oven until the whirls are tinted a golden brown.

When cold, the lemon meringues should be placed in paper cases ready for use as a variety in a selection of fancies.

Brioche

Although very rarely seen in this country on everyday sale, the brioche is very light and rich. Whilst the price that must be charged for these goods is perhaps a little high, orders do come in for special functions, and it is always useful to have a recipe handy.

The one below will be found to give a really satisfactory article and has the added advantage of being a quick, commercial dough, saving

M

the many hours of lying about in bulk called for in some recipes.

2 lb. 4 oz. flour	1 lb. egg
$\frac{3}{4}$ oz. salt	10 oz. butter or margarine
$3\frac{1}{2}$ oz. yeast	3 oz. milk
$1\frac{1}{2}$ oz. sugar	

Place the sugar, salt, malt, and yeast into a suitably sized hand-bowl which already contains the cold milk, and whisk to dissolve. Add the egg, whisk to amalgamate and, finally, add the flour, afterwards transferring to the bench. Rub down really well to produce a very smooth dough. The butter, which should have been previously beaten to a smooth plasticity, is now added in two portions, each being well beaten into the dough. When a really smooth, soft dough has been produced, scrape all together, and place in a greased hand-bowl of suitable size in a warm prover. Allow the dough to ferment for 1 hr, knocking well back three times during this period.

At the end of this time take to the bench and scale into suitably sized pieces, depending on the size required. For patty tins or medium-sized, deep, fluted frangipane tins $1-1\frac{1}{2}$ oz. will be ample.

When all are scaled, mould round, and then, using the sides of the hands, remould to leave a small piece about the size of a marble, whilst yet joined to the main piece of dough. Place the large piece into the well-greased tin, make an indentation with the moistened fore-finger where the small piece joins, afterwards placing the latter in the indentation.

This method is infinitely quicker than the one where two pieces of dough are required to be moulded.

Proving should be accomplished in gentle heat and without steam, and after approximately 10 min. the pieces should be removed and given a good egg-wash.

If desired, four deep cuts may then be made, taking in the top and edges and using a pair of scissors dipped constantly in hot water. The brioche should then be returned to the prover to complete proof, afterwards baking at 480°F.

These goods are usually sold plain, but there is no reason why, to give further variety, some cannot be brushed over with hot water icing immediately on removal from the oven, afterwards dipping in roasted coconut or flaked almonds. For sandwiches produce finger shaped.

Florentines

Of all the items of confectionery that it is possible to produce, these are very high in any popularity poll. Although quite easy and quick

9.37. *Lemon meringues are suitable for use either as a sweet or in a variety of fancies.*

9.38. *An alternative to the lemon meringue–strawberry meringue, using strawberry purée in place of lemon cheese.*

to make, it is remarkable how few one sees offered and, on that score alone, it is of value to deal fully with their manufacture.

15 oz. margarine   1 lb. castor sugar
5 oz. cream ($\frac{1}{4}$ pt)

Place all in a suitable pan, bring to a vigorous boil, then add and stir well in:

15 oz. nibbed almonds   5 oz. chopped citron peel
$7\frac{1}{2}$ oz. flaked almonds   12 oz. chopped cherries
7 oz. chopped mixed peel

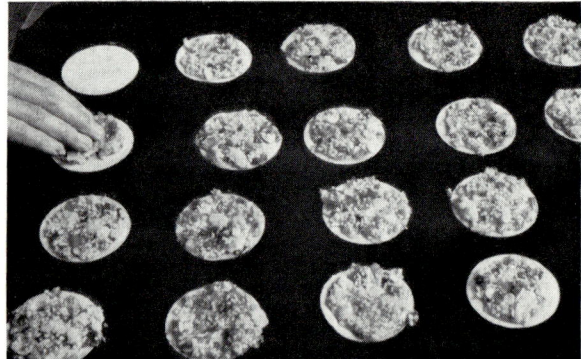

9.39. Setting out Florentine mixing on to wafer paper discs.

9.40. The alternative is to use silicone paper cases. Care should be taken when using these that not too much Florentine mixing is placed into each case.

Set the mixing on one side to cool.

Clean and grease lightly the number of sheet tins required, and here it should be pointed out that any mixing not worked off may be set on one side and kept over quite long periods. Set out on the prepared sheet tins discs of wafer paper, allowing some space between each disc.

Have available a bowl of lukewarm water and, dipping the fingers constantly into this to prevent adhesion, place a small heap of the mixing on each, pressing down just to approach the edges of the paper. Some "flow" will occur during baking, so take care that too much florentine is not used initially. It is now possible to purchase shallow paper cups of silicone paper in which they may be baked. The baking temperature is 380°F.

Immediately on removal from the oven, use a large plain cutter, dipped constantly in water, to draw in the edges and restore the florentine to the approximate size of the wafer paper. Set the sheets on one side to go cold.

To finish off the florentine, spread a piece of greaseproof or silicone paper with baker's chocolate or couverture, previously tempered, to a depth of ¼ in. thick. Into this place the florentines, and allow to set pressing well into the chocolate and giving space between each one for eventual cutting out with an appropriately sized cutter when the chocolate has hardened.

Recoat each, using a palette knife, and comb with comb scraper. When setting out on trays for a catering function, it is usual to alternate sides uppermost, as illustrated.

9.41. *If using the wafer-paper circles, it is necessary to draw the Florentine together immediately upon withdrawal from the oven, using a large-sized cutter, constantly dipped into water to prevent sticking.*

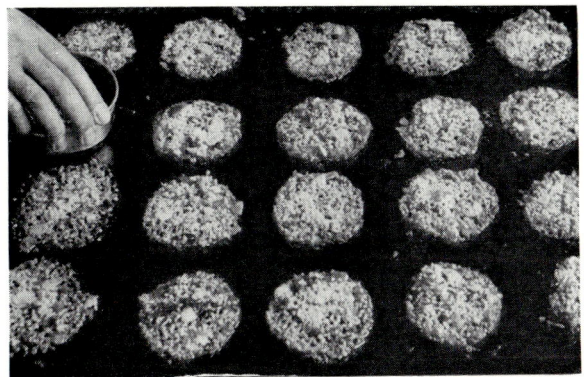

9.42. *Cutting the Florentines out of the chocolate into which they have been inset. All that now remains is to recoat with chocolate, comb, allow to set.*

9.43. *Setting out Florentines for display.*

Florentine Torte

Torte and gâteaux may be produced, using florentine as decorative media.

Cut out a disc of sweetpaste of the same size as the torte and half bake. Now cover the sweetpaste thinly with florentine and bake at 380°F. Use this for the top of the torte, the base of which could be plain, coffee or almond, previously split and filled with praline nougat buttercream. It is an advantage to segment the top before assembly.

9.44. *Florentine torte.*

The sides of the torte should be masked with buttercream and dressed with broken florentine, roasted nib or roasted flaked almonds.

Buttercream

Many and varied are the recipes available for the production of this item, but suffice for our purpose here to give one recipe, and that a popular one. The reader will doubtless have his own for, being creatures of habit, we tend to stick to that with which we are familiar, but, nevertheless, many recipes are in existence to produce a wide variety of types of fillings. Points to watch are, of course, flavour and keeping quality, this latter depending very much upon the type of fat available. Butter is generally considered the first choice.

4 lb. unsalted butter   4 lb. fondant (slightly softened)

Place the butter into the machine bowl fitted with beater, and start the machine on first speed. Break the fondant into reasonably sized pieces, adding each piece as soon as the previous one has been absorbed. When all has been added, change to fast speed and cream very lightly, warming in cold weather as is necessary. Add now 5 oz. egg whites or warm water and continue to beat to maximum volume. The resultant filling should have the appearance of fine velvet. Colours and flavours should be added as required.

Tea Scones, using Yeast and Powder Aeration

The recipe, as given, should produce approximately twelve-dozen scones:

An enriched type of tea scone may be produced using yeast and powder aeration.

In this case, the texture is slightly more open but, externally, a bolder, lighter article, with shorter eating properties may be produced. To offset the increased cost, the dough may be rolled slightly thinner, and this gives a greater yield.

6 lb. flour	1 lb. 4 oz. egg (1 pt)
4 oz. baking powder	2 lb. 8 oz. milk (1 qt)
12 oz. sugar	3 oz. yeast
12 oz. shortening	12 oz. currants

A little egg colour may be used, but every care should be taken to avoid a vivid yellow.

The dough may be produced by either rubbing in or creaming method.

Dissolve the yeast in the cold milk and mix, adding the egg to the milk and whisking well just prior to adding to the remainder of the ingredients. Clear really well and, finally, add the cleaned fruit, dispersing evenly through the dough. Work off by dividing into two, and commence rolling out the first portion, using a minimum of dusting flour, and constantly turning the dough round to prevent it sticking to the bench and to obtain an even thickness. Pin down to $\frac{3}{8}$ in., and cut with a 2-in. plain cutter, carefully, keeping the scrap down to a minimum.

Place the cut portions on a clean, lightly-greased sheet tin, taking care to keep the shapes quite round, and close together.

Press the cuttings lightly together, and place in the centre of the second piece of dough, enclosing by turning over the edges. Turn the dough over, to expose the smooth surface, and again repeat the pinning and cutting out process, afterwards transferring the cut shapes to the sheet tins.

The scrap may now be drawn together and rolled again.

Whilst a period of rest after the goods have been worked off is essential, they should be worked off immediately after mixing. To allow the mixed scone dough to stand whilst another job is completed is fatal.

Egg-wash carefully with a strong wash, allow the usual period of rest, egg-wash again, and bake on wires or an upturned sheet tin at 460°F.

Finally, I have preference for a dry heat, having found by experience that a much nicer article is produced if the work can be so arranged that the tea scones are the sole occupants of the oven during baking.

Cherry Scones

Variety, with good effect, may be introduced into what we can call the stock lines of scones, and I find that where introduced cherry scones have proved to be immensely popular.

5 lb. flour	12 oz. shortening
4 oz. baking powder	3 lb. 2 oz. milk
10 oz. sugar	12 oz. cherries

Mix as already detailed; the cherries, having been washed and dried, should be lightly chopped and dispersed throughout the dough.

Two types of finish are now possible. The first is to continue as for tea scones, using the method as detailed above, but, as this is an entirely different line, I advocate another finish.

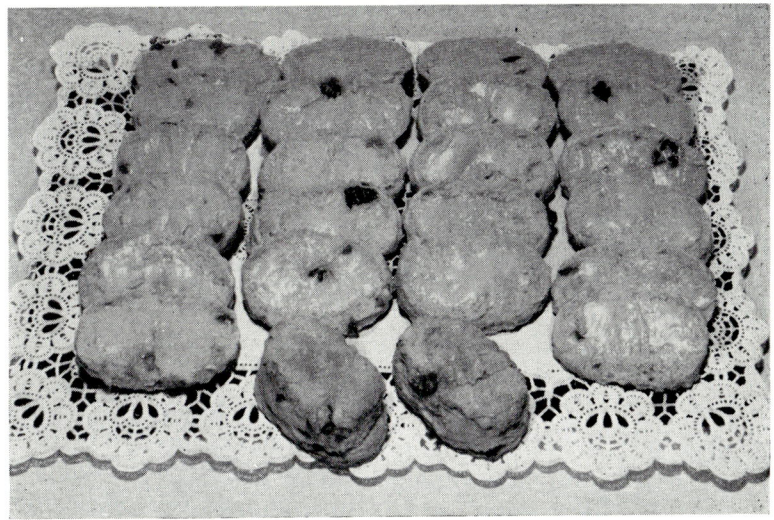

9.45. Cherry scones, ready for display.

For this, and using the minimum of dusting flour, pin out the dough to a rectangle, keeping the edges straight and corners as square as possible until the dough is approximately ½ in. thick. Brush over the surface with a mixture comprising half egg whites and half water, afterwards dredging lightly with castor sugar. Now, using a sharp knife, cut into strips 3 in. wide and divide, afterwards, each strip into individual pieces 1½ in. wide. Transfer carefully to a clean, lightly-greased sheet tin, and bake at 430°F.

Sausage Rolls

Whilst these are generally produced from puff paste, they may, of course, be produced from a good quality pie paste. Indeed, they may find greater favour using the latter, for when the puff paste variety are eaten cold, they do tend to have a rather greasy after-taste. For this job then, the first recipe (Chapter 11) produced by the cold process will give every satisfaction.

A study of the sausage meat to be used will well repay the time spent on it. I advocate the purchase of sausage meat as opposed to buying sausage and then skinning it. As is well known, to produce a good cake all the ingredients must be correctly balanced, otherwise unsatisfactory results are obtained. We are rather apt to regard sausage as "just sausage", yet this must be balanced in the same way as a cake mixing if we are to turn out a satisfactory article. Unless we

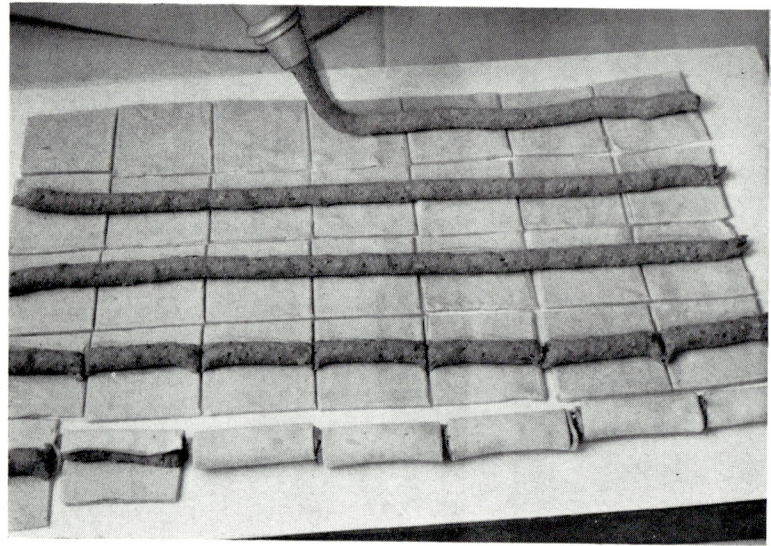

9.46. *The mechanics of producing sausage rolls.*

purchase sausage meat which has been correctly balanced by the manufacturer we shall not get the results we desire.

Excess fat will result in the meat disintegrating during baking, splitting of the paste and the sheet tin swimming with fat. Again, excess filler will result in a very dry roll, with the filling shrinking and pulling the roll badly out of shape. It may, of course, be necessary to purchase several manufacturers' products before an entirely suitable

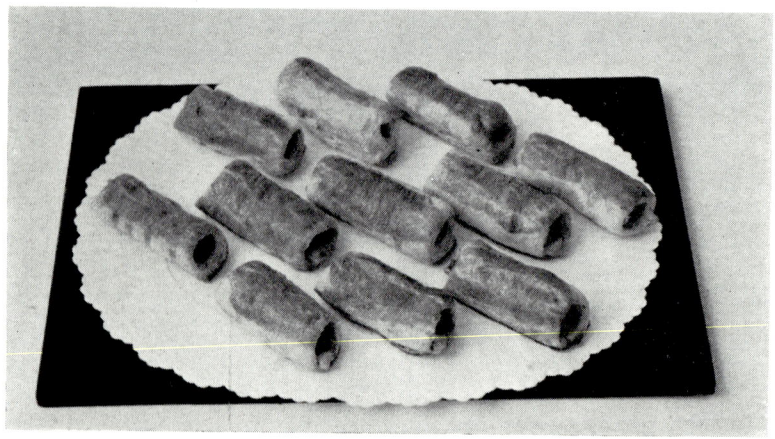

9.47 *Sausage rolls.*

meat is purchased, but buy for colour, flavour and baking properties. The meat should be used as purchased, without any addition.

Pin out the paste quite thinly, certainly no thicker than $\frac{1}{8}$ in., into a large rectangle. Using a seven-wheel pastry cutter set to the correct width, cut into strips vertically and then, using the same setting, horizontally, thus cutting the paste into squares of the desired size. Alternatively, of course, a stick of the correct width and a knife may be used, but I do think that the few shillings expended on one of these cutters is amply repaid in regularity and more speedy production.

Fit a savoy bag with a $\frac{1}{2}$-in. plain tube, place a small quantity of sausage meat in the bag and pipe in horizontal lines along the centre of the squares, working from left to right. When all the squares have been so dealt with, take a knife dipped constantly in cold water to prevent sticking and cut through the sausage to divide each rope into the size of the squares.

Wash the paste with water, take the top piece of the first square and fold on to the top of the sausage. Fold over again to totally enclose the filling, with the joint running along the middle of the underside. Place on to a sheet tin lined with greaseproof paper, and continue until all have been folded, placing them in neat rows on the sheet. Flatten gently by means of a rolling-pin, egg-wash, mark lightly with a fork if desired and bake at 440°F.

Sausage rolls are ideal subjects for deep freeze in the unbaked state.

CHAPTER 10

An Assortment of Sweets

It is in the production of sweets that the confectioner can really shine and create a good impression, women especially appreciating the unusual and different articles he is able to produce and present. A review of sweets that have previously appeared as part of the different menus, together with some variations that are possible, will be followed by further ideas and suggestions not mentioned before.

Suitable Sweets

(1) Fruit and jelly in individual soufflé cases or sundae dishes, either with or without cream, are more suitable for children's parties.

(2) Trifles may be produced in larger sizes, and should this be decided upon the finish should be most carefully considered, using, for instance, langue-du-chat biscuits and such decorations as meringue birds, roses, and mushrooms. It must be remembered that the production of trifle is well within the scope of the housewife; for this reason the article must have really good eating quality and present a first-class appearance.

(3) Pineapple savarins. The fruit may be varied according to availability and season, whilst an alternative to these is babas au rhum.

(4) Fruit salad and ice cream.

(5) Charlotte royale and charlotte russe, made by either the English or Continental method. The charlotte russe may be produced as an individual sweet.

(6) Petits Fours Glacés. These do not refer solely to our English version, comprising simply genoese of various shapes enrobed in differently coloured fondants, but to a wide variety, including othellos, with the accent on flavour.

(7) Gâteaux such as kirsch, rum, and Black Forest.

(8) Vacherin—again the type of fruit may vary with the season, and here one incorporating, for instance, fresh or frozen strawberries would be sure to find great favour. These, again, are suitable to produce individually.

(9) Gâteaux produced from a coloured and flavoured butter-sponge base, with the filling incorporating the appropriate chopped fruit, and finish including the crystallised fruit such as pineapple, pear, peach, apricot, etc. The accent here must be on flavour, and the medium used for flavouring the buttercream should be the syrup in which the fruit has been crystallised; this is far superior to essences.

(10) For cocktail parties, small petits fours and various chou-paste items, caramel fruits, marrons glacés, small cocktail-sized puff mince tarts in season and almond dessert, these latter comprising many varieties of small almond biscuits.

(11) Christmas pudding and rum sauce.

(12) Omelette surprise.

(13) Apple or other type of fruit tart and cream.

Now to further suitable dishes not previously mentioned.

Pear Salad

Allow two pear halves of reasonable size per portion, or cut the halves into two, then allow three pieces per guest. This latter method gives a more dainty appearance besides slightly reducing costs. If using fresh fruit, peel, core, segment and simmer gently in a simple syrup until tender.

Now, whether using fresh or tinned fruit, strain and add to the syrup an equal quantity of redcurrant jelly slightly above setting point. Re-strain, and when cold add sufficient good-quality port wine to give a decided flavour. Pour over the fruit and serve, if possible, well chilled.

Pineapple Fritters

Use pineapple rings of good quality, straining off the juice and drying the fruit.

Make a batter by sieving into a suitable bowl 8 oz. flour and a pinch of salt. Make a bay, add $\frac{1}{2}$ pt lukewarm water and 1 oz. oil or melted butter, beating well to produce a smooth batter. Finally, whisk up 4 oz. egg whites quite stiff and add, amalgamating gently but throughly.

Dip the drained fruit into the batter and deep fry to a crisp, golden brown. Serve with castor sugar and allow a portion of one ring.

Continental Sweets

Though relatively quite simple to produce, these sweets are really unusual in that the container itself is edible. After very little practice the confectioner will be able to produce them quite quickly, and they

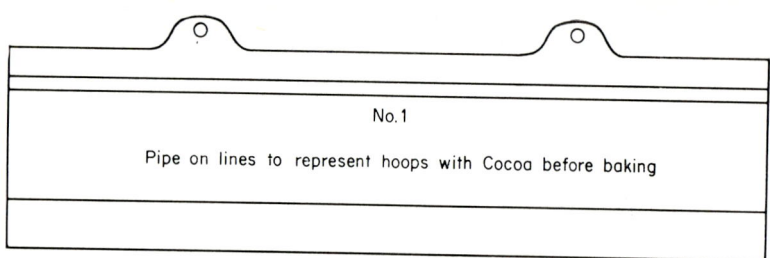

No. 1

Pipe on lines to represent hoops with Cocoa before baking

No. 1

No. 2

No. 3

No. 2

10.0. *Stencils required for Continental sweets. The actual size will depend upon the reader's choice.*

10.1. *Three unusual Continental sweets: Tub* (bottom left), *Casket* (top centre), *Butterfly Cup* (bottom right).

should prove a sound commercial proposition. In addition, they will bring a Continental flavour and atmosphere to the function and leave the guest with that good impression so necessary.

Illustration 10.1 shows the different types of sweets that can be produced and the diagram shows the stencils required. These can be made from stout, clean cardboard at the outset, and after the necessary experiments for size have been completed the reader could have these reproduced in either a plastic or suitable metal as being more permanent.

Hippenmasse

The paste required for the stencilling, namely hippenmasse, is easily produced by sieving together

10 oz. ground almonds	5 oz. flour
15 oz. castor sugar	

Add to this 6½ oz. egg whites and 3 oz. of milk to produce a smooth paste of spreading consistency. Stencil on to a greased and lightly floured sheet tin, baking off at 410°F.

When half baked, remove from the oven, allow to cool for a few moments and replace to complete the baking, thus ensuring even colour. Immediately on withdrawal from the oven, roll round a suitable wooden former such as a rolling pin, and press well to secure the joint. Allow to cool and then remove from the former.

Tub *(Illustration 10.1, bottom left)*

Produced from stencil No. 1, joining the sides to the base and painting inside with quick-set jelly. This is done to prevent possible softening by the filling. This latter comprises a russe cream, topped with strawberries glazed with a quick-set jelly, a whirl of cream, and a small piece of pistachio nut.

10.2. *Flowerpots.*

Casket *(Illustration 10.1, top centre)*

Produced from base and top round stencil No. 2, sides No. 1 minus handles. Both inside and out are painted with baker's chocolate; filling here consisted of ice cream and whirl of cream, with a half cherry shown in the opening of the casket.

Butterfly Cup *(Illustration 10.1, bottom right)*

The base here is an almond macaroon biscuit, with previously piped lines, before assembly, of chocolate. To do this, place the biscuits close together and, using a small bag of baker's chocolate, with fine aperture, pipe lines quickly back and forth whilst holding the bag high.

The sides are produced by using stencil No. 2 and sprinkling the hippenmasse lightly with fine flaked almonds before baking. The butterfly is again stencilled and bent on removal from the oven to give the necessary shape, whilst a piped line of chocolate will represent the body. The inside of the cup should be masked with quick-set

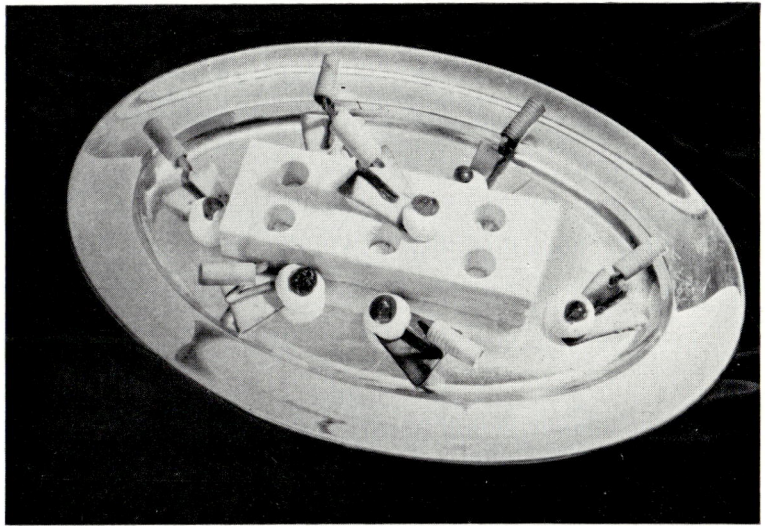

10.3. *The ice brick.*

jelly, and the filling consists of a russe cream containing a portion of chopped fruit, topped by a whirl of cream.

Flowerpot *(Illustration 10.2)*

Stencil No. 2 base, sides No. 3, the latter again being sprinkled with flaked almonds before baking. The filling may be any of those previously mentioned, topped with cream, the flower taking the form of a cartoon flower piped in chocolate.

Ice Brick *(Illustration 10.3)*

This is an extremely good illustration of the Continental idea of the unusual. Suitable for a function where the guests are predominantly connected with the building industry, the block of ice cream is a copy of the Continental brick, whilst the trowels are stencilled as detailed. being joined together with caramel sugar. Sufficient here, as shown by the trowels, for seven portions.

Black Forest Gâteau

A chocolate butter-sponge base is required. Split, layer with good-quality lemon-cheese and a reasonable amount of whipped and sweetened fresh cream. Replace the top, liberally mask both top and sides with the same material, and place on a cake board.

N

The traditional Black Forest gâteau has triangular pieces of cut chocolate placed in the cream in an upright position to represent the forest. It may be heresy to say so, but I feel that this finish is crude and, in this country at least, has no significance to the general public. Therefore I favour the finish as illustrated.

To do this, pour sufficient tempered-chocolate couverture, or preferably a baker's chocolate of good quality, on to a clean, dry, marble slab, working back and forth with a palette knife in the manner used to produce chocolate curls or rolls. Just before setting point is reached, trim the top, bottom, and two sides and, using a scotch scraper, scrape up the chocolate, going along the length of the rectangle. Pick up each scraping as produced and, if the temperature of the chocolate has been judged correctly, it is a simple matter to wrap round and over the top of the prepared gâteau, covering the whole entirely. As will be seen from the illustration, the form the chocolate takes during scraping is quite novel. To complete, place three or four strips of wood or cardboard across the gâteau and dredge with icing sugar, removing the wood or cardboard carefully afterwards.

Sponge Flans

The base for these is of the normal sponge sandwich, comprising:

1 lb. 4 oz. egg (1 pt)	2 oz. cornflour
1 lb. castor sugar	1 oz. warm water
14 oz. weak flour	

10.4. *Black Forest gâteau.*

Mixed in the normal way, the sponge is scaled direct into well-greased and floured large savarin tins and baked at 400°F.

On removal from the oven, reverse on to a clean cloth or sack and allow to go cold.

10.5. *Always popular, the sponge flan.*

To finish, split through the centre and layer liberally with cold, well-beaten vanilla custard. Replace the top and decorate the hollow portion with fruit, neatly arranged, as desired. These may take the form of tinned and well-drained mandarin oranges, cherries, peaches, apricots, pineapple, etc. Brush over with neutral, quick-setting jelly to preserve the glaze of the fruit, and complete by piping whipped and sweetened fresh cream around the raised edge, using a large star tube for the purpose.

It is, perhaps, not necessary to mention how popular this line is during the fresh strawberry season, when these luscious fruits are used.

Should large savarin tins not be available, it is, of course, possible to use ordinary sponge sandwiches, removing the centre after splitting with a large plain cutter. The flans are then produced as already detailed, whilst the cut-out centre portions can be used to produce miniature cream sandwiches.

Charlotte Russe No. 1

Two methods can be used to produce this, and the first to be described is that usually used in Britain.

The size to be produced will, of course, depend upon the number for whom the customer is to cater, but a plain, deep, round or oval tin with slightly sloping sides for use as a mould is to be desired.

After ensuring that the tin chosen is scrupulously clean, it should be rinsed out in cold water and well drained. Now prepare a table jelly in the usual manner and pour in sufficient to cover the bottom of the mould to a depth of $\frac{1}{4}$ in. Place in a refrigerator to set, then place the chosen fruits—well drained—in position on the jelly to form an attractive pattern, afterwards adding more jelly, now almost at setting-point, just to cover the fruit. Return the mould to the refrigerator to set. If he should be tempted to do this in one operation, the reader will probably find that the fruit will float and will, almost certainly, lose the pattern desired.

Using sponge fingers prepared and baked in the usual way, cut one end square and shape the sides to give a slight taper. When the jelly has set, remove from the refrigerator and place the prepared sponge fingers, upright, with the square end touching the jelly and each finger fitting exactly next to the other.

Now whip 1 pt fresh cream and approximately $1\frac{1}{2}$ oz. castor sugar to soft piping consistency.

Having previously soaked 1 oz. leaf gelatine in cold water until flabby place the gelatine into a clean saucepan and heat over a very gentle flame until liquid. Add to the whipped cream and amalgamate thoroughly and quickly, for the gelatine will soon commence to set and, unless the operation is carried out quickly, will set in strings, thus spoiling the cream. Pour immediately into the prepared mould, placing gently on top a sponge disc, previously cut from a swiss roll sheet to the size required. Replace in the refrigerator to set.

When required, trim off the tops of the sponge fingers level with the disc, immerse 1 in. of the base of the mould into a bowl of hot water for a few seconds only, remove, wipe off the moisture, place a suitable dish or tray on the top and reverse both together, afterwards lifting the mould clear. If desired, a narrow ribbon may be tied round the sponge fingers to complete the decoration.

In the foregoing, it will be noted that no mention has been made of flavours, though these are of great importance to give the charlotte russe good eating quality.

Combinations will come readily to mind, but a great favourite is orange jelly, with well-drained mandarin oranges inset, with the cream coloured a pale orange and flavoured with the liqueur, orange curaçao. So far as possible I would prefer a liqueur flavour with some of the fruit mixed in with the cream.

10.6. *An assortment of Charlotte Russes by the English method.*

Charlotte Russe No. 2

This, Continental in origin, is rather quicker to produce than the variety previously described, but, nevertheless, delightful to eat. Indeed, with the jellied cream in this instance being of rather softer character than the former, it may hold more attraction for many palates.

The mould is here dispensed with, and a hoop, size again depending upon the number to be catered for, approximately 1½ in. high, used.

From a sheet of Swiss roll, cut a disc to fit inside the hoop and spread with apricot jam, afterwards placing the disc upon a strawboard, rather larger in size than the hoop, to permit ease of handling. Now place the hoop in position round the disc of sponge.

Prepare sufficient savoy fingers by cutting to a height of approximately 2½ in., trimming the sides and standing upright inside the hoop.

To prepare the jellied cream, place 1 oz. leaf gelatine in cold water and soak until flabby.

Place 8 oz. whole egg and 8 oz. castor sugar into a suitable machine bowl and commence whisking to a full sponge, meanwhile bringing to the boil 1 pt fresh milk, afterwards adding the gelatine and stirring well to dissolve. Allow to go cold before adding to the sponged egg and sugar, whisking by hand to amalgamate, with a spot of egg colour and sufficient rum to give a good flavour.

Add 1 lb. 14 oz. by weight of fresh cream, previously whipped and sweetened, stirring well. Pour the mixture into the prepared hoops to within $\frac{1}{2}$ in. of the tops of the sponge fingers, and place in the refrigerator to set.

When this has been achieved, remove from the refrigerator and lift the hoop clear. Mask the base, where sponge fingers and disc join, with whipped and sweetened fresh cream, followed by roasted flake almonds. Mask top with cream.

To finish the top, pipe a basket-work pattern in whipped and sweetened fresh cream; this is simpler than it would perhaps appear from the illustration.

Using a small star tube, pipe the first line down the centre. Turn the charlotte russe at right angles to the body and pipe a loop over the first line at the far right-hand end. Leave a space sufficient for another loop, then pipe a further loop, and so on, until the other end of the line is reached. Turn the charlotte russe round to its original position, and pipe a second line from one end to the other, parallel to the first, and close enough just to hide the joint where the loops join the jellied cream.

Commence again with the loops, after once more turning the charlotte russe round, this time starting in the space between the original loops, continuing in this manner until one half is completed. Now turn the charlotte russe round, and complete the other half in a similar manner.

It should be mentioned that this operation is far easier and quicker to do than to describe!

To complete, place a pinch of green nib almonds in the centre.

Charlotte Royale

Cut a disc of greaseproof paper slightly larger than the hoop to be used, place on a strawboard, with hoop in position, as described for the second charlotte russe.

Starting in the centre of the hoop, place thin slices of small Swiss roll to cover the base completely. Around the sides place savoy fingers as previously described or, alternatively, a strip of sponge approximately $2\frac{1}{2}$ in. high cut from a sheet of Swiss roll. Using the jellied cream as previously described, pour in to within $\frac{1}{2}$ in. of the top, afterwards placing in position a disc of sponge cut from a sheet of Swiss roll.

10.7. *Continental Charlotte Russe.*

Allow to set in the refrigerator and, when required, cut the sponge fingers level with the disc. Reverse on to another strawboard, remove the greaseproof paper and hoop, and brush over the surface of the now exposed Swiss roll with boiled apricot purée.

Complete by piping round the edge with whipped and sweetened fresh cream and affixing a gay ribbon round the sides.

10.8. *Charlotte Royale which, like the Charlotte Russes, was made for organisations with Scottish connections, hence the tartan ribbon.*

Vacherin

This is the Continental type of filled and built meringue, the example illustrated being pineapple—always a popular choice.

The actual size will depend upon the number of servings required and a template is necessary; this can be conveniently cut from a sheet of stout, clean, cardboard.

Place the stencil on to a sheet tin, previously lined with greaseproof paper, add meringue, spread level and remove the stencil, making one for each vacherin required.

On another papered sheet tin, mark the outline of the stencil, and inside the marked line pipe a ring of meringue, using a savoy bag fitted with a ¼-in. star tube. Pipe lines diagonally across to form lattice work and, as they will not be seen in the finished article, it does not matter if they are a little rough. Once again, one piped circle will be required for each vacherin. Dredge all with castor sugar and dry out at 260°F in a steam-free oven.

To complete, take a silver strawboard of the size required and spread thinly with whipped and sweetened fresh cream. On to this place the piped lattice disc and spread thinly with cream, enough still to show the lattice work. Into each hollow place a segment of well-drained, tinned pineapple, and apply a further, slightly thicker, layer of cream. Place the disc on top, followed by a further layer of cream on the top and sides in a manner similar to icing a wedding cake.

10.9. *Large Continental Vacherin.*

Using a savoy bag fitted with a ½-in. plain tube, pipe parallel lines across the top and, using a star tube, complete the side decoration as illustrated. Place alternately, in haphazard fashion, half cherries and segments of well-drained pineapple across the parallel lines of cream.

To complete, at right angles to the piped parallel lines of cream sprinkle baker's chocolate, using a paper bag with fine hole and, holding the hand high above the vacherin, waving the bag from side to side.

The above is just one of the varieties that can be produced from cold meringue. In addition, there are such diverse lines as mushrooms, meringue birds, and roses, suitable for decorating large trifles, and other types of built meringue.

One of the latter type is the beehive, fruit and cream filled, which makes an extremely attractive after-dinner sweet.

Babas, Savarins and Marignon

The similarities here are that all are made from the same dough, which is probably amongst the richest that it is possible to produce, and that all are immersed in sugar syrup to produce a beautifully tender article. Because of this immersion, some confectioners produce them only once a week, the immersion taking away any tendency to dryness.

4 lb. strong flour	4 oz. yeast
3 lb. 2 oz. eggs (2½ pt)	1 oz. castor sugar
1 lb. 12 oz. melted butter	4 oz. warm water

Because of the richness of the dough, mixing must be accomplished so that the relatively large amount of butter is not allowed to retard fermentation. Total yield of this mixing is in the region of six dozen, depending upon type and size of tin used.

Place the flour into a machine bowl fitted with hook, add the warmed eggs and yeast, this latter previously broken down in the small quantity of water. Beat well to produce a tough but fairly soft smooth paste. Splash the surface with warm water, cover with polythene or clean cloth, and place in a draught-free place for 25 min.

At the end of this period, restart the machine and add the butter (previously melted to a warm, *not* hot, oil) in small portions, beating well in between each addition, until all is incorporated, the result being a really tough, smooth paste. Using a savoy bag and large plain tube, pipe the batter into:

(*a*) Savarin tins, well greased and, if desired, dressed with flaked almonds. Size of the tins must depend upon portion control and the type of function for which they are required. If required to enhance a sweet buffet, then they may be produced in large sizes, but for outside catering generally it has been the writer's experience that the individual sizes are more convenient. Whilst piping out the paste, a bowl of water should be to hand in which to dip finger and thumb and cut off the paste.

(*b*) Boat-shaped tins to the confectioner, barquette moulds to the caterer; they should be well greased. Into them pipe a line of the dough from end to end.

(*c*) Babas are usually produced in dariole moulds, previously well greased. Although this is the conventional shape, there is no reason why they should not be produced in other tins, as custards or fluted frangipanes, to choice. Babas contain fruit, and this may take the form of currants, sultanas and peel, or certain types of fresh or tinned fruits, such as apple, pear, pineapple, etc., but not citrus fruits, which would exude all moisture into the dough, merely odd pieces of skin being left. To the quantity of dough given above, a total of 1 lb. would be required.

Whichever variety is being produced, three-quarter fill the tins. Prove in gentle heat without steam to the tops of the tins, baking at 470°F, with a slightly cooler oven for larger sizes. On removal from the oven, empty from the tins and allow to cool on a clean cloth.

For babas and savarins, prepare a simple syrup by boiling together 2 lb. sugar and 2½ pt water. Skim, turn off the gas, and when the first heat has left, flavour most definitely with rum, then immersing the goods individually for 10–12 sec. Lift out of the syrup and lay on

10.10. *Babas.*

10.11. *Savarins, showing two different sizes.*

10.12. *Marignons.*

to a wire, placed over a tray, and allow to drain. If costs permit, and as an alternative to flavouring the syrup, more rum may be added by means of a bottle fitted with spot cork. Glaze with boiled apricot purée, splitting the babas, piping in a line of whipped fresh cream.

To finish the savarins, after glazing place dessert fruit into the hollow, covering with a whirl of fresh cream and decorating with glacé fruit as applicable. Serve these with the addition of fresh fruit salad, or fruit cocktail, allowing something like 2–3 oz. per head, depending upon the size of the savarins.

Marignons

To complete these, prepare a syrup in the normal way by boiling together:

2 pt water	Two sticks of cinnamon
1 lb. sugar	Juice of two lemons
A few coriander seeds	

then allowing to simmer gently for 10 min. Skim, strain and immerse as for savarins.

Glaze the boats with boiled apricot purée, reverse them, split open with a sharp knife, piping in a reasonable quantity of whipped fresh cream.

Decorate by inserting several mandarin orange segments into the cream. If it is estimated that the goods will have to stand for some time before serving, it is advisable to glaze the fruit lightly with quick-set jelly.

Fresh Fruit Salad

Allow a total of 5 oz. per head, to include juice.

Make a sugar syrup by boiling together 2 pt water with 1 lb. cube sugar, remove any scum that appears and allow to go quite cold. Add the juice of two lemons and a variety of fruit, studying colour as well as flavour, to give eye appeal.

ORANGES

Peel and segment the required number, at the same time removing pips. If the oranges are large, cut the segments into reasonably sized pieces. Tinned mandarins are very good here, including the juice.

GRAPEFRUIT

As above.

APPLES AND PEARS

Slice thinly after peeling and coring.

BANANAS

Slice thinly after peeling.

GRAPES

Black and green—cut into two and be sure that the pips are removed.

CHERRIES

Fresh, if in season, otherwise a good sample of tinned. Halve, and remove the stones after washing if fresh.

STRAWBERRIES

Remove the stalks and wash. If small, use whole, or cut into pieces of reasonable size.

MELON

Either small cubed, or scoop out the flesh and "ball". The melon case itself may be used as a buffet decoration. For this, cut off about a quarter way from the top, and scoop out the fruit, making sure that the skin is not damaged in the process. Both of the cut surfaces may be serrated, so that the top may be replaced. When ready to set out on the buffet, fill with fruit salad and tie a ribbon round the widest part of the melon, serving, of course, from this as the meal proceeds.

All the fruit should be covered by syrup to prevent discoloration taking place, and, to this end, it is a good plan to put the citrus fruits in the syrup first. The fruit will not discolour in an acid medium. If costs permit, the addition of port or sherry is popular, and the salad may be made the previous day, storing in a refrigerator overnight. This may be served with fresh cream, whipped to soft piping consistency, or, better still, with:

Lemon Ice

| 4 Lemons | 1 qt water |
| 1 Orange | 14 oz. sugar |

Bring the sugar and water to the boil and skim. Drop in the zest of three lemons and one orange, boil gently for 5 min. and place on one side to cool. Now add the juice of the lemons and orange, strain and freeze.

Orange Ice

| 12 oranges | 1 lb. sugar |
| 1 qt water | |

Method as for the lemon ice.

Both of the foregoing recipes may be improved by the addition of two egg whites, beaten to a stiff meringue, together with 2 oz. castor

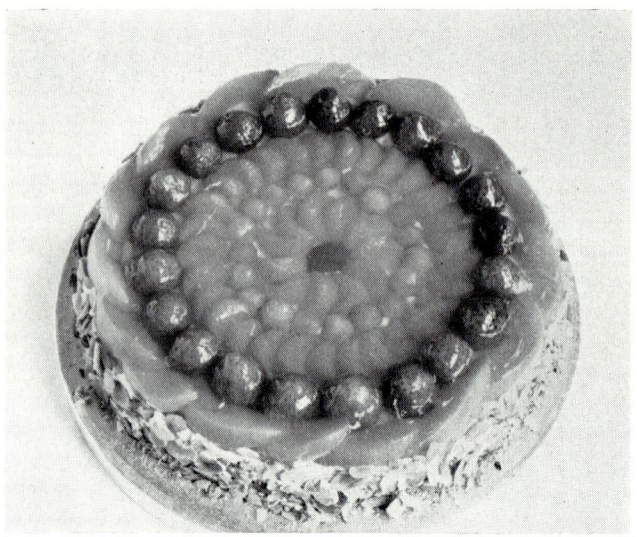

10.13. *Fruit torte.*

sugar. Add to the water ices after freezing, but just prior to stopping the machine, ensuring that the machine has taken the meringue through the mix.

Ice Cream

The rules for the production of this commodity are extremely stringent, and a caterer contemplating production should take every care that his premises are within local bye-laws.

8 oz. castor sugar	Two teaspoonfuls vanilla essence
8 oz. egg yolks	Two sheets gelatine
2 lb. 8 oz. milk (2 pt)	

Soak the gelatine in cold water

Make a custard in the usual way, add the essence and gelatine, stir well in and freeze, after allowing sufficient time for the custard to cool.

If cream ice is required, add ½ pt cream to each quart custard.

RASPBERRY OR STRAWBERRY ICE CREAM

1½ pt fruit purée	Juice of two lemons
1½ pt milk	Four sheets gelatine
1 pt cream	French pink
1¼ lb. castor sugar	

10.14. *Small orange and strawberry Vacherin. Stencilled out in meringue, those for orange are round, with oval for the strawberry. Pipe round the perimeter of the shapes with meringue, using savoy bag and star tube, dredge with castor sugar and dry out. Fill the cases with the chosen fruit, piping on the top fresh cream, double for preference as it does not weep to the same extent as single. Decorate strawberry Vacherin with a fresh strawberry, and the orange with a disc of crystallised orange peel, cut out with fluted cutter, and angelica diamond to form floral motif.*

10.15. *Cake or sweet? However presented, Marron Chou Rings are popular. A ring of chou paste is split after baking and a generous portion of marron paste/apricot purée is piped in, followed by whipped fresh cream. Complete by masking the tops in coffee fondant and immediately into roasted flaked almonds.*

Heat the milk and dissolve the sugar. Add the previously soaked gelatine and stir well until dissolved.

Allow to cool, add the purée, colour and lemon juice, followed by the cream.

Freeze normally.

Fruit Torte

This is an ideal sweet for a buffet, for it makes an immediate impact on the guests. This is probably one of the most popular of all sweets, yet it is so very easy to produce.

The base is a butter sponge, size as desired. Split this twice, sandwich with a good layer of jam and fresh cream and replace. Mask top and sides thinly with the same whipped cream and allow to set in the deep freeze.

To finish, pattern the top with fruit, either fresh in season, or tinned. Start in the centre in concentric circles, working to the edges, covering the cake entirely. Types of fruit used should be carefully considered, to gain the maximum amount of eye appeal, using mandarins, black and green grapes for contrast (halved, with pips removed). Cherries similarly and, in season, strawberries whole or halved as necessary. When the pattern is completed, glaze with a quick-set jelly, hot or cold. Re-mask the sides and dress with roasted flaked almonds.

Despite the number of sweets that have been suggested, many more are possible by variations. The craftsman can really enjoy himself by devising these, including, whenever possible, motifs peculiar to the organisation for whom he is catering, for these little details count and bring further orders. In compiling a menu the caterer should always bear in mind the serving entailed. For instance, if the function is to comprise a cold meal, plate service, then a sweet requiring portioning could be used; for hot meals an individual sweet would assist in keeping labour to a minimum.

Where, however, a buffet is being served, the caterer should go all out to make a lasting impression. Nothing will enhance his reputation more than large, colourful sweets of enchanting and delicious flavour.

CHAPTER 11

The Picnic Trade

THIS is a splendid opportunity for the baker and confectioner to supply pre-packed meals. This service can, with sufficient drive and enthusiasm, be extended to cover airports, railway and coach stations, and coach and long distance bus companies could be approached with a view to supplying them with pre-packed meals and snacks to be consumed en route.

The object of this chapter is to suggest ways and means of going about this new type of business, and to show how to produce some suitable lines.

Let us now consider one or two of the general aspects. First, is it profitable? This, of course, is a question that only the reader can answer for himself. Costings should be very carefully worked out.

A variety of lines should be priced and listed, so that a potential customer can be shown the list, and the type of meals suitable for her requirements. These may be pre-packed meals on cardboard plates, and placed on a cardboard tray, previously covered with a suitably sized white doily.

Before dispatch, each plate should be placed in a heat-sealed, moisture-proof, cellulose film bag. The complete tray should then be similarly covered and sealed to give the best possible eye appeal when collected by the customer.

The cardboard plates are specially treated to give an egg-shell finish. Should the reader shrink at the thought of "cardboard" then it should be borne in mind that the modern plate is not of the low grade pulp board that we used to get, but is a really high quality job available at something less than 1d. for a medium-sized plate. Several sizes are available in a variety of patterns and colours.

There should be included with each meal, where necessary, a plastic knife, fork and spoon.

Each pre-packed meal should include a paper serviette and here the reader may do a little advertising, by having his name and address, and perhaps telephone number, printed on it.

As, quite often, a meal and a reputation are made or broken on the "trimmings", great care should be taken to include those applicable. For instance, for many people a meat pie is spoiled unless mustard is

o

available. Therefore, mustard, in tube form, should be packed with the lunches. Similarly, pickled onions may be packed in sealed moisture-proof transparent cellulose bags when cheese is offered, and so on.

In many of the photographs some ancillaries are shown as a reminder of their importance.

As any one who has accompanied children on a picnic will know only too well, "drinks" are of great importance. One idea is a flagon of soft drink together with disposable cardboard cups. Like the plates, each cup costs about 1d. and to supply several extra cups would, I feel sure, be greatly appreciated. It should be quite possible for the baker and confectioner to obtain soft drinks to order from the wholesaler and thus obtain another source of revenue.

Should coffee be requested, then it should be possible to fill two flasks, previously supplied by the customer. Ensure that these are clean, then fill one with hot coffee, and the second with hot milk, supplying cube sugar and plastic spoons. Never mix the coffee and milk together for, all too often, discoloration takes place. Similarly, if tea is required, keep tea and milk separate.

One could also include a paper tablecloth, if desired. The modern examples are quite good and, again, prices are not prohibitive.

Finally, a plastic sponge, wetted and supplied in a polythene bag, can be a positive life saver when there are children in a party!

Individual packing is more suitable for supplying to those travelling by coach, bus, plane, or rail.

Here, the meal is placed on a plate, wrapped and sealed as before, and placed in a collapsible box. A serviette is included together with a tomato—do not forget the salt!—and fruit. This, again, is only a suggestion, but fresh fruit is popular with a great majority of people, both after a meal and during a journey, and can assist in making the meal more enjoyable and help, from the suppliers' point of view, to make it more profitable.

First, and most important, is that every item supplied by you must be in a first-rate condition as it leaves your premises. It is appreciated that you have no jurisdiction over when the meal will be consumed, so every effort must be made to see that it is "just right". For instance, the finger rolls from yesterday are not good enough, neither are over-baked scones or eccles cakes. Every item must be as near perfect as possible. Quality, and the maintenance of quality, is of vital importance.

Secondly, use only items that can be expected to travel reasonably well. "Squashy" cream goods are not acceptable. Also chocolate

*11.1. An individual
pack, suitable for
passengers travelling by
coach, train, etc.*

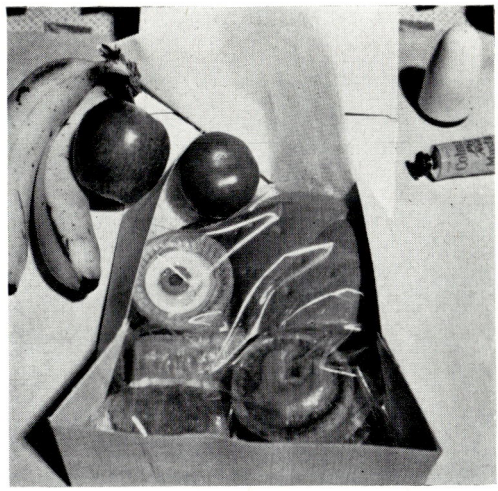

goods should be somewhat restricted. Try to imagine the effect of a few hours' travel on such goods on a warm sunny day.

One of the things I suggest you avoid when catering for the picnic trade is the preparation of ordinary sandwiches, when, with a little extra trouble, it is possible to turn the same materials used in a sandwich into something far more acceptable and tasty.

Ham Gipfels

One suggestion is that you make ham gipfels, which, basically, are straight croissants, with a ham filling. The following recipe will make 36 of them.

1 lb. 12 oz. strong flour	1¼ oz. yeast
1 oz. butter or cake margarine	1 lb. 4 oz. milk (approx.)
½ oz. salt	

Sieve the flour and salt together, and rub in the butter and make into a dough. Put on one side, covered with a clean cloth or sack, to recover for a few minutes. Meanwhile take 6 oz. butter, and 6 oz. pastry fat.

Pin out the dough into a rectangle, placing the butter and fat over two-thirds of the area. Fold into three as for puff paste, and give three half turns in all, allowing, if possible, a short resting period between each half turn. None of the resting periods should last longer than 10 min. at the most.

Place the dough into a polythene bag and leave in a refrigerator for at least 2 hr.

To work off, pin out the dough and cut on the divider, thinly pinning out each piece to a triangular shape.

Moulding of these is a knack soon acquired. Place a clean sack on the bench, transfer the first triangular shape on to it, with the point nearest to you and the wide part running parallel to the edge.

With the ball of the thumb, flick the centre of the wide edge, which will cause it to curve upwards and over. Now, using the flat of the right hand, commence rolling towards you, meanwhile stretching the point with thumb and forefinger of the left hand to ensure a tight roll. Place on to a lightly greased, cleaned, sheet tin.

Eggwash and prove very gently. When almost fully proved, transfer the sheet tin to a refrigerator to set the dough and arrest fermentation, so that a second, good eggwash may be applied. Bake in a dry oven at 450–470°F.

The knack of producing these goods properly lies partially in the baking. Do not remove from the oven until the gipfels are really crisp. Allow to go cold before finishing.

To finish, split each with a sharp knife and spread with well creamed butter, to which has been added sufficient dry mustard to give a pronounced flavour. Insert a finger of roasted or boiled ham. Replace the top.

These are really delightful to eat, and are quite suitable for buffet catering as well as for picnics.

11.2. Ham gipfels—acceptable at all times.

Meat pies always go down well on a picnic. Easy to carry, serve and eat, they require minimum fuss on the part of the consumer.

The pastry should be firm enough to hold the juicy filling, yet short enough for good eating. Hard, flinty pastry is not acceptable. The pie should have a clean, bright appearance, and should have been eggwashed to give it a rich, golden tint.

The meat should be a natural colour and it should be remembered that wet, soggy bread and rusk can never be passed off as meat, no matter how cunningly seasoned. I feel that pies should be well made and charged for accordingly. A cheap and badly made article reflects badly upon the producers. The customer will not remember the price, but the flavour and quality.

Jelly, of course, is all important, both for flavour and moist eating, and all pies should be jellied twice—the second time after the first has been absorbed.

For pie pastry, should the hot or cold process be used? Both points of view have their own followers. The recipe given here is suitable for either the hot or cold process.

10 lb. flour	$2\frac{1}{2}$ oz. salt
4 lb. 12 oz. fat	2 lb. 8 oz. water

The fat may be in the form of shortening if desired, and could include any good pork or beef dripping.

For cold paste, sieve together the flour and salt, and rub in the fat until the mixture has the consistency of bread crumbs, then add the water.

To use the same recipe for the hot process, place the water, salt, and half the fat into a suitable pan and bring to the boil. Meanwhile, rub the other half of the fat into the flour and make a bay. Pour all the boiling liquid into the bay and commence mixing, using first a scotch scraper and then completing by hand after the first heat has left the paste, which should be allowed to cool somewhat before use.

The following recipe is somewhat cheaper:

4 lb. 8 oz. compound fat	4 oz. salt
4 lb. 8 oz. flour	

Cream quite lightly, heating as necessary during cold weather. Add 7 lb. 8 oz. flour, and mix to "bread crumb" consistency. Then add 3 lb. 12 oz. cold water, and clear until paste leaves sides of bowl cleanly.

In many ways, it is an asset to use this type of cold paste, not the least being that all scrap paste may be creamed again in the first stage, thus making it possible to use fresh pastry all the time. The greatest fault here is that too many operatives fail to get stage one light enough, hence finishing with a tough paste.

The seasoning is an important part of the pie. So many variations are possible, that only general guidance may be given.

A pre-mixed seasoning is probably the most satisfactory and accurate weighing is essential, for you should always strive to produce a pie of regular flavour. Probably nothing destroys a pie trade quicker than irregular flavouring.

A good basis for a pre-mix is 2 lb. 4 oz. salt and 1 lb. white pepper. Sieve them together several times and store in an airtight tin. To this may be added 1 oz. ground ginger and/or $\frac{1}{2}$ oz. ground nutmeg. For pork pies a little rubbed sage or thyme could be introduced to produce a local speciality.

11.3. *The small bridge pie, popular at picnics, and equally at home on a buffet.*

The meat is preferably purchased by the joint, so that the baker has some control of lean/fat percentages, the coarseness of cut, and proportion of waste incurred. It is generally better to "coarse chop" the meat, for finely minced meat too often "balls" or settles too firmly, in the pie.

To each 6 lb. meat, $\frac{1}{2}$ pt cold water should be added, together with 2 oz. pre-mixed seasoning (allow $\frac{1}{3}$–$\frac{1}{2}$ oz. seasoning per lb. meat). Whilst local tastes vary, this quantity will, if carefully weighed out, be found quite satisfactory.

For picnic purposes, the size of pie you make will probably be between the small bridge pie, and the 1 lb. family pie.

The latter will require a base comprising 8 oz. pastry, moulded round and pinned out to a size large enough to enable a 6 in. sandwich tin, cleaned and lightly greased, to be blocked without excess scrap. Fill with the meat, beef, pork or veal and ham (and hard boiled eggs if required). A total of 8 oz. meat for this size is needed.

1 oz. pastry should be sufficient for the lid, rolled out quite thinly, with the edges neatly notched. Pastry leaves may be added if desired, but a perfectly plain one, with a nice eggwash, is usually acceptable, and gives a nice home made appearance for picnics.

Much the same, with a reduction in ingredient quantities, may be said for the smaller pie. In both cases a steam escape hole should be inserted into the lid.

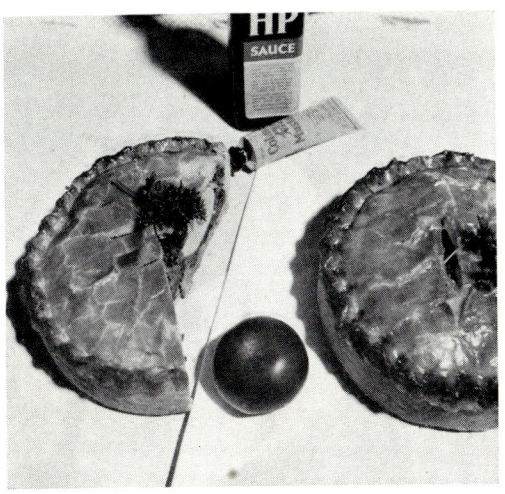

11.4. *Pork or other meat pies containing eggs are always welcome.*

Bake off at 420–440°F depending on size, and ensuring that the filling is allowed to boil vigorously for at least 5 min. before removal from the oven.

The pies should be emptied from tins, placed on wires, and jellied with a pie jelly of the same temperature. This is most important, for hot jelly in a cold pie (and vice versa) could be disastrous.

The best way to make the jelly is to simmer together for several hours pork bones and rinds to produce stock. The resultant liquid should then be strained, carefully seasoned with salt and pepper, with enough gelatine added to produce a reasonable set.

To test the set, place a teaspoonful into a clean patty tin, afterwards popping the patty tin into the refrigerator. The "gel" strength may then be quickly ascertained.

Where it is not convenient to produce jelly from stocks in this way, boil a 1 oz. strip agar agar in 1 gal. water, seasoning with salt and pepper to taste.

Alternatively, soak 8 oz. leaf gelatine in 1 gal. water, bring to the boil, remove immediately from the gas, and add the seasoning.

Whichever method is used, great care is needed to ensure absolute freshness, and to this end it should be made and used daily.

The smaller pies should be placed in greaseproof paper cases, and should be packed for transit as recommended.

Chicken and Mushroom Pies

A line for which a necessarily high price will be required, it is, nevertheless, popular wherever offered. The filling can be used for pies or vol-au-vents, and either of two methods may be used, depending upon price obtained and amount of trouble that the reader is prepared to expend.

For the first method, clean one boiling fowl, 4–5 lb., in the normal manner. Place into a suitable pan of cold water, bring to a gentle boil and skim. Now add 2 oz. whole onion, 2 oz. whole carrot, washed and peeled, together with six peppercorns and a bouquet garni. This generally consists of a little parsley, thyme and bay leaf, usually tied inside pieces of celery and leek. Season with a little salt and pepper and simmer all together until the fowl is cooked through, which may be tested by a trussing needle in the leg, and ensuring that no blood is visible inside the bird.

Make a velouté by melting 4 oz. margarine in a copper pan. Now add 4 oz. flour, mix well in over the gas and cook to a sandy texture over gentle heat without allowing the mix to take on colour.

Allow the roux to cool, replace on the gas and add 1 qt boiling chicken stock, which will be the liquid in which the chicken has been cooked. Stir until the mixing boils, then allow to simmer very gently for one hour. Pass through a fine strainer, then add and stir in 5 oz. dairy cream.

Well wash 8 oz. button mushrooms, cut into quarters and cook in a little stock with a few drops of lemon juice and a small pat of butter, about $\frac{1}{2}$ oz.

To make up the filling, remove the skin of the chicken, carving and cutting the flesh into reasonably sized pieces. Add this to the velouté, together with the strained mushrooms, adjusting seasoning as required. Fill the blocked pies or vol-au-vents in accordance with costings.

Should it be intended that the pies are to be eaten hot, a puff pastry lid could be used, eggwashing as usual to give an attractive glaze.

ALTERNATIVE METHOD

A quicker and cheaper method is to cook the chicken as detailed, carve and dice, then add to reconstituted mushroom soup, made thicker by adding only three-quarters of the recommended quantity of water to give a thicker base. Costs may be varied by increasing or decreasing the quantity of chicken in relation to soup.

Of the two fillings, the first should score heavily on colour, by virtue of the method of cooking the mushrooms. The second will be somewhat discoloured by the mushrooms in the soup.

Baking temperature is 420–440°F, depending on size.

Chicken Flans

For popularity, chicken flans take some beating. To make them, line the required number of small sandwich tins, foil or cardboard flan cases, with the pie paste, trim carefully, dock well, and allow a short resting period for recovery. Bake thoroughly at 430–440°F, and allow to cool.

Spread a reasonable layer of sage and onion stuffing in the bases of the flans, topping with thin slices of cold roast chicken. Place the

11.5. *Small chicken flans.*

flans on a wire, and fill with almost cold aspic jelly. Garnish with parsley, and set in the refrigerator. Then re-jelly. When set, the flans are ready for despatch. The reason for jellying over the parsley is to preserve its fresh appearance.

The quantity of chicken used can be varied according to costings. Small individual flans may be made as shown in Fig. 11.5.

Stuffing may be used in the flans if required, according to individual taste. A good recipe for the stuffing is as follows:

1 lb. 8 oz. chopped onions	8 oz. shredded suet
2 lb. 4 oz. breadcrumbs	5 oz. milk
$\frac{3}{4}$ oz. powdered sage	$\frac{1}{2}$ oz. baking powder
$\frac{3}{4}$ oz. rubbed thyme	$1\frac{1}{2}$ oz. lemon paste
4 oz. egg	seasoning to taste

Chop the onions, and boil until tender. Then strain and mix with the rest of the ingredients including onion water as required. Bake in a tin greased with hot dripping at 400–410°F until the top is crisp and brown.

The requisite amount could be added to the flans before baking. Alternatively, it can be beaten to a smooth consistency, and added to the baked flan cases.

If lemon paste is not available, then the zest and juice of a fresh lemon will do.

Cornish Pasties

Whilst cornish pasties may not be acceptable when cold to everyone, they are sufficiently popular to be offered.

A cold pie pastry is preferable, and should be rolled to about $\frac{1}{4}$ in. or slightly less. Cut out with a plain cutter of 4 in. or 5 in. diameter, and into the centre of each place sufficient of the fillings.

3 lb. diced fresh potato *or*	1 lb. diced swede
1 lb. dried and 5 pints water	1 lb. chopped onion *or*
1 lb. 12 oz. diced stewing steak	4 oz. dried, hydrated
2 oz. salt	$\frac{1}{8}$ oz. pepper

The filling is used raw, and care should be exercised that the ingredients are cubed small enough to cook during baking at 400°F.

Splash the filling with water. Wash round the perimeter of the cases with water, draw up the edges to the centre and over the filling, pinching together firmly and then notching with finger and thumb. Eggwash, make a steam escape hole in the top and bake at 400–410°F, allowing about $\frac{1}{2}$ hr to ensure that the filling is thoroughly cooked.

11.6. *Large chicken flans. Note the accompaniments.*

Cheese and Onion Pasties

To make cheese and onion pasties, line the number of baking plates (foil, tin or cardboard) required with pie pastry.

Three ways are popular for making the filling.

The first, and probably most simple, is to mix together 2 parts grated cheese to 1 part of finely chopped raw onion. Divide it out evenly amongst the lined plates.

11.7. *Cornish pasties.*

The second method utilises the same ingredients, with the same proportionate mixing, but the onions are partially cooked first with sufficient seasoning. Strain off most of the water, then add the cheese, which should be of good flavour and in fairly large flakes. Stir well together and adjust seasoning as desired.

The last method utilises well boiled pudding rice. Obviously, as a filler, the amount used will depend upon costings. It should be washed, placed in a pan, covered with water, and seasoning added. Allow to simmer very gently until quite soft and tender.

Using again 2 parts of strong cheese to 1 part raw onion, mince, using the coarse plate. Add this mixture to the boiled rice, stirring thoroughly to amalgamate. Any surplus may be refrigerated for future use. Should this then be too stiff, add sufficient fresh milk to adjust the consistency.

To complete our cheese and onion pasties, place sufficient of the filling on each lined plate, washing round the edges with water.

Roll out virgin puff paste quite thinly, cut with the appropriate cutter, place in position and lid in the usual manner. Allow a resting period.

Eggwash, insert a small steam escape hole and bake at 400–410°F.

Cheese Straws

Just watch how, quite unconsciously, a person will eat one cheese straw after another. These should find a welcome in any picnic basket.

Using virgin puff pastry, roll out to approximately $\frac{1}{4}$ in. thick. Wash with weak eggwash, and liberally grate full flavoured cheese over two-thirds of the surface. Fold the untreated third half-way over the treated portion. Fold over again in a manner similar to giving the paste one half turn, and pin out to a rectangle $1\frac{1}{8}$ in. thick and approximately 6 in. wide, afterwards cutting into $\frac{1}{4}$ in. wide strips. Place on to a clean sheet tin, allow a period of rest, eggwash carefully and bake at 410°F

If desired, the ends of the straws may be twisted before placing on the baking sheet.

As with all savoury items, seasoning is important so, whilst the straws are still warm, dust lightly with celery salt (see Fig. 11.8).

Sultana Loaf

It may seem quite a jump from cheese straws to sultana loaf, but this is the only item in Fig. 11.8 not dealt with. The cake is of reasonable quality, yet only lightly fruited, which is generally quite acceptable for a picnic.

11.8. *A simple picnic meal for three or four people—individual chicken flans, cheese and onion pie with tomatoes, cheese straws, cake and a beverage.*

Prepare 16 1 lb. bread tins by thoroughly cleaning and greasing—particularly in the corners. Dust with flour.

Prepare the batter by sugar batter method, scaling at 12 oz. for each cake.

The recipe is as follows:

1 lb. 8 oz. margarine	2 lb. 4 oz. sultanas
2 lb. castor sugar	8 oz. mixed peel
2 lb. 8 oz. egg (1 qt)	$\frac{3}{4}$ oz. baking powder
8 oz. golden shortening	egg colouring
3 lb. flour	

After scaling, spread level with moistened hands and bake at 360–370°F for 40–45 min.

Upon withdrawal from the oven, empty immediately from the tins and allow to go cold. For picnics, it is probably wisest to wrap these in moisture-proof heat sealing film to ensure that they are not dry when required.

Incidentally, the flask has been included in Fig. 11.8 as a reminder to offer to fill flasks when the order is collected.

A Simple Meal

Figure 11.9 has been included to serve as a reminder that perhaps not everyone will require a number of items. Some customers will even express a desire for just this kind of simple food.

The bread is possibly most suitable in the form of fancy shaped dinner cobs. These have been packed in pairs, with two cheese portions included.

To produce the dinner cobs, make a straight dough at 78°F from:

10 lb. strong flour	2 oz. sugar
5 lb. 8 oz. water	2 oz. salt
10 oz. compound	8 oz. yeast
8 oz. milk powder	

The dough should be firm, yet quite lively to the touch. Give bulk fermentation time of 1 hr, knocking back after 45 min.

Scale at 3 lb. 6 oz. for a 36-piece dough divider. Mould round, allow to recover, and re-mould into fancy shapes. Place on a lightly greased sheet tin, eggwash with a good glaze, prove and bake at 480–490°F.

The pickles can also be supplied in bulk, pre-packing in the small plastic cases now available complete with lid. Cocktail sticks would be useful here for "spearing" the pickles. If insufficient are required to warrant the use of the plastic holder, then a small film bag, moisture-proof, will contain a smaller number of pickles quite successfully.

Whilst the traditional beverage is something stronger than milk to accompany bread and cheese, it has been pictured in Fig. 11.9 as an alternative—especially where children are to be included.

Previously in this chapter the production of gipfels, which are really straight croissants, was dealt with.

Figure 11.10 shows what conventional croissants, with a few additions, can look like. Speared on wooden cocktail sticks are alternate pieces of smoked vienna sausage and gherkin, with small silverskin onions on top (these could almost be called cold kebabs). Two of these sticks accompany each croissant, which may be packed as soon as prepared into sealed polythene bags, and they should retain their moistness.

Alternatively, the customer can be supplied with the tinned sausage and the requisite number of gherkins and pickles packed in the plastic disposable containers. I would suggest that cider would be a good drink to have with these.

Perhaps not so much preparation in the bakery would be required for the goods in Fig. 11.11. Continental travel has made customers

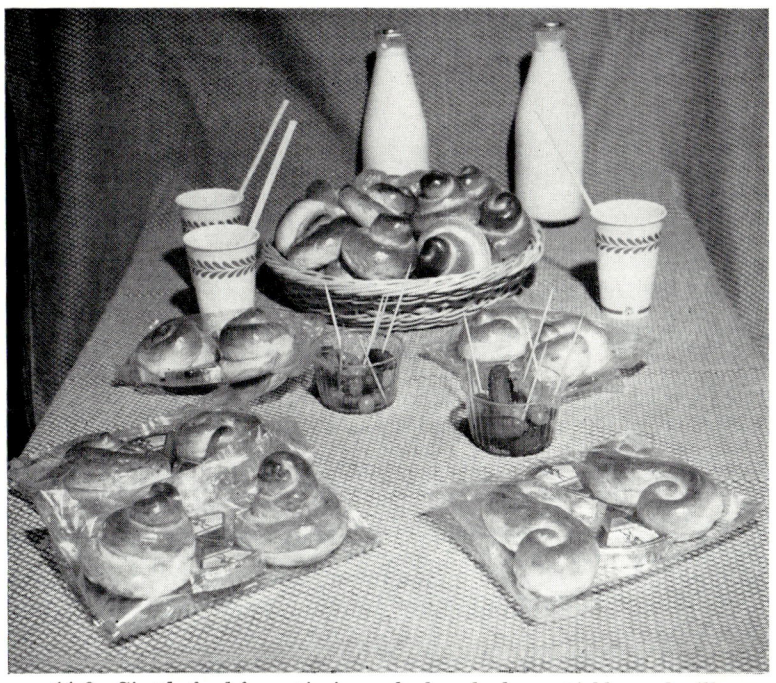

11.9. *Simple food for a picnic meal—bread, cheese, pickles and milk.*

11.10. *Croissants—with a few additions.*

conscious of the existence of the many different types of Continental meats. Here are shown slices of salami, accompanied by salad, assorted cobs (including vienna cobs) and butter.

The meat should be provided sliced and wrapped in individual portions, unless you are requested to provide a set number of meals already prepared on plates. In the latter case, place the meat portion on one side of each of the plates, and place the lettuce beside this with the remaining salad tastefully arranged. Immediately each meal is completed, seal in a polythene bag.

Distribution of the various items in their right proportions is rather difficult so I have prepared a list which should give you a rough guide as to the various amounts to allow.

Allow: one lettuce between eight people, one tomato between two, one hard-boiled egg (sliced) between four, one box of mustard and cress between 15, and one bunch of watercress between 10.

It should be stressed that the above guide is only to be followed when the food is prepared on the plates. When supplying the food in bulk, one egg and one tomato per person would normally be required. Avoid beetroot, for this so often stains other food, spoiling the appetising appearance.

Flavourings

Salt and pepper should be provided, and the customer questioned as to whether pickles, salad cream, salad oil, and vinegar is required.

11.11. *A salad, incorporating salami.*

11.12. Wholemeal farl with cheese, salad and pickles.

Farls

In Fig. 11.12 is a wholemeal farl and cheese. Many of the salad items I have already mentioned go well with these items.

The farl is quickly and simply made, and eaten fresh will certainly be enjoyed. Mix the following ingredients into a lactic batter:

  1 lb. 3 oz. wholemeal flour   1 lb. 9 oz. cold milk

Allow to mature for 30 min. Should the milk be on the turn or sour, so much the better. Then you need:

  1 lb. wholemeal flour   2 oz. lard or compound
  ½ oz. salt   1 oz. syrup
  1½ oz. baking powder

Mix all the dry ingredients together, rub in the fat, make a bay, and add the lactic batter and syrup. Mix all well together, but do not overwork. Scale at 4 lb., mould round and pin out to approximately 12–13 in. diameter. Deeply mark the farl into four. Wash with milk and dust lightly with wholemeal flour. Allow a recovery period of 20 min. or so, then bake at 400–410°F for about 40 min.

Break into four pieces along the marks made when it has been baked. Of course, the farl would be supplied uncut if it was to be taken away for a picnic. Provision would then have to be made for a cutting knife.

Finger rolls are included as a reminder that not everyone wants a complete meal on a picnic, and that you should be prepared to serve finger rolls with quite a variety of fillings.

To list but a few: fish and meat pastes, egg and cress, salad (tomato lettuce, cucumber, etc.), salmon and cucumber, meat (ham, tongue,

P

beef, etc.), chicken and stuffing, cheese (varieties with pickles), sandwich spreads, crab or lobster, and sardines. The list could be continued indefinitely (see page 109).

The roll itself should be spongy, light, not overbaked, and very fresh. The filling should be nicely seasoned where necessary.

Use butter on the rolls—many people *can* tell the difference.

Sausage rolls (shown in Fig. 11.13) are very popular. I would advocate the use of pie pastry in preference to puff pastry for a sausage roll which is to be eaten cold.

Good sausage meat is necessary, whilst one or other of the pie paste recipes which have been given already would be satisfactory.

Pin out the paste to about $\frac{1}{8}$ in. thick, and cut into 3-in. squares. Fill a $\frac{1}{2}$-in. savoy bag, fitted with a plain tube, with a small quantity of sausage meat, and pipe in lines along the centres, working from left to right. When all the squares have been dealt with, take a knife and cut through the sausage to divide each "rope" into the size of the squares. It is necessary to dip the knife into water from time to time to prevent it sticking.

Wash the paste with water, take the top piece of the first square, and fold on top of the sausage. Fold over again to totally enclose the filling, with the joint running along the middle of the underside.

Place all the folded rolls in neat rows on a sheet tin lined with greaseproof paper. Flatten gently with a rolling pin, eggwash, and bake at 440°F.

Figure 11.14 illustrates a simple picnic tea for six people, and consists of croissants (with butter), jam, cheese, wheatmeal sultana

11.13. *Sausage rolls, produced from pie paste.*

11.14. *A simple picnic afternoon tea, comprising croissants with butter and conserve, cheese, wheatmeal sultana bread, frangipane tart, jelly and fruit.*

bread, frangipane tart, and jelly and fruit.

The making of croissants has been dealt with previously. The butter is perhaps better supplied in bulk, and it should be packed in a plastic container, complete with lid and knife. The jam should be packed in fairly small quantities so that each guest at the picnic may have his or her own choice.

Besides strawberry, raspberry and apricot jam, offer more unusual varieties such as pineapple, apple and gooseberry, rhubarb and ginger, etc. Instead of lemon cheese offer orange curd, and make the customer realise that all these different varieties do exist. Even though most people are extremely conservative, it will create a favourable impression if a wide choice is offered.

In our trade we are in the unique position of not only being able to buy in bulk, but we can utilise any surplus materials in any one of a hundred different ways. Boldness can pay dividends. Even the lemon cheese can be supplied in varying quantities and types.

Wheatmeal Sultana Bread

The wheatmeal sultana bread is something a little bit different, and a 14 oz. loaf, sliced and wrapped, amply provides for six people.

The following recipe will produce six loaves, scaled at 1 lb. The recipe may, of course, be multiplied to suit individual requirements.

3 lb. wheatmeal	2 oz. yeast
2 lb. water	1½ oz. fat
1 lb. sultanas	1¼ oz. castor sugar
1½ oz. salt	

Produce by the straight dough method, with a dough temperature of 76°F. Bulk fermentation time is 1 hr, knocking back and adding the sultanas after 35 min.

Scale, mould, and place into 1 lb. lightly greased loaf tins. Prove and bake at 460–470°F.

Frangipane Tarts

The frangipane tart, shown in Fig. 11.14 on a cardboard plate, should really be produced in a foil case, so that the customer can transport it with a reasonable chance of it arriving on the picnic table in one piece.

The basic requirement for these tarts is a good sweet paste, and for this you need:

2 lb. weak flour	4 oz. egg
1 lb. butter or margarine	egg colouring as required
8 oz. castor sugar	

Produce by the rubbing-in method. A 7-in. diameter foil case (approx. 1 in. high) should give a large enough tart for six people.

Line the case with a thin layer of sweet paste, then cover the bottom with raspberry jam. Retain a little of the sweet paste, rubbed down to piping consistency (with water added), as you will need this to pipe on the lattice work.

Frangipane filling is often desecrated today with the addition of varying quantities of cake crumbs, but nothing can disguise such a filling so that the customer will not realise what it is. I would emphasise that the small baker's best policy is to produce the highest quality article he can, and charge a price commensurate with that quality.

For top quality frangipane filling you need:

1 lb. castor sugar	1 lb. egg
1 lb. butter or margarine	1 lb. ground almonds
1 oz. flour	

1 oz. of lemon paste could be added if thought necessary, but otherwise no colouring or essence is needed.

Produce by the sugar batter method, taking very great care not to overbeat the batter, for frangipane tart should be very moist.

Pipe the required quantity into the cases, spread level, pipe on the sweet paste lattice work, and bake at 350–360°F. When cool, glaze with boiled apricot purée and thin water icing, or hot fondant.

For the baker who requires a slightly cheaper filling, without losing too much quality, the following recipe is quite satisfactory.

1 lb. 9 oz. persipan	5 oz. flour
1 lb. 4 oz. margarine	6 oz. milk
1 lb. 3 oz. castor sugar	vanilla essence
13 oz. egg	egg colouring

Produce by the sugar batter method, again taking great care not to overbeat. Complete in the same way as the method given for the previous recipe.

At the end of this chapter I hope to give recipes and methods for producing your own jellies, but all you need to do to make the delightful jelly and fruit mixture (shown in Fig. 11.14), is to place some tinned fruit in a disposable plastic container, and fill with an ordinary packet or crystal jelly, made in the usual way.

Depending upon the weather, a little whipped and sweetened cream could be piped on the jelly prior to fixing the lids on the containers, and packing for despatch.

Tea Cake Sandwiches

Tea cake sandwiches (shown in Fig. 11.15) are suitable for customers who merely want "something to eat".

A great number of different fillings are possible, a number of which were dealt with in a previous chapter. "Double decker" sandwiches can be made, using two fillings together.

To make the tea cakes you need the following:

10 lb. water at 104°F	4 oz. sugar
3 lb. strong flour	10 oz. yeast
8 oz. milk powder	

Whisk the ingredients together to dissolve the yeast, cover, and place in a draught-free position. Allow to rise and fall (which should take about 45 min.).

Meanwhile, weigh out the following ingredients:

14 lb. flour	1 lb. 8 oz. compound
8 oz. sugar	3 oz. salt

Add them to the mixture to produce a light clear dough, which should not be too sticky.

Allow to ferment for 1 hr, giving a good knock back after 30 min. Scale at 5½ lb., and cut in a 36-piece divider. Mould round, and after a short recovery period, pin out to about 4 in. diameter. Place in lightly greased, warmed sheet tins, dock, and prove, baking at 480°F.

TOO SWEET?

Some people might find these tea cakes a little sweet, especially as they are to be used in conjunction with savouries, and as an alternative you could make muffins, for which you would need:

20 lb. flour	7 oz. yeast
12 lb. 8 oz. water	8 oz. milk powder
5 oz. salt	10 oz. compound
3 oz. sugar	

Produce a straight dough at 78°F, giving a bulk fermentation time of 1½ hr, knocking back after 1 hr. The dough should be quite light and lively, yet not sticky.

Work off as detailed for the tea cakes, but during baking (and when set) draw the sheet tins to the front of the oven, and reverse the dough pieces. With a good oven at 480–500°F, the dough should be set enough to commence this operation after 3 min.

Scones

In most picnic baskets, scones of one type or another may be found (see Fig. 11.16). Too often these are badly made, and providing the basic rules are observed, there should be no difficulty. The rules are as follows:

1. Never use guesswork (use the scales and stick to the recipe).

2. Do not be afraid of mixing the dough (clear really well, either by machine or by hand).

WORK OFF IMMEDIATELY

3. Work off immediately the mixing is complete (do not go off for half an hour break, and expect the baking powder in the mixing to take a break as well. It will not—to the detriment of the finished product).

4. Do not try to obtain a greater yield than the mixing is capable of giving.

5. If using eggwash, make certain it *is* eggwash—not 1/10th egg, 2/10ths milk, and 7/10ths water.

6. Bake off in a good, hot, dry oven, preferably on biscuit wires or upturned sheet tins.

11.15. *Tea cake sand-
wiches.*

11.16. *Currant afternoon
tea scones, yeast and
powder aeration.*

The recipe is as follows:

6 lb. flour	12 oz. shortening
3 lb. 12 oz. milk (3 pt)	12 oz. currants
12 oz. castor sugar	4½ oz. baking powder

Mix by the rubbing-in method, and pin out to approximately ⅜ in. thick. Cut with a 2 in. plain cutter to give a yield of 12 doz. Place quite closely together on lightly greased sheet tins, eggwash at the beginning and end of a 20 min. recovery period, and then bake at 470–480°F. (see rule six).

SLIGHT ADJUSTMENT

A slight adjustment to the recipe gives an improved, bolder, softer article.

6 lb. flour	12 oz. compound
3 lb. 2 oz. milk (2½ pt)	3 oz. yeast
12 oz. sugar	12 oz. currants
10 oz. egg (½ pt)	4 oz. baking powder

Mix and work off in the same way as given in the previous recipe. If this line received as much care and attention as many of the "glamour" lines did, I am certain that sales would increase tremendously.

Bacon and Egg Pie

Ever-popular picnic lines are bacon and egg or cheese and onion pies. Whilst these are generally made round in shape, usually for four or six portions, quite a novel effect may be obtained by producing them in the trough shaped tins (Fig. 11.17).

These tins have quite a wide variety of uses, and, though they may quite possibly have to be made to order, they are well worth the trouble incurred. Useful measurements are 30 in. long, 3 in. wide, 1 in high.

Whichever pie is being produced, line the tins with a good quality pie pastry, recipes for which appeared earlier.

Lightly grill or fry the bacon before rolling and placing across the tins, bearing in mind that each slice, when baked and cut, should contain a roll of bacon: a slice of approximately 1½ in. will be about the average.

Prepare the egg filling by measuring into a suitable bowl 1 lb. 6 oz. fresh shell egg.

Whisk to break the grain, but not to cause a froth, then add 2 qt fresh milk stirring constantly.

Season with salt and pepper, always bearing in mind that the bacon can, often, be quite salty.

Fill the troughs to within ¼ in. of the top, baking off immediately on the oven sole at 420–430°F until the filling has set—somewhat in a similar manner to custards.

Allow to cool before tipping from the tins and slicing.

Cheese Bread

Figure 11.18 depicts what is probably the simplest possible picnic meal—cheese bread, butter and salad.

11.17. *Bacon and egg pie, produced in long tins to permit cutting to size as required, served with salad and cordial.*

11.18. *Cheese bread, either white or wholemeal, for flavour.*

One of the difficulties in selling cheese bread in my experience is the price that must be charged for normal retail sale. In the context of picnic trade, however, it should be quite possible to charge the extra. Make no mistake about it—once purchased, the customers will return again and again, for the flavour of these breads is entirely different.

The cheese recommended is that specially prepared for bakers' use. Obtainable in several flavours, it is easy to use, giving a loaf of extreme tenderness, good bulk, pleasing golden crust and soft, short-eating property.

As an extra, try slicing in fingers, slow frying to crisp, rolling into powdered cheese and, when cold, bagging in convenient-sized, moisture-proof packs. Presented thus it is ideal both for picnic and licensed house snack trade.

FERMENT AND DOUGH

Whisk all the following ingredients together and allow to stand in a comfortable place for 30 min.:

3 lb. 12 oz. water (3 pt) 104°F	4 oz. yeast
2 oz. sugar	1 lb. strong flour
2 oz. milk powder	

Dough up with:

4 lb. strong flour	2 oz. shortening
2 oz. salt	1 lb. baker's cheese

80 min. bulk fermentation, knocking back after 40 min. Scale at the desired weight, and here it would perhaps be advisable to produce as a sandwich loaf. Prove and bake at 440°F.

CHEESE BREAD (STRAIGHT DOUGH)

10 lb. flour	4 oz. salt
8 oz. yeast	2 oz. sugar
4 oz. milk powder	2 lb. baker's cheese
4 oz. shortening	7 lb. 8 oz. water (6 pt)

Finished dough temperature 80°F. Bulk fermentation $1\frac{1}{2}$ hr, knock back after 60 min. Scale and mould. Bake at 440°F.

WHOLEMEAL CHEESE BREAD

5 lb. wholemeal	2 oz. salt
1 lb. baker's cheese	4 lb. 6 oz. water ($3\frac{1}{2}$ pt)
3 oz. yeast	

Straight dough temperature 80°F. Bulk fermentation 1½ hr. Baking temperature 440°F.

Whichever recipe is produced, an alternative addition could be concentrated tomato purée.

It is perhaps advisable that the bread be supplied sliced (not too thinly) and wrapped, to give less work at the venue. Butter can be supplied in bulk and goods for the salad polythene-wrapped after preparation. Pickles could also be supplied, together with salt and pepper in cheap, plastic containers.

Castonets

Here is something quite different, crisp and tasty, every bit at home at either picnic or smart cocktail party.

The size can be determined by each caterer, but, to commence, eggwash a knob of butter the size of a walnut shell and roll it in bread crumbs. Brush again with eggwash, roll in bread crumbs and repeat the process three or four times, until the diameter is of the required size.

Using a 1-in. plain cutter, cut through half-way, leaving the disc in place.

Fry until golden brown in cooking oil at approximately 340–350°F, making certain that the exterior will be crisp.

When taken from the fat, and again using the 1 in. cutter, remove the "plug" and empty out the butter from the centre which, by now, will be in a molten condition. Allow the cases to become cold. The butter should be retained for use later.

11.19. *Castonets—something different for picnic or buffet.*

FILLING

Mix 1 lb. baker's cheese, 1 lb. warm water to a paste.

Beat well with 2 lb. butter to a cream, then add 2 lb. chopped ham and mix well in.

Using a savoy bag and a ⅝ in. plain tube, pipe into the bases and replace the "plug." Spear a cocktail onion and olive on a cocktail stick, placing sideways into the filling. If for immediate consumption, a sprig of parsley will garnish.

Simple Meal

Figure 11.20 illustrates a meal of great simplicity.

Kebabs are the main item (foreground) and consist of various items of meat, i.e. steak, kidney, chop, liver, and so on, all affixed to a skewer for ease of handling. In our case, for picnics, the meats should be ready cooked, but for barbecues, the meats should be supplied raw and cooked on the spot.

To accompany the meats, pickles, sauces, mustard should be provided.

Croissants and butter, with a variety of individual portioned cheese, complete the savouries.

"Afters" are supplied in the form of wheatmeal or proprietary sultana bread and fresh fruit.

In the main, sweets have not yet been considered—at least separately. Cakes, mentioned in a previous chapter, should be confined to those that will carry well, are reasonably easily packed and will remain unaffected by hot weather. But what of other types of individual sweets?

Figure 11.21 depicts strawberries as an example, but these could be substituted by any other fresh fruit in season. Every care should be taken to see that the fruit is cleaned, packed, and supplied to the customer ready to eat, and in perfect condition. Sugar, where necessary, should be supplied in suitable quantity.

Bavarois Cream

Russe cream, or, as our catering friends would describe it, a bavarois cream, is shown in the glacine cases. This can be produced at the bakery, kept under refrigeration, supplied, complete with lid, in individual portions. There are several ways of producing it but my favourite is as follows.

Place 1 oz. leaf gelatine in cold water, soaking until flabby. Whisk to a full sponge

8 oz. shell eggs   8 oz. castor sugar.

11.20. *A simple yet expensive meal, depending upon the customer's taste and purse.*

11.21. *Bavarois and fresh strawberries as a sweet.*

Meanwhile bring to the boil 1 pt fresh milk, afterwards adding the soaked gelatine and stirring well to dissolve.

Allow to get cold before adding the sponged egg and sugar, whisking by hand to amalgamate, with a spot of egg colour to brighten and any liqueur desired to flavour.

Now add 1 lb. 14 oz. by weight of fresh cream, previously whipped and sweetened, stirring well in.

Pour into the glacine cases and, as mentioned, refrigerate.

A less complicated method is as follows:

Soak 1 oz. leaf gelatine until flabby, then transfer to small pan and heat over very gentle flame until liquid.

Now add to 1 pt fresh whipped cream (to which has been added 1½ oz. castor sugar when whipping). Amalgamate quickly, otherwise the cold cream can cause the gelatine to set quite quickly in "strings". Divide amongst the glacine cases.

Individual tastes vary, but it is my opinion that this one is improved greatly by adding fruit to the cream for, if lacking flavour, it can taste almost like foam rubber!

Other ideas here can be rice moulds, using a variety of flavours and colours, blancmanges using two or three different flavours to each case. This idea is especially popular with children. Custard rice, with or without the addition of fruit, is again popular.

Fruit Pies

Depicted in Fig 11.22 is a plate apple pie, together with a variety of individual pies.

Some readers may raise their eyebrows at the cheese accompaniment, but apple pie (or is it tart?) served with cheese is quite the "done" thing in many parts of the North.

The first requisite is, without doubt, a really nice short pastry, to eat almost like a biscuit.

My first recipe is done by the "rubbing in" method, and is as follows.

5 lb. flour	15 oz. sugar
2 lb. 8 oz. shortening	15 oz. water
1 oz. salt	egg colour

The second recipe utilises the creaming method, and is a little cheaper but, properly handled, will produce a good pastry, suitable for hand or machine.

Any scraps may be added in the first stage.

Stage One

3 lb. flour   3 lb. shortening

11.22. *Fruit tarts are always welcome as a sweet. Foil cases are recommended for withstanding knocks in transit.*

Stage Two

1½ oz. salt   12 oz. water
12 oz. sugar   egg colour

Stage Three

5 lb. flour   1½ oz. baking powder

Place the materials in group one in a machine bowl fitted with a cake beater, start the machine on slow speed until a paste-like consistency is obtained, afterwards changing to fast speed to cream quite lightly, warming as necessary.

Meanwhile, dissolve together the ingredients in group two, and sieve together group three.

Scrape Down

Scrape down bowl and beater as necessary, and when the mixture has attained the indicated lightness, add group three now running the machine at slow speed until the mix has attained the consistency of fine breadcrumbs. Pour in the liquid (group two), and commence mixing on slow speed, changing finally to second speed, clearing until the paste leaves the sides of the bowl quite cleanly.

I must here express personal preference for the raw (fresh, bottled or tinned) fruit for the fillings, as opposed to pre-cooked fruit.

Having said that, some time ago I found myself in the position of being able to use a fair quantity of fruit pie fillings and listening to customer reaction at first hand. The result was, to me, rather surprising for every comment, entirely unsolicited, was favourable. Flavours used included cherry, pineapple, peach, raspberry, strawberry, blackcurrant and bilberry. The favourite, by a short head, was undoubtedly the cherry, where quite a proportion of actual fruit was discernible.

CUSTOMER REACTION

To the reader who, perhaps like the writer, has been prejudiced, it may well be worth while to try a little of the fillings and obtain customer reaction.

Fruit Flans

A good sweet pastry is a "must" for fruit flans, and the recipe for this was given previously.

Foil cases are again to be recommended, lining up in the usual way and baking empty at around 410°F. The cases may be lightly docked to prevent "blowing" or alternatively, may be filled with dried peas.

After baking and cooling, mask the base with quick set jelly or boiled apricot purée to stop seepage from the fruit softening the pastry.

Arrange tinned dessert fruit tastefully in the case and cover the fruit entirely with quick set jelly (see Fig. 11.23).

Table Jellies

Table jellies are extremely simple to produce and are made basically from a sugar syrup to which gelatine, colour and flavour have been added. It is possible to purchase flavour/colour compounds specially for use in jellies, and these are to be recommended rather than using the normal confectionery essences. The basic mix is as follows:

7 lb. cube sugar	1 oz. glycerine
12 oz. glucose	$\frac{3}{4}$ oz. citric acid
6 oz. gelatine (leaf)	2 lb. 8 oz. water (1 qt)

Soak the leaf gelatine in cold water until quite flabby. The cold water as referred to here is not, of course, that mentioned in the recipe.

Boil together the cube sugar, glucose, glycerine and the quart of cold water to 260°F in the normal way. Remove from the gas, allow

11.23. *Fruit flans.*

the temperature to fall to 200°F, then add the soaked gelatine, acid, flavour and colour. Stir well to amalgamate, finally pouring into suitable tins to a depth of 1 in. Trough tins, previously mentioned in this book, are ideal.

When set, immerse the tins in hot water for a few moments to release the contents, and cut into blocks 5 oz. each. If not for immediate use, the block may be wrapped in wax paper and stored under normal conditions.

METHOD

To make up, take one of the 5 oz. blocks, add ¾ pt (15 oz.) hot, not boiling, water, dissolve throughly and use as desired.

Well, that is the basic recipe, and the following flavour and colour additions should only be taken as a guide, remembering that different manufacturers produce essences of varying strengths.

When checking the flavour by tasting the basic, it is a good idea to reduce the strength as previously indicated, e.g. in the proportions of 3:1, to taste the flavour the customer will receive.

Lemon jelly. 3 oz. lemon essence, ½ oz. liquid lemon yellow.

Orange jelly. 1 oz. orange essence, ½ oz. liquid orange colour.

Pineapple jelly. 4 oz. pineapple essence, ½ oz. liquid lemon yellow.

Cherry jelly. 5 oz. cherry essence, ¼ oz. pink colour, 2 oz. liquid orange colour.

Q

Blackcurrant jelly. 5 oz. blackcurrant essence, 3 oz. pink colour, ¼ oz. black jack.

Sherry jelly. 6 oz. sherry essence, 2 oz. black jack, 1 oz. spirits (wine).

Strawberry jelly. 5 oz. strawberry essence, 3 oz. pink colour, ½ oz. orange colour.

Cordials

Cordials are, again, extremely simple to produce, and similar to the jellies in that, basically, the cordials are produced from a simple syrup.

One of the advantages of producing these oneself is that flavour strength and sweetness can be varied to give a really first rate article.

For the picnic trade, it could be supplied in bottles, either concentrated as produced, or ready for drinking.

For a basic cordial simple syrup you need:

8 lb. cube sugar	12 oz. glycerine
2 lb. glucose	10 lb. water (1 gal.)

Place all the ingredients into a suitable copper pan, and bring to the boil, holding to the boil for approximately 5 min. Skim off all impurities that may arise.

Remove from the gas, add flavours and colours desired, allow to cool, bottle and cork.

From the flavour point of view, the most popular in my experience are lemon, orange and lime. In each case, the flavour is supplied by the fruit paste.

Lemon cordial. 1 gal. simple syrup, 8 oz. lemon paste, 1¼ oz. citric acid, lemon yellow colour.

Orange cordial. 1 gal. simple syrup, 8 oz. orange paste, 2 oz. tartaric acid, orange yellow colour.

Lime cordial. 1 gal. simple syrup, 7 oz. lime paste, 1 oz. citric acid, lime green colour.

Peppermint cordial. 2½ oz. essence peppermint, 1 gal. simple syrup. (No colour or acid required.)

To the above may be added raspberry, strawberry, blackcurrant, etc.

Well, here are some ideas upon which to build a picnic trade. So very many alternatives and local specialities exist, that one can only hope to point a way in the general direction. Enthusiasm, knowledge and ingenuity on the part of the individual can, it is certain, build this section of his trade, at least during the summer, into well worthwhile propositions.

CHAPTER 12

Retardation and Deep Freeze

OVER the years, man has developed many different techniques for food preservation: the first probably was the smoking of meat, closely followed by the use of spices, salts.

Food industries as a whole have, since the war, expanded at a tremendous rate, and with the rising standard of living the demand for convenience foods has increased.

We should, first, define the difference between retardation and deep freeze.

A dictionary definition of "retard" gives: "to hinder progress; to make slow or late; to impede," so we can summarise the work of this type of refrigeration as a means of delaying, within limits, the process of fermentation. Compared to deep freeze, the delay in a retarder is for relatively short periods only.

Retarders normally operate at temperatures of from 33° to 38°F, with a relative humidity of 85 per cent or thereabouts. These are used chiefly to retard the fermentation of small goods such as croissants, danish pastries, conventional and fancy shaped dinner cobs and rolls, and goods of the sweet dough variety, such as cream cookies, chelsea buns, swiss fingers and doughnuts (of the fermented type), etc. Thus has the retarder been useful to enable the baker and confectioner to lengthen the time between actual working off and baking off of the doughs. The use of equipment of this type is to iron out the weekly production peaks, so may some—or all—of the lines mentioned be produced in standard daily quantities during the latter part of the morning and during the afternoon. Withdrawals from the retarder are made each morning to the shops list, with proving, baking and finishing completed quite quickly. Thus, for the smaller baker, night baking as regards the "small" lines can be obviated, and production during the day can be planned to the extent of producing larger mixings which, as all practical readers will agree, are far more economical from all points of view.

In the writer's experience, retardation has proved a very practical possibility when the doughs have been worked off, but bulk doughs, such as danish pastry, have not been as successful. The reason is quite obvious—a retarder is just not cold enough to reach the middle of the bulk dough, which continues to ferment from the centre. Should it be desired to retard bulk doughs, then they should be rolled out to a thickness certainly no greater than 2 in. maximum. Having said that, it is still the writer's considered opinion that it is preferable to work off the doughs. Tests have shown that doughs in bulk entering the retarder may take several hours at 35°F to reach their lowest temperature, and, as can readily be imagined, some deterioration can set in over such a period.

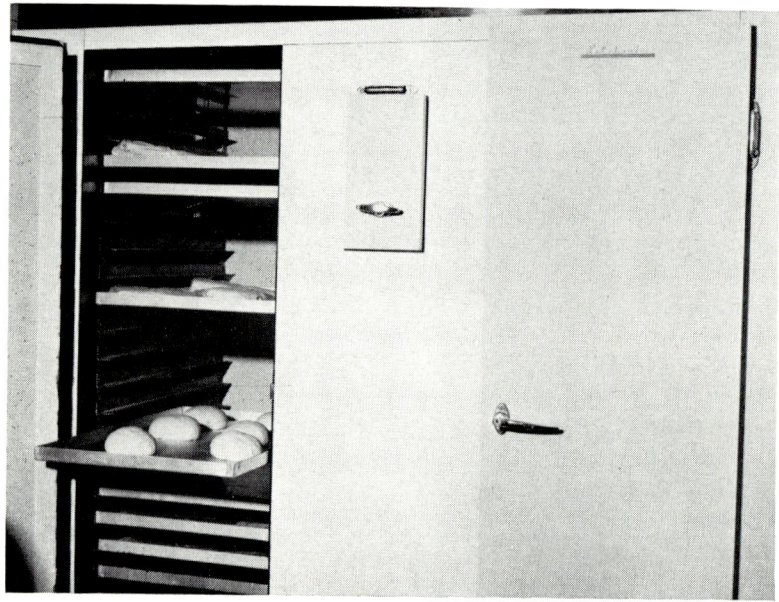

12.1. *The conventional dough retarder which, in this case, combines a normal refrigerator.*

It can generally be said that any usual dough recipe may be satisfactorily retarded. In some instances, it has been found advantageous to reduce the yeast and slightly increase the salt quantity in order to assist in retarding fermentation, but there are so many variable factors that no set rule can be applied.

It could be that the dough pieces, now worked off and set out on sheet tins, show discoloration of the undersides after retardation and baking. This is caused by the action of acids within the dough upon the metal of the sheet tin, and usually occurs when the sheets are aged. The remedy is renewal of the tins, re-tinning or the use of silicone paper.

Perhaps as great a contribution as any that retardation can make is that, apart from the alleviation of night work and the ironing out of production peaks, goods are so very handy to produce and finish quickly should any sudden rush of trade warrant it.

Three simple rules should be followed at all times:

1. The door should not be opened any more than is absolutely necessary, for constant opening and closing of the door can make it difficult for the equipment to maintain the required temperature.

2. The equipment should be able to maintain a temperature below 38°F even when fully loaded.

3. Doughs should never be retarded for longer periods than 72 hr.

To sum up, the retarder is useful for made-up pieces for approximately three days before baking (maximum). A "holding list" should be worked to, to keep the cabinet replenished, with daily requirements extracted in strict rotation. Doors should only be opened for the absolute minimum.

Deep Freeze

The freezing of all food must be brought about quickly, because slow freezing causes the slow formation of ice crystals, squeezing the molecular structure and breaking and bruising both internal and external cell walls. This results in general deterioration, loss of flavour and, in the case of baked goods with which we are primarily concerned, more rapid staling. Only food in perfect condition should be frozen, and this accomplished as rapidly as possible, especially between temperatures 26–22°F, and down to below 0°F. The ideal holding temperature is between $-5°$ and $-10°F$. Indeed, where large quantities of food are being processed, the products are laid on flat trays, passed along an insulated tunnel through which a blast of air at a temperature of minus 40°F is circulating, i.e. 72°F of frost.

What may deep freeze be used for in the context of our industry?

1. Completed baked products, such as cream sandwiches, bread, tea cakes, rolls and goods of similar type.

2. Uncompleted bases, such as genoese, sponges and butter sponges, either of the classical or modern types, using stabiliser.

3. Unbaked goods—danish pastry, fruit tarts, sausage rolls and

other types of savoury pastries, such as steak and kidney pies, made-up puff pastry goods, vol-au-vent cases, etc. Such goods should be allowed to rise to bakery temperature generally before baking off. Possibly the best way to accomplish this is to remove the goods from the deep freeze the day previously, and gently de-frost in the retarder. The time then required to bring to bakery temperature is comparatively short.

Care must be exercised as to what stage in manufacture the goods are deep frozen. In the vast majority of instances the goods are perfectly satisfactory, but it has never been the writer's experience that the "oven fresh" quality is enhanced by deep freezing.

In the case of storing Parisien croissants unbaked, for instance, it is my experience that the goods, after baking, lacked oven spring, bloom and lightness, this being the result of several experiments. Conversely, storage of the dough in bulk over quite a long period, followed by working off in the normal manner and, in some instances, retardation of the moulded pieces for not longer than 72 hr, resulted in satisfactory goods, every bit as good as any produced in the normal fashion.

Refrigeration of any type is not a "cure-all" and care must be taken at all times that any specific item of equipment does not become a "dumping ground". Another malpractice to be frowned upon is that of placing goods into the deep freeze after a day in the shop window, then expecting to be able to sell the same goods the following day as "fresh". An item coming out of the deep freeze will be no better than it was when it went in, and strict control should be exercised overall. It will be found to be of advantage to place such equipment in the care of one responsible person, who would attend to all facets of use, care and strict rotation of stock.

Obviously, in a chapter of this type, we may only generalise, for no two businesses are the same, and much will depend on output, type of production and space available. The reader deciding on an installation will surely obtain at least two or three quotations together with ideas from competitive firms.

The general estimate regarding capacity is to allow approximately 1 cu. ft of cabinet space to each 2 lb. weight of article to be frozen. Whilst the refrigeration engineer will advise, remember that deep freeze owners are rather like keen gardeners with greenhouses—they never have sufficient space, so allow for one as large as possible.

What type of cabinet should the reader purchase?

For the smaller producer, I would consider the "walk in" most un-economic. It is inclined to take up far too much space for value, and

12.2. *A small deep freeze unit, suitable for a kitchen or, if fitted with runners, a bakery. Of stainless steel construction, the unit incorporates air circulation.*

constant opening of the necessarily large door puts much strain on the freezing unit. Generally, the cabinet types with runners to accept wire trays and sheet tins peculiar in size to those in use in the reader's own bakery are to be recommended.

The unit should be *overpowered* with the blast of cold air directed into the cabinet from the top. Thus, as goods are placed in the deep freeze, they are put on the upper runners, the cold blast freezes them quickly, and they may then be removed to the lower runners.

Regular checking of the cabinet is essential, the temperature being checked with a max./min. thermometer, this being placed between the food and *not* near to the freezing unit, or plates.

Goods should not be stocked above the recommended capacity, and the insurance broker should be consulted to obtain adequate cover against losses occurring in the event of a breakdown of the installation; this is quite a normal business procedure.

Obviously, positioning is a most important decision to make, and not one to be arrived at hastily, since incorrect siting will lead to much unnecessary movement, thus increasing labour costs.

Factors that must be considered are size and capacity of the unit, which must take into consideration space required. Needless to say, the equipment must be in close proximity to the bakery, yet, ideally outside, where dust and heat will not have a deleterious effect on the electrical components. The really large coldrooms require a separate recovery room after the goods have been extracted, but this chapter is aimed rather towards the smaller producer.

The use of a larger room also requires consideration to the flooring upon which the unit will stand, for, if racks are to be wheeled in and out, a level approach is desirable. Indeed, where a ramp exists, all too often does one find that condensation takes place when the door is open, causing the ramp to become dangerously slippery, especially when one takes into consideration the fact that most operatives find bakery materials clinging to the soles of the shoes. The evidence points to the fact that ramps should be avoided if at all possible.

We have all seen the effect of prolonged frost upon the pavement flagstones of our towns and cities. The same could occur under a deep freeze unit. To obviate this, it is usual to insulate and, quite often, to lay an under floor heating unit of suitable low temperature. Without this, damage could occur to the deep freeze unit as well as to the floor. Low temperature heated door frames are also generally fitted to prevent freezing and, again, consequent damage.

To work at maximum efficiency, the equipment should be defrosted regularly and cleaned out weekly. Most manufacturers provide the equipment with automatic defrosting, the interval depending on a number of variable factors, including actual size and weight of goods held. Goods in the deep freeze should be stored in such a way that any roof condensation does not, during the defrosting process, fall upon them and create waste. In this connection, the use of polythene sheets and bags is to be recommended.

From the smaller producers' point of view, it would appear that several cabinet type deep freeze units, situated in different parts of the bakery, would be preferable to a large one. Thus one may be installed in the decorating room, where bases of genoese and gâteaux, etc., may be stored ready for use at any time. Part of this could be set aside to retain certain types of goods and fancies ready for immediate despatch at any time. In this connection we should also include after-dinner sweets, for, quite often, the customer would purchase say a charlotte russe or charlotte royale if she was aware that items were obtainable without prior order, as is so often the case. So not only may deep freeze be able to assist in a more even flow of production, but it could also assist in the development of a hostess service, widening the scope of the business. And who has never had to cope with the unexpected guest?

Freezing of Baked Goods

Baked goods should first be allowed to cool naturally to 80°F, and this may be accomplished in the usual bakery rack. Small goods will obviously cool—and freeze—quicker than, say, large loaves. Actual freezing time, that is time taken to reduce the bakery goods temperature, will depend on several factors, including:

1. The amount, or weight, of produce in the deep freeze.
2. Refrigerating capacity of the equipment.
3. The free and rapid circulation of the cold air.
4. The type of tray being used to hold the goods.

Dealing with the latter point, wire trays or baskets are obviously going to allow the circulation of cold air quicker than wooden packing boards, which are bad conductors of heat. Nesting wire baskets are the most popular for the larger units, are light in weight and are "stackable".

Physical size of baked goods is reduced upon freezing, but this is compensated upon thawing. It may be as well to mention again the importance of keeping the door closed as much as possible, accomplishing both loading and unloading in the minimum amount of time.

THAWING OUT

Correct thawing out is every bit as important as freezing, and if space and conditions—including time—permit, it is often sufficient to place the goods in a warm part of the bakery, allowing them to warm quite naturally at a temperature of 75–80°F. Small items require $\frac{1}{2}$ to $1\frac{1}{2}$ hr with a small loaf taking 4 hr and a large up to 6 hr.

These times may be speeded up by placing the goods in warm air, with a relative humidity of between 50 per cent and 60 per cent. The use of the prover will be immediately apparent to the practical reader, together with just a trace of steam. The prover should be at approximately 100°F. Here, I have heard the opinion expressed that time allowed for complete thaw should be 1 hr per lb. weight of article.

Whilst some bakers like to use the oven to speed the process even more, it is all too easy to sell a loaf feeling "oven fresh" which, if immediately cut, would show a solidly frozen centre.

Goods that may be Deep Frozen

Whilst we have already given some details of goods that may be deep frozen, it will be to the reader's advantage if, perhaps, we enlarge on the list a little.

1. Baked bread, fermented buns generally and rolls.

2. Sponge cakes and swiss rolls, baked and cream filled.

3. Plain and fruit cakes of all sizes. This would exclude wedding and heavily fruited type of cakes that should be individually wrapped in greaseproof paper and stored in a cool cellar, or zinc-lined cupboard in a cool place.

4. Danish pastries, worked off, but left ready for finishing with cold beaten vanilla custard and baking off. This would take place after the pastries were de-frosted, of course.

5. Scones, preferably baked. If unbaked, the scones are better made using yeast and baking powder aeration.

6. Powder aerated counter goods, baked.

7. Some types of sweet and short pastry goods; for example, undecorated frangipane tarts, both large and small. Unbaked fruit tarts are better to deep freeze than when baked. Unbaked mince pies are quite satisfactory, especially when blocked on the foil cases. On the other hand, custards are quite useless deep frozen after baking.

8. Puff pastries, cut-out and not baked. Into this class would come vol-au-vents, both large and small, eccles and banbury cakes. Puff pastry in bulk.

9. Babas and savarins, baked but awaiting soaking in rum syrup and finishing.

10. Some types of genoese afternoon tea fancies, with a butter-cream finish.

11. Savoury pastries, such as steak and kidney pies, unbaked.

12. Meat pies, unbaked.

Goods Unsuitable for Deep Freeze

1. Vienna bread. Even though the crust may be crisped by limited rebaking, the toughness very soon becomes apparent.

2. Chocolate, fondant and other type icings that sweat upon removal from the deep freeze.

3. Custards.

4. Fruit flans. Deep freeze breaks down the jelly, causing this to crack.

5. Goods surrounded by marzipan or almond paste, such as battenberg, which are affected by condensation. These goods are better to be given an extended shelf life by the use of moisture proof, heat sealing transparent cellulose.

6. Meat pies, when baked, jellied and cool. These goods are best transferred to, and sold from, a refrigerated counter.

The usual, normal recipes for goods that are amenable to deep freeze should be satisfactory, and perhaps the greatest saving of time can come from the provision of a wide variety of bases that can always be to hand for the confectioner, where genoese, gâteaux and torte bases may be held indefinitely. Indeed, the ideal is to treat the deep-freeze unit as a bank, decide what working balance is required and see that the stocks do not fall below that level. Remember that, properly maintained, goods may be kept for days, weeks and months.

Obviously, use of such equipment necessitates rethinking of production schedules, for no longer is immediate output geared to immediate—or immediate shop future—needs. Mixings and doughs can be geared to oven space rather than immediate requirements so it is reasonable to expect that production per man should increase. This in turn should lead to a reduction in overhead expenses, an increase in gross profit, and, ultimately, an increase in net profit.

In addition, it should be possible for the shops to be stocked first thing in the morning, with no tiresome (for sales staff) wait for individual items. This, in its turn, should make for an increase in shop sales, for the customer will soon become aware that a wide variety of first-class goods is available from first thing each morning.

Obviously, such equipment as has been mentioned is expensive and must be paid for, but it is estimated that any installation should pay for itself within 1½ years at the most. This figure must, of course, be only taken as a guide, for much will depend on the correct use and common sense.

What type of equipment should be purchased?

In the preparation of this chapter I have discussed the various types with refrigeration engineers, and all have stressed that each installation is built separately from standard components. Whilst the different parts are standardised, each cabinet or cold room is tailor-made to suit the individual baker and confectioner's requirements.

Take as example a frozen foods cabinet, as may be seen in any grocer's shop or supermarket. Here the goods arrive ready frozen, so the unit is only required to prevent *external* thawing. Let us now assume that the same cabinet was going to be used to deep freeze and hold goods peculiar to our industry. It is at once obvious that a greater degree of cooling is required in the second case to reduce the *internal* temperature beyond the staling stage. Thus would a larger cooling unit be required than in the first instance.

CHAPTER 13

Conclusion

IN CATERING, four parties must be satisfied if any function tackled is to be successful. They are:

1. The customer
2. Owners and caretakers of the venue
3. The caterer's staff
4. The caterer

Taking the individual parties in order, the customer is the most important. It is through him, or her, that any business thrives, so at all costs must the customer be satisfied. Any reasonable—and, indeed, at times unreasonable—requests must, if at all possible, be fulfilled. No hint of rush or panic should be apparent, the service at all times being as unobtrusive as possible. At every function, each guest is a customer and a potential means of introducing further business.

Full details of every booking must be made, and the first detail is to ensure that the customer's name and address are known, together with telephone number.

The type of function, e.g. wedding party, dinner-dance, should be noted together with the place where the function is to be held: included here must be the name and address of the caretaker, with details as to when he may be contacted. Details will include approximate numbers, with a request that exact numbers will be supplied two or three days beforehand.

Required time of commencement of the meal should be noted, together with full details of menu and service required. It will be stressed at the time of booking that the price given will be subject to fluctuations. Any special requirements such as wedding or other celebration cake, piano, band, etc., should be carefully recorded. Some guests may not eat meat on Friday, whilst Jewish guests or vegetarians may require special consideration. These are the details that should be mentioned at the time of ordering, so that it should be possible for all guests to be offered something that they may enjoy.

The person ordering is generally very appreciative of attention being drawn to details that may so very easily be overlooked. To this end, it is worthwhile considering the production of a brochure, setting out in broad outlines the types of catering accepted, giving sufficient relevant detail. A pro forma duplicate book could be used solely for catering, or a foolscap diary, one page to one day, utilised. None of these ideas are to any avail, though, unless they are consulted daily, so that any necessary preparation may be put in hand.

All too often does the caterer find that he has no control over the venue. By care, courtesy and consideration to the caretaker, manager, steward, landlord or proprietor, he can very soon have a friend and worthy ambassador, as well as a person who will help to oil the wheels when the caterer is on the premises. He can also assist by bringing in further business, so his efforts should be appreciated. Needless to say, any of his equipment used by the caterer should be left in as good a condition as he found it.

Now and again, the caterer is called to cater at a venue that, for one reason or another, is unsuitable or, let us face it, is just not up to the required standard as regards cleanliness. The answer to this one is not to accept further bookings until a change has taken place. Rather than say this in so many words to the customer, it is preferable to say that, on that date, it is regretted that you are fully booked.

The caterer's staff have the success of any job very much in their hands, and their attitude is a reflection of the management's attitude. In the matter of amenities, they should be given every consideration. They must work as a team, and any difficult member, or one that does not wish to conform, should be weeded out, as should any that do not give 100 per cent effort on every job. There is no room for the one not prepared to fit in. Uniform clothing, kept particularly for catering, should be provided, maintained and laundered by the firm.

Of management much could be written. They must be bold and imaginative, yet always ready to listen to suggestions from any quarter. Humble enough to roll up sleeves and work with the staff, they should yet be ruthless at the odd times necessity demands. Because they are prepared to be this, the staff realise, and the necessity very seldom arises.

In catering, we are dealing with commodities that must be produced, displayed, admired, eaten and enjoyed all in one day. Time is precious, so every minute should be spent in planning, organising and producing so that each and every function accepted will be a success.

Far too many people in management fail to give the necessary lead, drive and enthusiasm required. Complaints of any sort are the responsibility of management, and all too often arise because of inadequate or poor supervision on their part. Decisions are required at once, and to delay these often means frustration to the staff, with consequent deterioration in their attitude. NOW is the time to get things done.

It is not a good sign if staff are constantly changing, unless for perfectly valid reasons. To pay them well and give good strong leadership will mean a happy team. Discipline is always acceptable if properly given, and the staff made to feel wanted and part of a team.

A strict rule should be that any complaint, however trivial it may appear, should be handled immediately by the senior person present. Forest fires can often be prevented if the initial spark is extinguished. No expense should be spared to see that the complaint is rectified to the customer's satisfaction.

A positive approach by the staff should be encouraged at all times. If a guest has to ask for the obvious, then a mistake, on someone's part, has occurred. Let us take as a simple example, a menu including roast beef. Mustard should be provided automatically, and no guest should have to ask for it. The responsibility rests with the person in charge to see that all these things are attended to prior to the arrival of the guests.

Careful watch should at all times be kept on costings, adjusting prices down, as well as up, providing that the profit margin is satisfactory.

Purchasing should also be carefully studied. One caterer known to the writer, for instance, makes heavy purchases of turkey immediately after Christmas, when prices are generally low. As these take up quite a large amount of deep freeze space available when raw, he cooks them and allows them to go cold, after which they are carved. He then wraps ten portions in foil, before storing in deep freeze until required. If being served hot, the turkey is heated in thin stock, only sufficient for requirements being removed from deep freeze at any one time. When the turkey is required to be served cold, it is served straight from the foil, allowing defrosting to take place at normal room temperature. His one very strict rule is that, once removed from deep freeze, the turkey is never put back.

Speciality and convenience foods abound in plenty, so many, in fact, that one could become almost bewildered by the wide choice. Should one use them, if so which, and for what course? All these foods must have a place in modern catering, and only the reader having studied well all angles can be in a position to decide.

Costs and Costing

Absorbing and interesting as undoubtedly outside catering is, the confectioner is in business to make a living. This branch of our trade is hard work and the labourer is worthy of his hire. His quotation should include a reasonable margin of profit. This trade is one that does too much for the customer for nothing, and this is undoubtedly wrong, for I have known customers to ask for a quotation and then hedge in the hope that the confectioner will reduce his price. Some, I know, do just this because they fear a competitor may otherwise get the order. This is utterly wrong. If a job has to be skimped and is not going to prove profitable, then I would say "forget it".

I would ask the reader to pause for a moment and cast his mind back to the last occasion when he had workmen, such as builders, plumbers, electricians, and decorators, in either his home or bakery. The price quoted was, perhaps, stiff, but if this had been mentioned, the attitude of the person concerned would undoubtedly have been: "That's my price, think it over." In other words: "Unless our margin of profit is met, we are not interested in the job." Needless to say, when the bill is presented it is quite often in excess of the quoted figure!

I firmly believe that the caterer should give value for money; give first-class service; and make a profit on all jobs tackled.

EXAMPLES

In the introductory chapter to this book the reader will recall that, in costing, I recommended that all goods used from shop or bakery should be charged for at full retail price, and that in costing a meal he should charge at least twice the cost of food. It should be noted that the words are "at least twice".

Let us now extend this a little further and consider costings for a meal, our imaginery function being for 50 people, and the cost of food at 5s. per head. The first example is by charging twice the cost of the food.

50 guests at 10s. per head: £25

Food cost (50 per cent)	£12 10s. 0d.
Wages at 25 per cent	£6 5s. 0d.
Costs =	£18 15s. 0d.
Revenue	£25 0s. 0d.
Deduct costs	£18 15s. 0d.
Leaves balance of	£6 5s. 0d.

or 25 per cent.

Let us now compare the above figures with the following, now charging two and a half times the cost of the food, otherwise a food cost of 40 per cent.

50 guests at 12s. 6d. per head: £31 5s.

Food cost (40 per cent)	£12 10s. 0d.
Wages at 25 per cent	£7 16s. 3d.
Costs =	£20 6s. 3d.
Revenue	£31 5s. 0d.
Deduct costs	£20 6s. 3d.
Leaves balance of	£10 18s. 9d.

or approx. 35 per cent.

In both costings it will be noticed that wages have been allowed for at 25 per cent which, I feel, is about average. When catering for buffets this figure may be reduced somewhat, but it is folly to skimp on staff, both in numbers, quality or wages paid. Every member taken to a function holds the success of the firm in his or her hands. Remember that you have many customers gathered together and criticism either good or ill can have lasting repercussions.

From the balance of each example must come such charges as petrol and transport; floral decorations; laundry; detergents and cleaning materials; commission to third party who introduced the business; sauces and condiments, unless allowed for in food costings and often overlooked; equipment replacements, etc.

It will be noticed that in the second example the wage percentage allows higher wages. This allows the caterer to employ either more or better types of waitresses and give extra prestige to his business.

Allied to these figures are very many details such as extra floral arrangements and cotton gloves for waitresses; both items incur expense, and yet call forth favourable comment and stamp a business with the necessary individuality. It should be possible for the caterer to set aside a percentage of profit from each job to enable him to purchase further equipment and silverware, each time stocking first-rate equipment to further enhance the functions at which he caters.

I suggest, too, that costs should be worked out after every function, for it is all too easy to prepare set menus, sometimes costed originally months previously, and work from those costs. He can all too easily find himself working for very little.

The portions served should also be very carefully watched, for extra heavy portions can be overfilling. Similarly, too small portions should be avoided, for this can brand the caterer as "mean". The portions given throughout the whole of this book can be rigidly adhered to, for they have proved very satisfactory.

Catering has many forms, some of which I have tried to show in this book, including some of the pitfalls. By careful attention to detail, both on his own side as well as the customer's, can the reader ensure that it is, indeed, profitable to all concerned.

R

Index